IMAGES
of America

TRAILBLAZING WOMEN OF TAMPA BAY

On the Cover: Margaret Clark Miller welds metal at McCloskey & Company at Hooker's Point Shipyards in Tampa on September 18, 1943. By that year, 16 million women made up 65 percent of the US workforce. At McCloskey & Company, under the direction of Matthew H. McCloskey, they built concrete ships for World War II. On this day in September, three new ships were christened, and McCloskey & Company hosted a celebration. Miller, a 21-year-old welder, was chosen by the other female welders to launch one of the vessels, the *Richard Kidder Meade*, and fellow welder Nell Sivacoe was on hand to assist. Shipbuilding boomed during World War II, and 23,000 workers, including women, were employed repairing and building ships in Tampa. Renowned welder Opal Brown won a welding competition at Hooker's Point. By 1945, there was little need for shipbuilding, and the Florida legislature established the Tampa Port Authority, acquiring holdings of McCloskey & Company along with 131 acres of waterfront. (Burgert Brothers Collection, Tampa–Hillsborough County Public Library.)

IMAGES
of America

TRAILBLAZING WOMEN OF TAMPA BAY

Madonna Jervis Wise

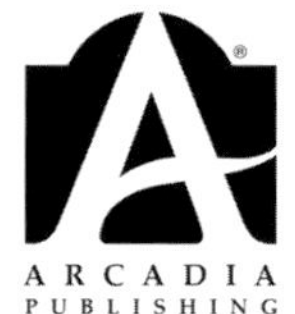

ISBN 978-1-4671-0755-6

Published by Arcadia Publishing
Charleston, South Carolina

Printed in the United States of America

Library of Congress Control Number: 2021947207

For all general information, please contact Arcadia Publishing:
Telephone 843-853-2070
Fax 843-853-0044
E-mail sales@arcadiapublishing.com
For customer service and orders:
Toll-Free 1-888-313-2665

Visit us on the Internet at www.arcadiapublishing.com

Dedicated in honor of a trailblazer who has saved lives and made a difference, Margarita Romo, and to the remarkable ladies who have enriched and fulfilled my purpose in life: Mamie Venita Jervis Wise, Rachel Beth Jervis Wise, Blakely Jane Wise, Nell Louise Cleveland, Emily Humphries Wise, and Audrey Fern Cleveland. You are my inspirations!

Contents

ACKNOWLEDGMENTS

Thank you to the following for their contributions: Margaret Angell; Tammie Adams Arias; Imani Asukile; Shelby Bender; Jennifer Bexley; Scott Black; Stephanie Black; Pat Carver; Heather Culligan; Nancy Dalence; Danielle Dannemiller; Florida History & Genealogy Library at the John F. Germany Public Library of Tampa–Hillsborough County Public Library; Robert Gorden of Henfield Museum in London; Dixon D. Gutierrez of Florida Memory; Division of Library and Information Services, Florida Department of State; Shannon Harmer of PARS International; Clinton Inman; Natalie Kahler; Jan Knowles; Ellen Lynn of The Spring of Tampa Bay; Jeff Miller; Geneviève Noël, archivist and director of the Central Archive Departement, Sœurs des Saints Noms de Jésus et de Marie; Clemmie C. Perry; Sally Redden; Sr. Ann Regan; Richard K. Riley; Margarita Romo; Nancy C. Ryan, special projects producer, WFLA; Mary Katherine Mason Sauter; Lauren Gonzmart Schellman; Adam Smith, director of communications, City of Tampa; Drew Smith, associate librarian, University of South Florida Libraries (USF); Tampa Bay History Center; Tampa Historical Society; Jeanette Thompson; University of Florida Digital Library; Andrea Gonzmart Williams; Emily Wise; Mamie Wise; and Rachel Wise.

Introduction

Although Ponce DeLeon is credited with naming the tropical paradise and lush peninsula with the moniker la Florida in 1512, reportedly while he gazed at the thick, colorful foliage, Florida women from the earliest days have served metaphorically as Lewis and Clark–type pathfinders. The plucky audacity of individuals and groups who chose to break the mold to improve life and defy the unthinkable has impacted and enhanced the trajectories of women who see contemporary careers and aspirations that are limitless. Twenty-first-century women stand on the shoulders of their extraordinary forebearers who took incredible risks and traversed unchartered paths.

Since human occupation, which dates to 14,000 BCE in Tampa Bay, indigenous women have shouldered burdens of subsistence. Eternity holds and whispers the anonymous names of the women who were nurturers of the sustenance of life for their families. The abundant lithics found throughout Tampa Bay offer glimpses of the work of women in planting, gathering, hunting, and tending homes while facing challenges of hardships brought on by scarcity and circumstance. Shell and burial mounds throughout the Tampa Bay area suggest the utter sophistication and developed community structure of the early indigenous people whose first encounters with explorers ultimately brought disease and eradication of their unrecorded lives. From the Seminole Wars spanning from 1816 to 1858, continued hardship was evidenced as land became a precious power commodity that determined destiny.

The Armed Occupation Act of 1842—and later, the Homestead Act of 1862—shone additional light on agriculture and ranching as families migrated to the area and received a quantity of land with specifications for improvement to make it their very own. Many of the Tampa Bay communities began to emerge in the 1840s as settlers arrived with their families. Maps of Tampa Bay in the 19th century are peppered with rugged homesteads that were dependent upon open range and makeshift agriculture. To succeed, a family required both husband and wife to plant and till the land and manage wild hogs, cracker cattle, and the like. Brewing up a meal of swamp cabbage, grits, and wild meat was the task of the household, and preserving, tanning, weaving, sewing, and laundering clothing required ongoing tasks from dawn to dusk, with unbridled stamina and ingenuity of frontier women. Accounts of women on horseback silhouetting the tasks of their husbands, brothers, and fathers were abundant. In addition to this, the role of the midwife and the knowledge of homespun medical care kept families thriving, although the loss was unceasing as childbirth and infant death rates were sky-high.

The identity of women during frontier eras was largely based upon their father or husband. As genealogists who uncover records can attest, locating the first name or maiden name of women in the 18th- and 19th-century records is at times challenging. Laws supported this anonymity as women did not have legal rights of property ownership or business entrepreneur or management roles. The successful working women did it under the auspices of their husband or father or were somewhat renegade and careful enough to circumvent the rules. The sheer fearlessness of women in the early 20th century and before to advocate for women's rights and women's suffrage took daring beyond belief as they were ridiculed and ostracized.

By the late 19th century, real Florida towns were emerging with identities. The railroads brought travel and a new level of refinement or at least creature comforts. Gazing at Tampa, Plant City, Brooksville, and Dade City, for example, photographs and records of hotels, churches, and society were forming the essence of the various communities while some areas remained vastly rural and unique to their origins for decades. For example, Wesley Chapel in 1840 had merely 14 settlers tucked into remote areas and often connected only through Fifth Sunday Sings or a visit to the general store. Other Tampa Bay area communities, such as Zephyrhills, emerged from unique foundations such as the Union Civil War soldier retirement haven that came from the recruitment by the founder, Capt. Howard Jeffries, of soldiers throughout the United States, or the socialist Common Good Society, which bought land for a cooperative of settlers who renamed Jarve Springs to Crystal Springs.

After the Civil War and by the late 1800s, because of the impact of the war that cast women into commercial work positions previously held by men, women began to find a community voice. Institutions such as the Woman's Club, Garden Club, Eastern Star, and Grange offered opportunities for leadership and growth, and with new conveniences, women could spend a portion of their time on endeavors that were not for life and death survival at the basic instinctual hierarchy. Their attention focused on social welfare and education.

Newspapers document activism with female involvement in the early 20th century and before. Logically, there was a desire to participate in a government whose constitution talked of the free. Suffragettes emerged but did so at personal cost. There was a stigma associated with that level of activism, and participation was limited to certain socioeconomic groups. Prominent women particularly shunned association. For the Tampa Bay area, Ella Chamberlain, Elizabeth Askew, Elizabeth Robins, and Mary Dreier Robins were incredible role models who worked tirelessly for the passing of the 19th Amendment.

As the 20th century beckoned, industry was flourishing, only to be halted and impacted by World War I, the Great Depression, and World War II. A new surge of change was wrought as women entered nontraditional workforce roles and persevered to preserve their families once again. With the right to vote, a few women were seeking political activism and office, and the Tampa Bay area history chronicles women in council roles, mayoral positions, and state legislative roles. Their entry into professional careers had begun.

Perhaps the next logical extension of woman's empowerment was being able to serve on a jury, which occurred in 1949; however, until 1967, women were still required to contact the clerk of the county court to ask that their name be added to the jury rolls. The emancipation act was introduced by Florida trailblazer Mary Lou Baker, the sole woman in her law school class of 1938. Previously, women were under common law coverture. The Married Women's Rights Law gave married women the right to manage property, enter contracts, and execute documents. After eight weeks of debate, the House passed the bill 46 to 38. It was a huge step, but there was still work to be completed. As Baker ran for her third term in the legislature, she was attacked for being a feminist because she continued to use her maiden name.

Male-controlled sports were still largely exclusionary until mid-century, when women began to risk involvement in those areas as well. Title IX, the federal civil rights law in 1972, marked another step in the evolution of women. Prohibiting sex-based discrimination in education and sports was a monumental change that helped to open doors for women.

Trailblazing Women of Tampa Bay provides a look into courageous women, famous and unknown, who took risks, and offers just a few examples. Countless women were and continue to be trailblazers—particularly the unnamed and marginalized groups who did not have light shone on them by way of photography and news coverage and should be remembered. This book offers just a sample of the trailblazing women who took risks, opened doors, and acquired their voice for equality. As you review these inspirational accounts, I hope that you will reminisce about the trailblazers in your own life and the ones you are nurturing for the future.

One

Nameless Women Who Paved the Way

The experience of the frontier was diverse and unique, often fluctuating according to birth, background, socioeconomic status, and environment. Minus recorded histories of nameless indigenous women of antiquity, knowledge gleaned through artifacts, burial mounds, and oral history discloses hazy sagas of their primitive lives. Throughout Tampa Bay, hunters of lithics discern objects such as knives, dishes, and utensils that were often uncovered by the Seminoles and repurposed from indigenous forebearers. They radiate the continuity of a major life purpose of women transcending time as nurturers.

This brief compilation of images includes a phenomenal Dali painting that triggers one to contemplate the interpretations that have evolved about the indigenous ancestors. A glimpse of a burial mound from the late Weeden Island period in Tampa Bay is just one of the hundreds that existed. Included as well are some accounts of Native Americans in later generations as they were depicted in festive native dress, performing mundane but necessary duties of daily life. The imposed sacrifices upon the Native Americans in the Trail of Tears disclose the dogged path of Manifest Destiny on emerging Tampa Bay. With the unfolding Armed Occupation Act of 1842, brave frontier woman of rugged, unsettled Florida were immigrants on a peninsula that held incredible charm but offered tumultuous obstacles.

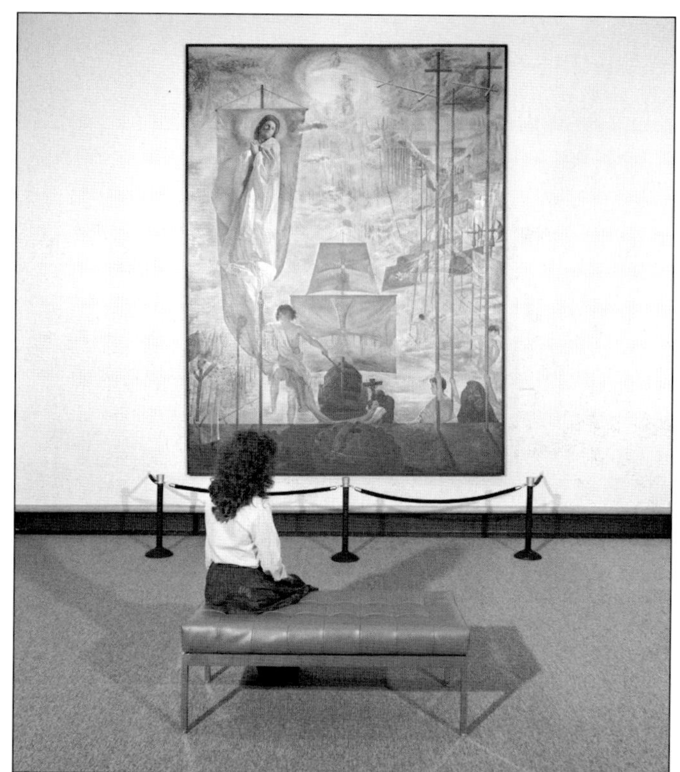

As a metaphor of reflection regarding women and their role in exploration and settlement, a female art enthusiast ponders a metaphorical painting at the Salvador Dali Museum in St. Petersburg. The painting depicts explorers and indigenous peoples as they may have appeared in the earliest of explorations. This 1982 photograph is by Robert M. Overton. (Florida Memory.)

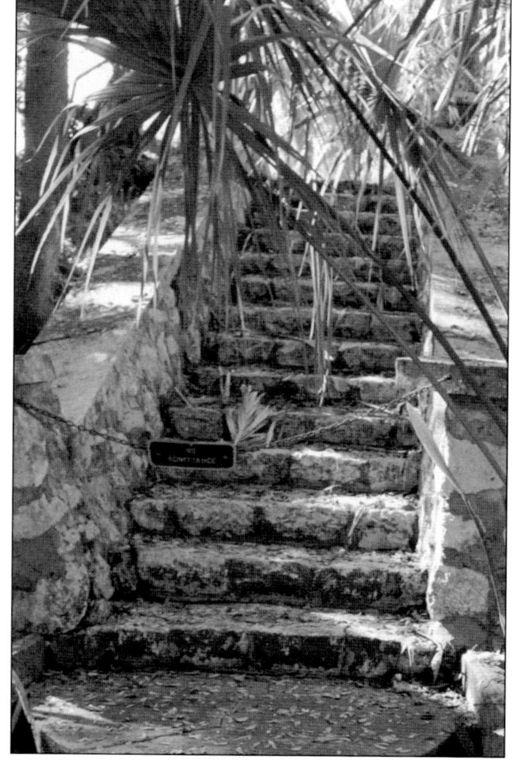

The Eschaskotes Mound, also known as the Oelsner Mound in New Port Richey, is a remnant of indigenous peoples from the late Weeden Island period, about 1000 CE. The mound was preserved by its owner, Martha Oelsner. Along Tampa Bay, over 15 villages have been acknowledged along the Gulf Coast from southern Hernando County to northern Sarasota County, including Tampa Bay. The developed communities are uncovered via lithics such as tools, weapons, and pottery. The temple and burial mounds hint at the impact of early women's contributions to their families and communities. (Author's collection.)

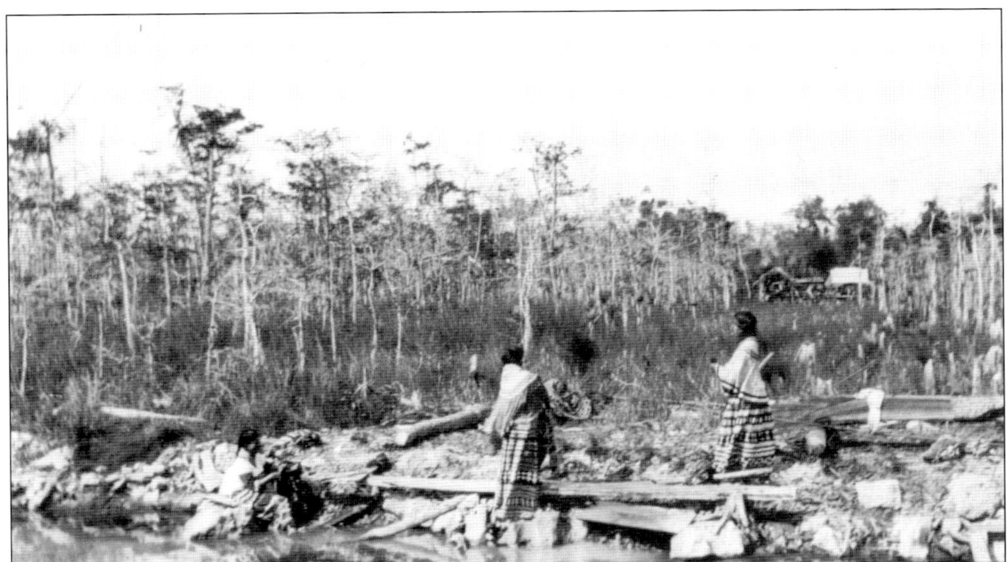

This photograph of 20th-century Seminole women provides a glimpse into the Seminole culture, which began when bands of Creek Indians from Georgia and Alabama migrated to Florida in the 1700s. By 1817, conflicts between settlers and Seminoles resulted in three major conflicts—the Seminole Indian Wars. (Tampa Bay History Center.)

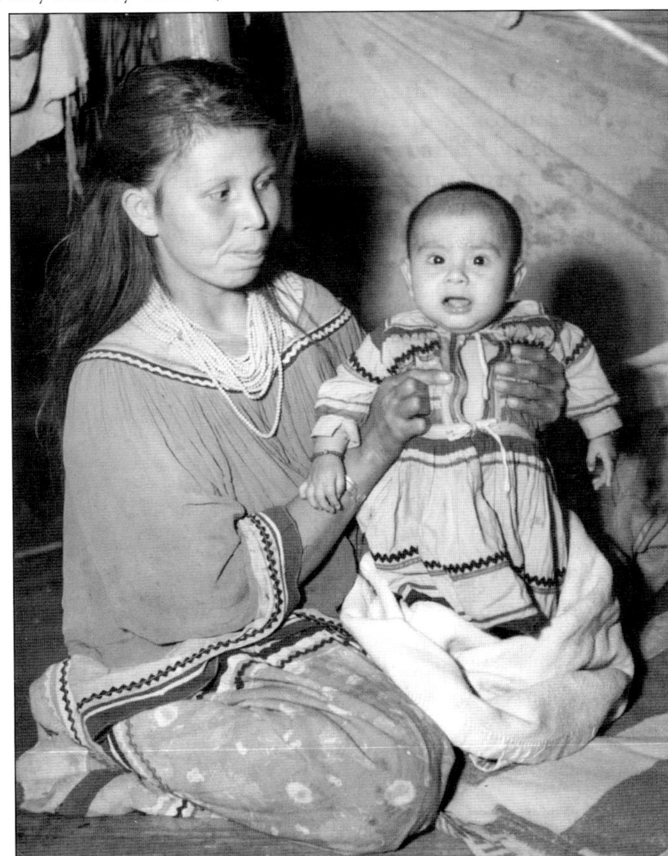

The Indian Removal Act of 1830 was a relocation of Seminoles to Oklahoma, which provided the impetus for the Second Seminole War. Seminole genealogy is passed through the mother, as the children belong to her and to the clan she represents. The maternal figure rules the household. (Burgert Brothers Collection, Tampa–Hillsborough County Public Library.)

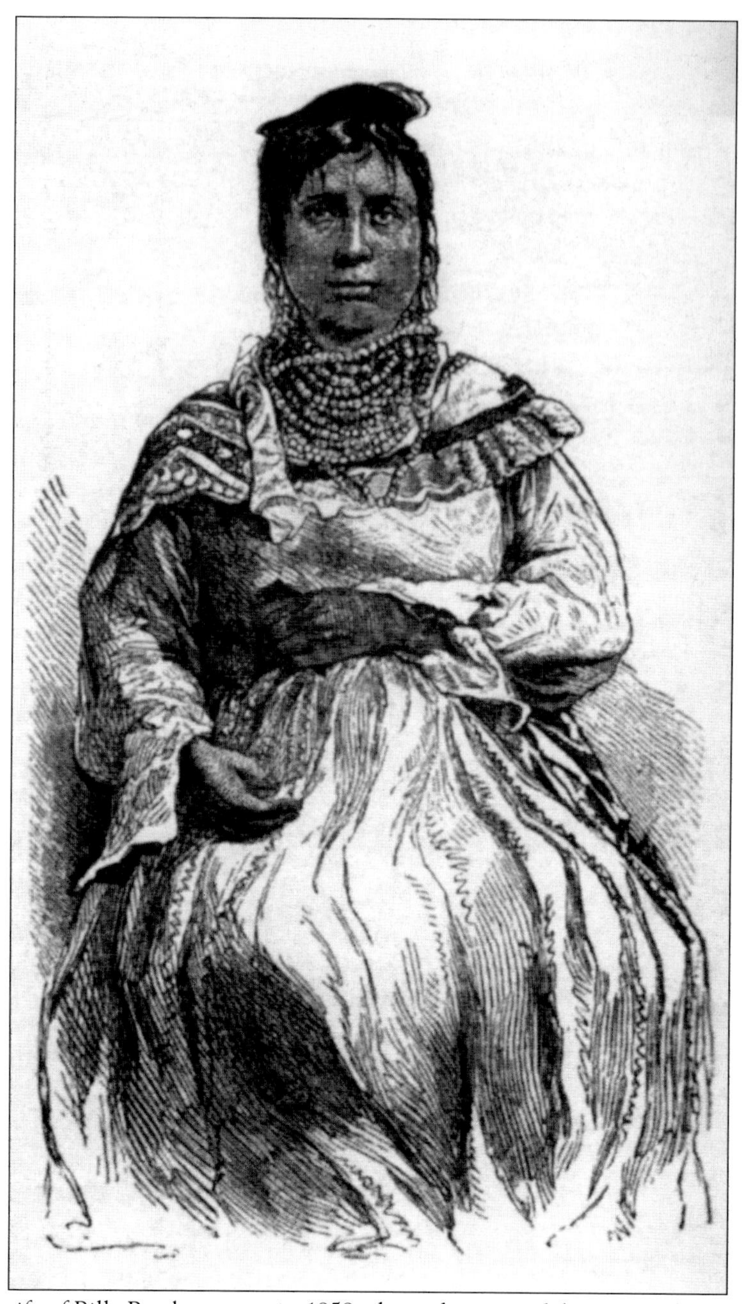

The second wife of Billy Bowlegs poses in 1858, about the time of the Seminole surrender in the Third Seminole War. Multiple marriages were permitted in Seminole culture. Billy Bowlegs's first wife was the sister of Nocose Emanthla (Bear Leader), one of his warriors who signed the peace agreement in 1842. His second wife was the sister of Fasatchee Emanthkla, his lieutenant. Bowlegs was the principal Seminole leader in the Third Seminole War (1855–1858). He and his war-weary band surrendered on May 7, 1858. Thirty-eight warriors and eighty-five women and children, including his wife, boarded the steamer *Grey Cloud* at Egmont Key on May 7, 1858, to begin their journey to Indian territory in the Trail of Tears. Bowlegs died soon after his arrival. (Florida Memory.)

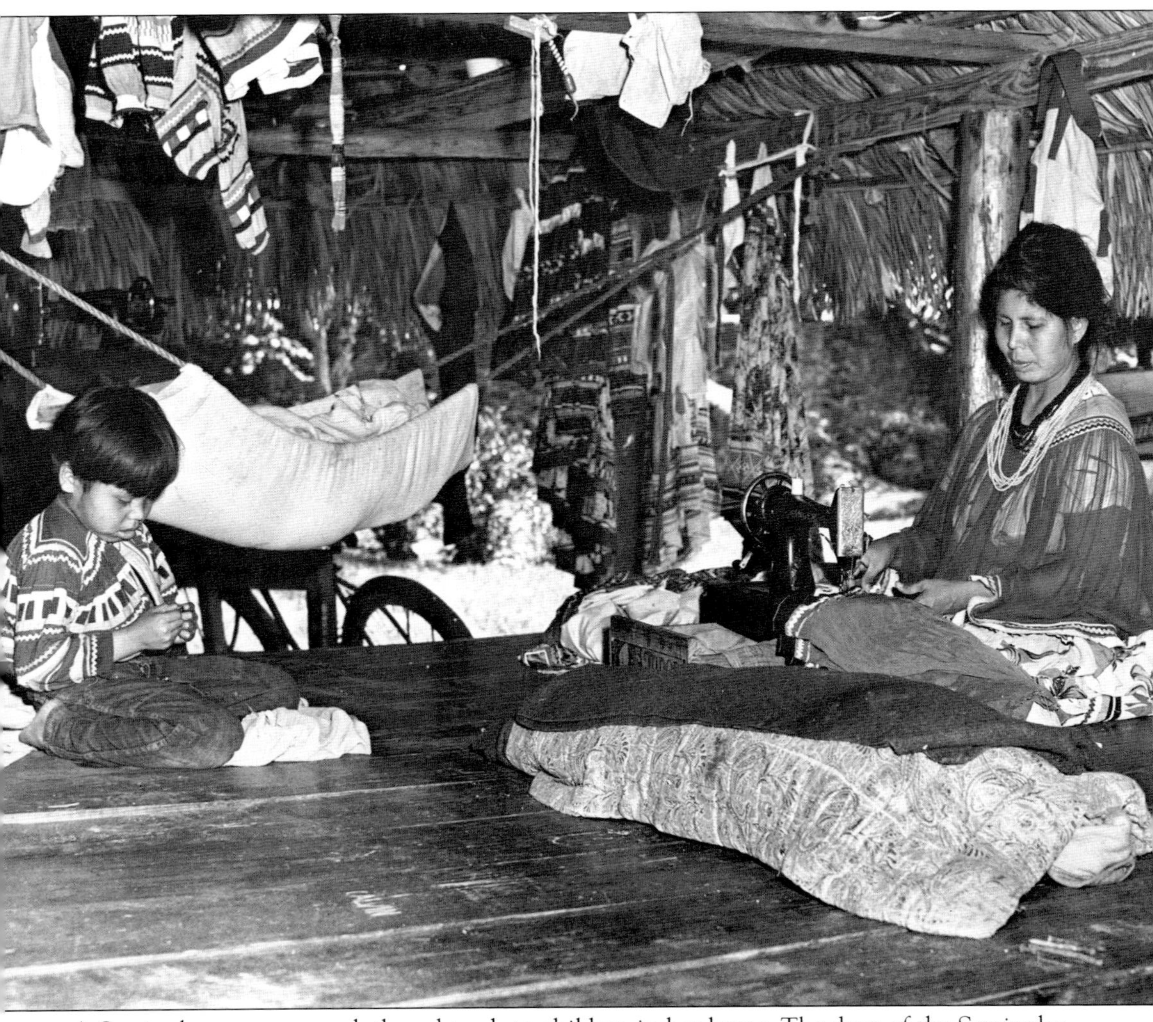

A Seminole woman sews cloth and tends to children in her home. The dress of the Seminoles includes intricate designs of various vibrant and contrasting colors, which date to the early 1800s. Beads carried symbolism that was linked to age and status. Pedal sewing machines were used as early as 1880 and added the familiar patchwork designs. Like the varied designs, the Seminoles arrived in Florida before 1750 and came from various culturally related tribes. (Florida Memory.)

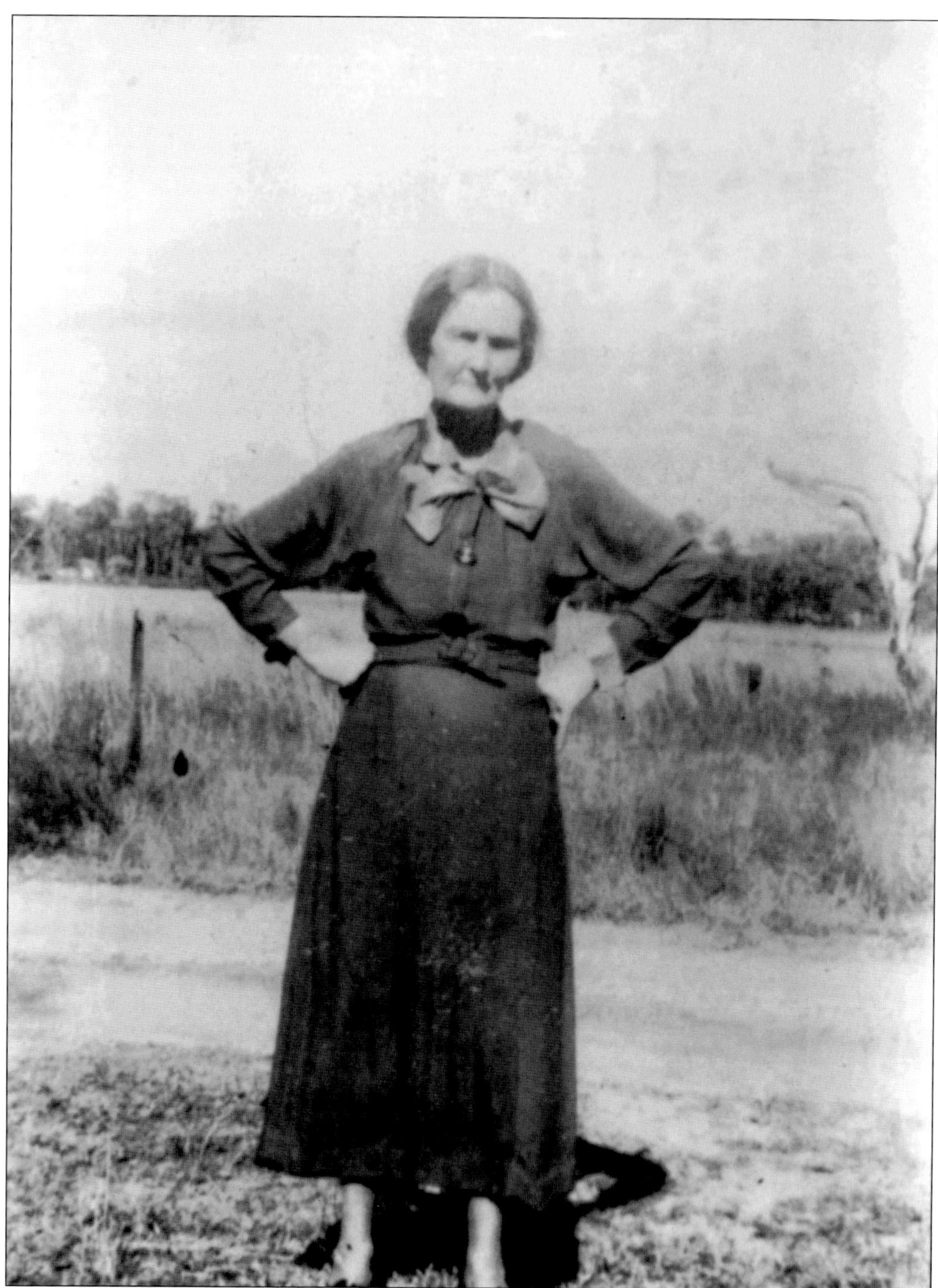

Frontier women worked tirelessly in domestic and agrarian tasks. Rarely were their leadership skills formalized in work outside the home, but there were the occasional trailblazers who were acknowledged. Pioneer Florida Museum volunteer Wayne Sweat shared that his grandmother Roxie Ann "Missouri" Spivey Wells was one of the first frontier women to hold a government position. After her husband, Dee Wells, passed away, she was appointed by the governor and then later elected to a local position of supervisor of registration. (Wayne Sweat.)

Two

Movers and Shakers

After the Civil War, women underwent changes in perceptions, work, and prospects for their future. Florida women tended the homesteads while their husbands were away at war and grieved losses. Estimates assert 16,000 Floridians fought in the Civil War and 5,000 were killed. Women toiled to provide foodstuffs and goods as Florida supplemented clothing, iron, crops, and precious salt, which was essential to preserve foods. Women collected and shipped items to the troops and were there to pick up the pieces when loved ones returned home.

Although they had unremitting fortitude as frontier women, their perceptions were altered by the Civil War, and a sense of empowerment was spawned.

From the mid- to late 19th century, giving the vote to women was written about, dreamed of, and debated. By 1892, Elleanor "Ella" Collier McWilliams Chamberlain of Tampa organized the Florida Woman Suffrage Association, which lasted five years. The subsequent years brought some hesitancy, but later, Tampa Bay women rejoined the effort through the development of the Florida Equal Franchise League. Although the 19th Amendment did not pass until 1920, it was many years in the making. By 1919, the unprecedented concept of giving women the power of election was infiltrating the psyche of both men and women throughout the area.

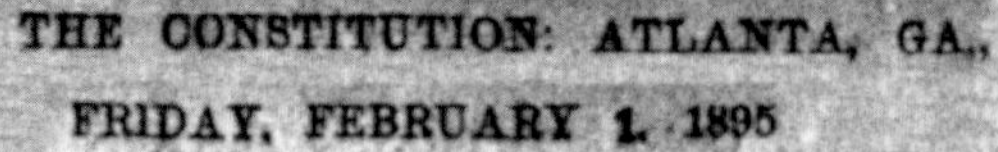
THE CONSTITUTION: ATLANTA, GA.,
FRIDAY, FEBRUARY 1. 1895

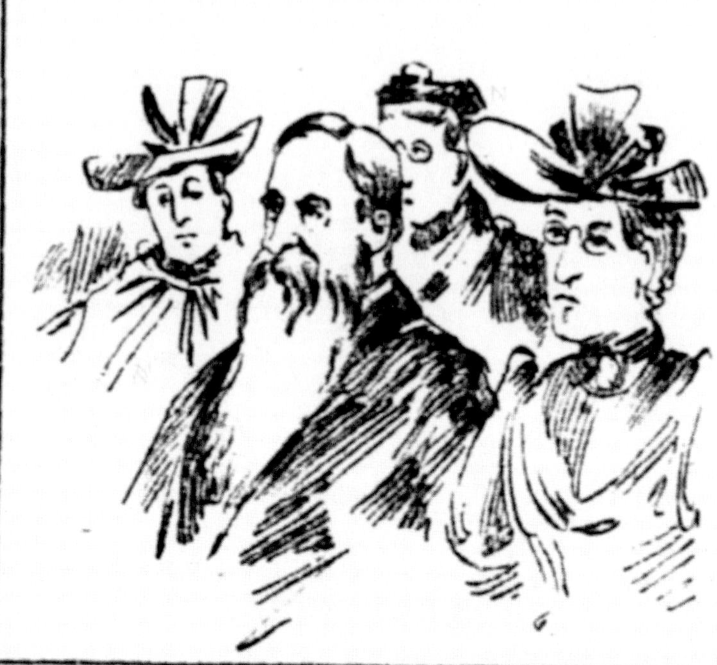

THE WHISKERED DELEGATE FROM FLORIDA.

Several Reports Read.

Several interesting reports were next read from the auxiliary states.

Among these a splendid showing was made by Mrs. Chamberlin, of Florida, and by Mrs. Virginia D. Young, of South Carolina.

Ella Chamberlain spearheaded Florida's women's suffrage movement. Born in Iowa, she lived a very extraordinary life, teaching school, owning caves in Indiana, writing for newspapers, and championing social causes such as prison reform that enriched and saved lives. Chamberlain lived in the Tampa Bay area for 51 years and worked diligently on the passage of the 19th Amendment. This sketch of Ella and her husband, Fielding Chamberlain, appeared in the February 1, 1895, edition of the *Constitution* newspaper as part of coverage of the National Suffragette Convention in Atlanta. Ella credited her husband with bringing her into the fold of woman's suffrage, and he, in turn, jokingly referred to himself as the "whiskered suffragette." (Library of Congress.)

Historian Leland Hawes claimed that the best-known piece of writing from suffragette Eleanor McWilliams Chamberlain, the first woman to speak on woman's suffrage in Florida, was a poem entitled *Cherokee Rose*. It was printed on the first page of Ernest L. Robinson's *History of Hillsborough County*. Chamberlain was one of Susan B. Anthony's favorites because of her intellect and tenacious fervor. It was rumored that Chamberlain sent Anthony a box of oranges annually from Florida. (Florida Department of Commerce Collection, Florida Memory.)

Legend of the Cherokee Rose
by Ella Chamberlain

A Seminole warrior wooed for his bride,
A Cherokee maiden, his foeman's pride;
As they fled together, the trembling maid
For a last long look at her home stayed.

On the rude lodge roof the blossoms white
Glowed like stars in the soft moonlight;
With tears in her eyes, the Indian bride
Broke a spray that grew by the portal's side.

To a Florida home she bore it then
To brighten her lodge in the stranger's glen,
And oft to her children the tale she told
Of the alien and the lover bold.

And whenever the waters go stealing by
In that land of bloom and cloudless sky,
The Cherokee rose wreaths the forest wild
And dreams it shelters the Indian child.

A hundred years and warrior and bride
In forgotten graves lie side by side;
Yet over them climbs and blooms and grows
The lover's flower, the Cherokee rose.

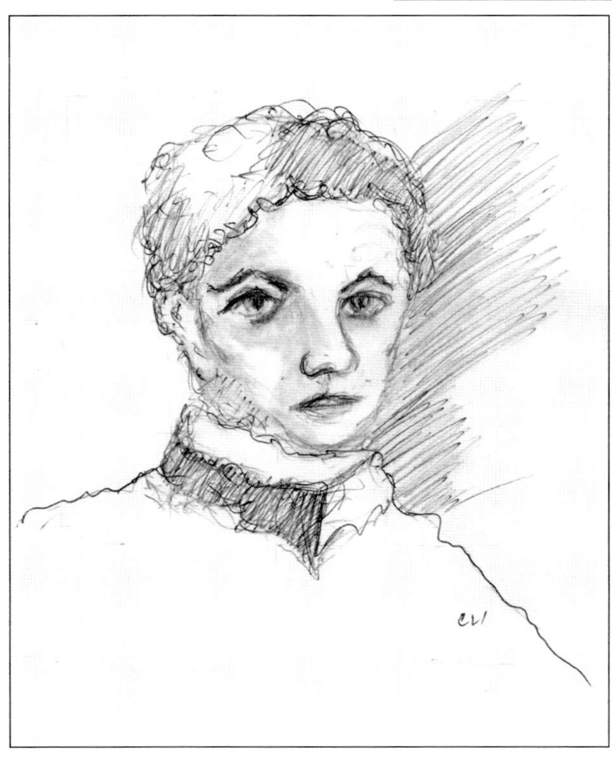

Born in the anti-slavery western part of Virginia in 1858, Elizabeth Askew moved with her family to Tampa in 1894. Leader of three woman's clubs, she was a founding member of the Tampa Civic Association and later secretary and president of the Woman's City Club that advocated for the needs of working women, declaring their crowning achievement a hot lunch program for public schools. In November 1913, when the Florida Equal Suffrage Association was founded, Askew was its secretary. A year later, she was one of the Florida delegates to the convention of the National American Woman Suffrage Association in Washington, DC, in December 1915. This is an interpretative sketch from a *Tampa Times* article published on April 30, 1930. (Sketch by Clinton Inman.)

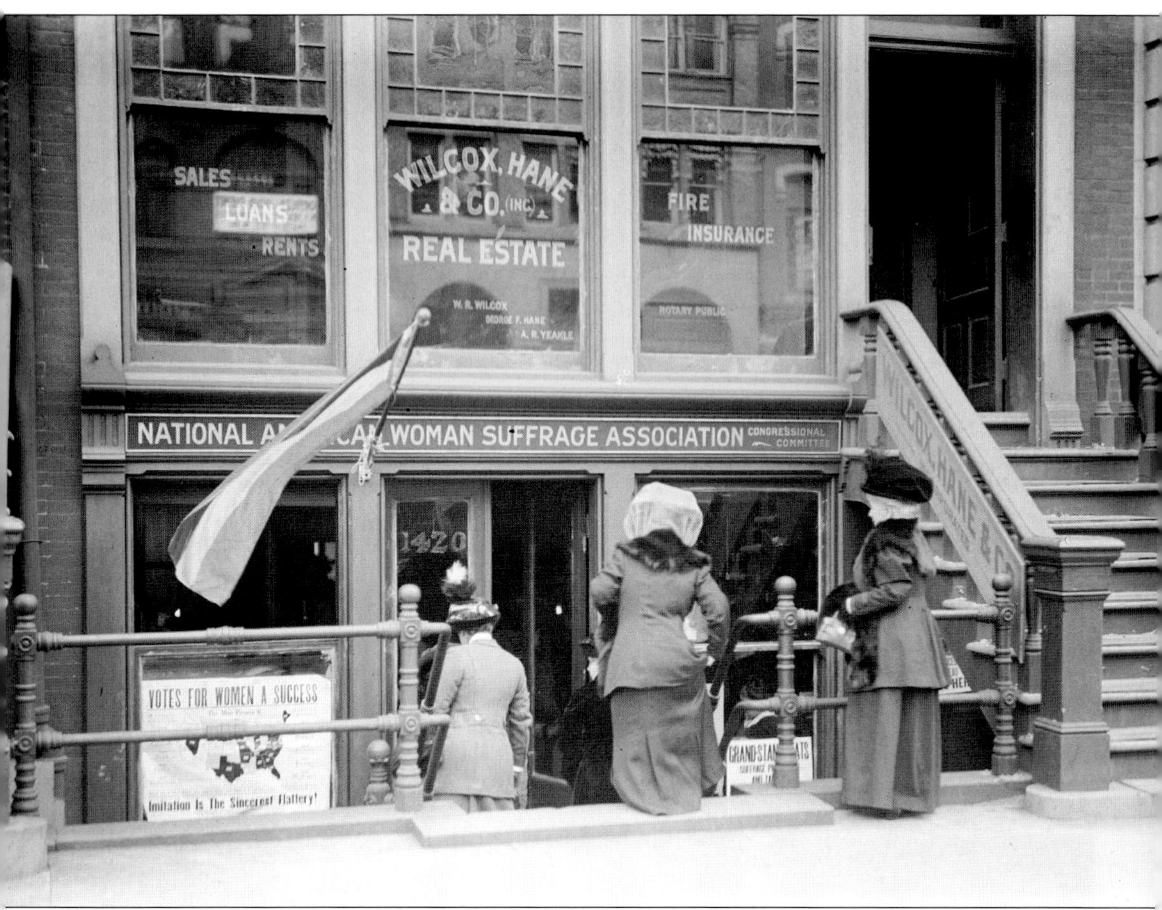

Elizabeth Askew was the first woman to hold the position of stenographer in a Tampa bank, where she worked just after the bank had weathered the Great Freeze. A staunch suffragette, in April 1917, in her speech about the world war entitled "Back to the Farm," she told the Webster Woman's Club in Sumter County, "For the nonce is become the war cry in place of 'Votes for Women' " Yet she noted that American women were hopeful that their government would grant women the right to vote—"as the champions of world democracy, it can scarcely do less." Askew traveled to Washington, DC, regularly for suffrage meetings and lived there sporadically. This 1913 photograph shows the headquarters of the National American Woman Suffrage Association, which Askew frequented for planning meetings. (Harris & Ewing Collection, Library of Congress.)

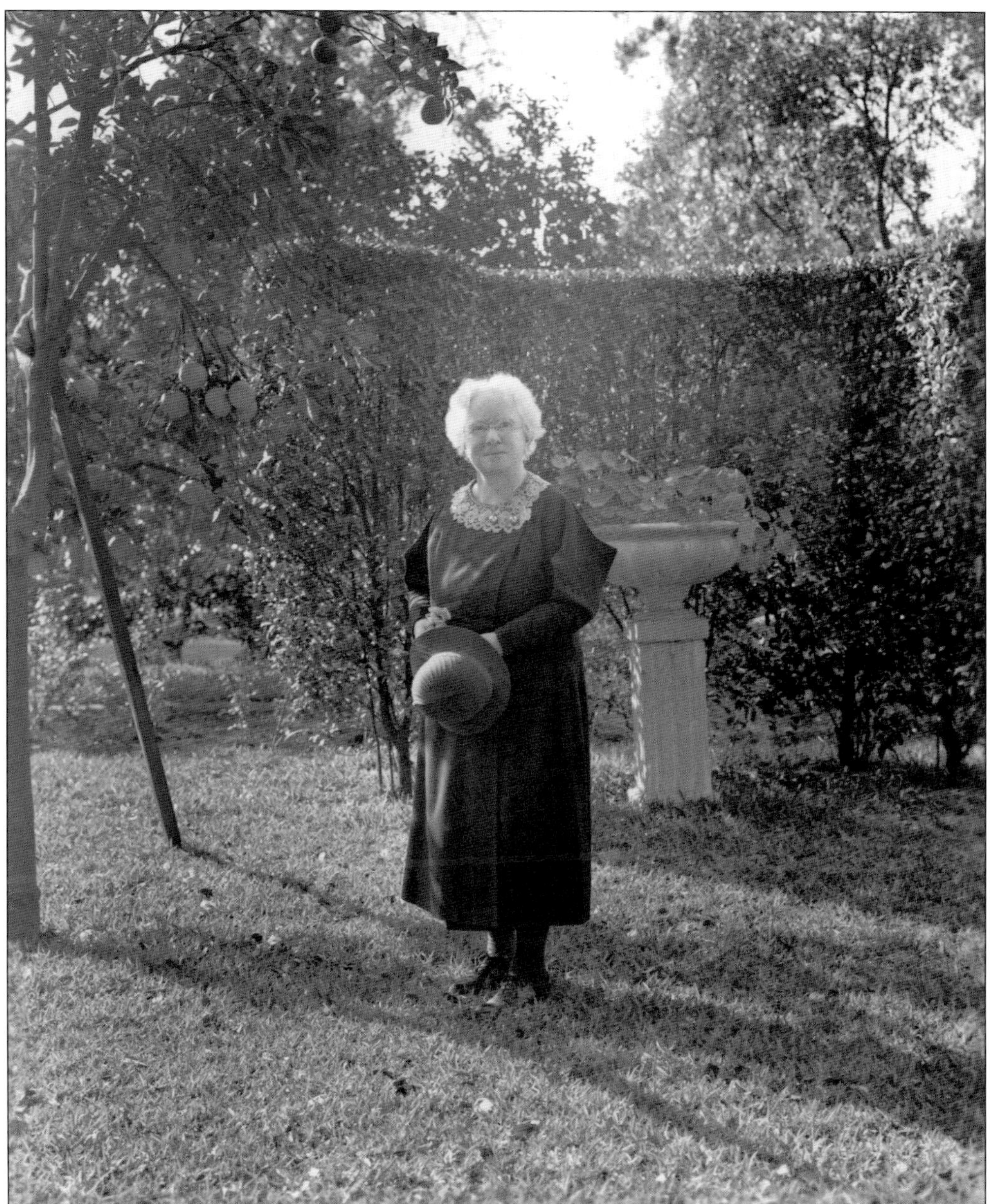

Kate Veronica Jackson was the founder and president of the Tampa Civic Association in 1911. Her efforts in club work and advocacy contributed greatly to women's rights, although she was cautious of overt involvement for some time in the suffragette movement. In 1919, she more demonstratively joined the suffragettes publicly when she hosted events at her home for the Florida Woman's Suffrage Association, which she and friends were careful to point out had nothing to do with the more militant National Woman's Party. A March 16, 1919, *Tribune* article announcing an event at Jackson's home read, "Now is the time for the women of Florida who have been backward in suffrage work to come forward and join in the march of progress or else they will sooner than they realize, find themselves in the behind-the-time-old-fogy class." While her father and brother were mayors of Tampa, Kate Jackson contributed comparably as an advocate and philanthropist. (Tampa Bay History Center.)

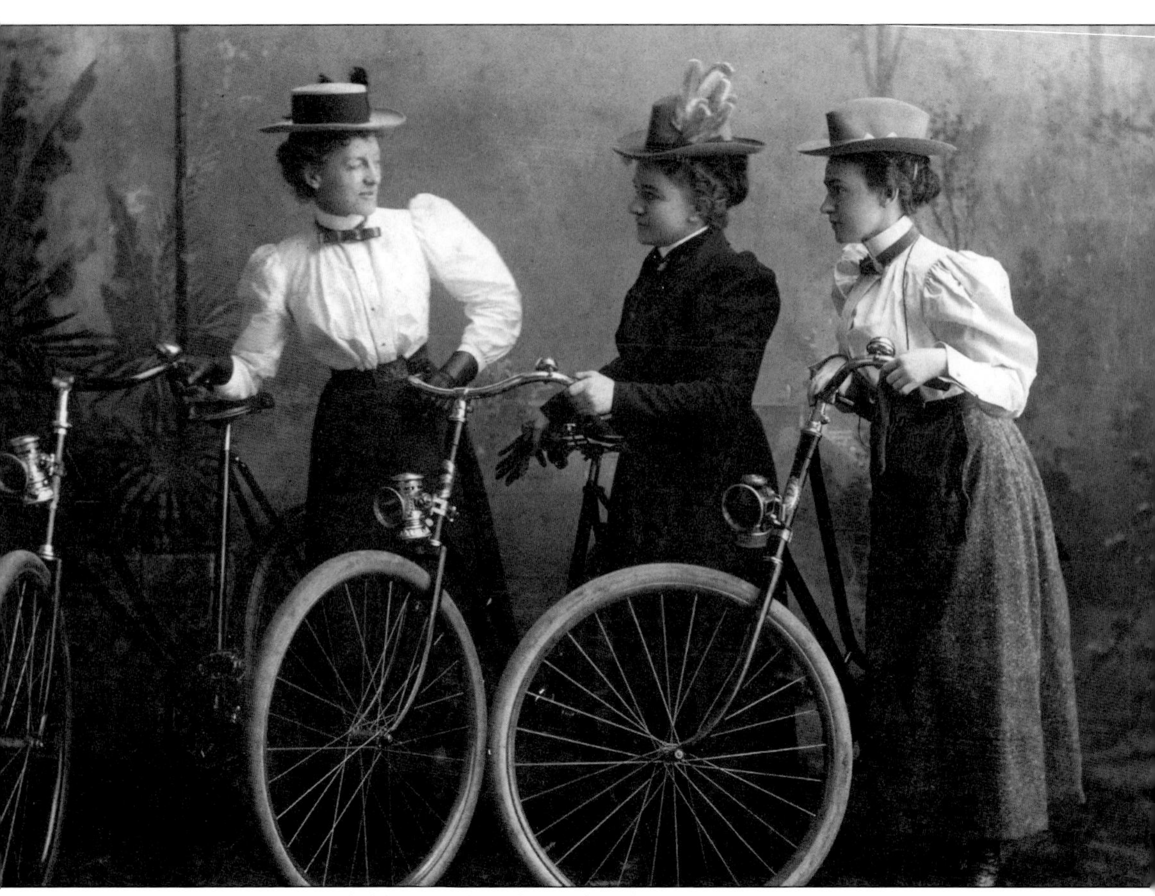

Kate Jackson is surrounded by two friends on their bicycles in Tampa. A 1925 interview in the *Times* chronicled her life of service: "Women from time immortal have rushed in where men fear to tread. A valiant little band of club women with Jackson as leader, took the long upward trail." Not only was Jackson the first president of the civic association, she served for over 50 years to better the city of Tampa as commissioner of the Girl Scouts, Business and Professional Women's League, Catholic Woman's Club, and nearly every woman's group in Tampa. (Tampa Bay History Center.)

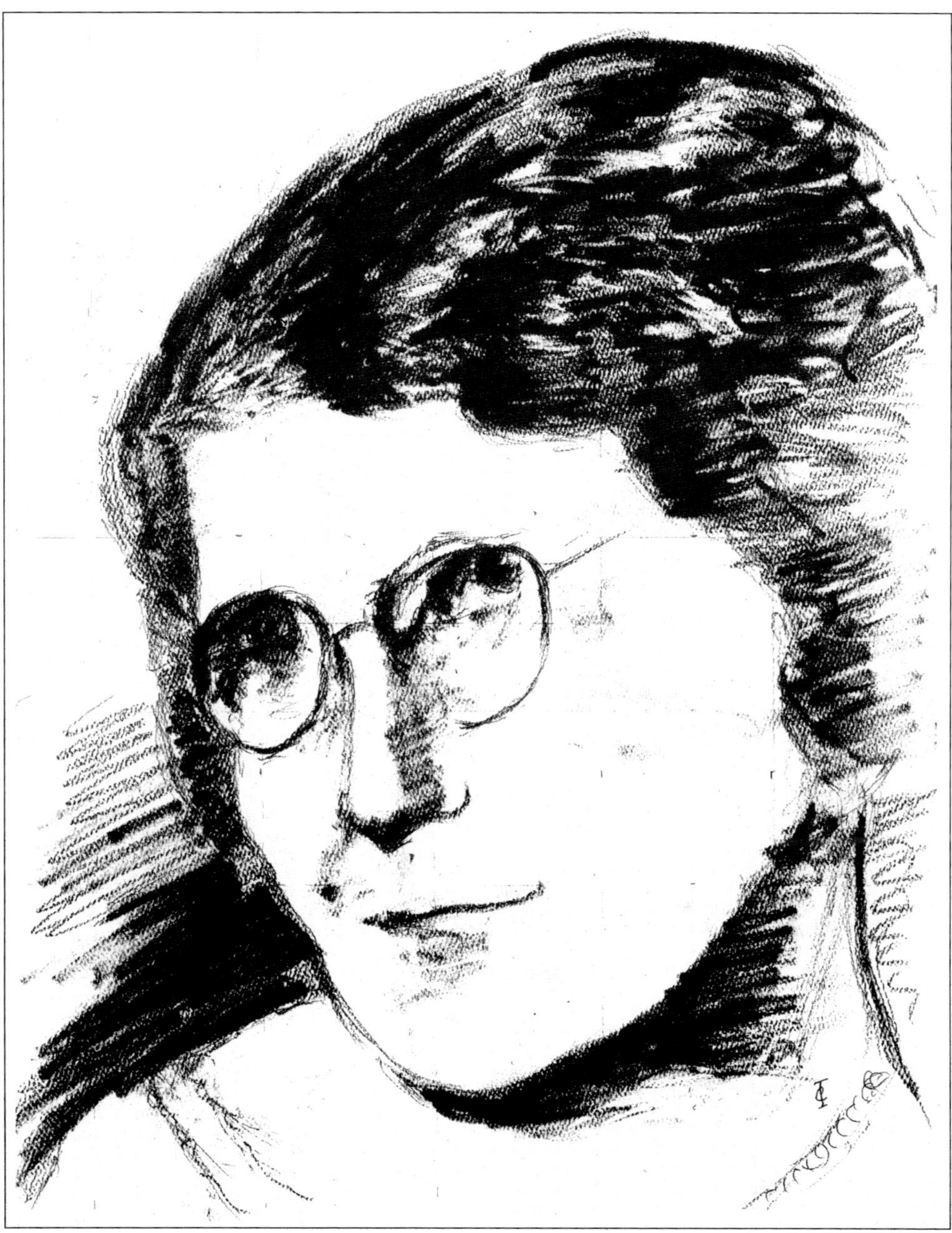

Martha Ada Price, president of the Tampa Equal Suffrage League, delivered a zealous keynote suffrage speech in January 1919 at the Hillsboro Hotel. The audience applauded Helen Ring Robinson, who had served two terms as a state senator from Colorado, and Ellen Spencer Mussey, organizer of the first Washington, DC, Woman's Law College. Other officers were Mabel C. Bean, Sarah Chapman, Jane A. Davis, and Alice Eugenia Snow. Club representatives included Kate Jackson from the Tampa Civic Association; Leo Browning Hamman of the Clearwater Woman's Club; Sarah H. Downs of the Tampa Woman's Club; and Lillian A. Rushing of the Pinellas Federation of Woman's Club. Dr. Mary A. Safford of Orlando, state president, and Elizabeth Skinner of Dunedin, district chairman, were also on hand. This sketch is based on an image from the February 16, 1939, *Tampa Times*. (Sketch by Clinton Inman.)

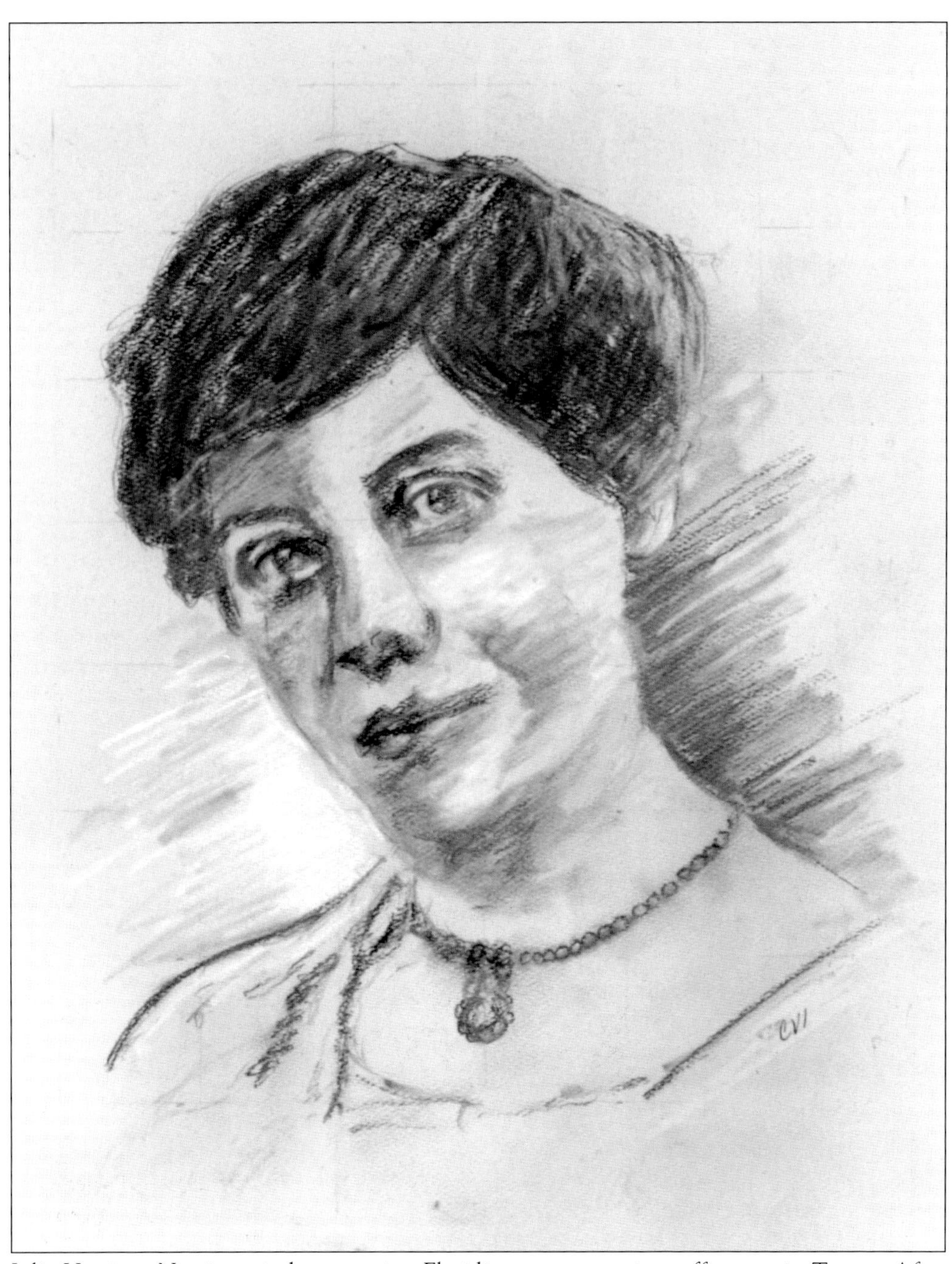

Julia Harrison Norris, a sixth-generation Floridian, was an active suffragette in Tampa. After the right to vote was obtained, she committed herself to politics. She fostered changing the city government of Tampa into a commission and headed the Civil Service Board for 18 years. Integral to the Red Cross chapter during World War II, she had leadership roles in the Tampa chapter of the Daughters of the American Revolution and Tampa's Woman's Club, and was national honorary president of the United Daughters of the Confederacy and organist for her church. This sketch is based on an image from the February 16, 1939, *Tampa Morning Tribune*. (Sketch by Clinton Inman.)

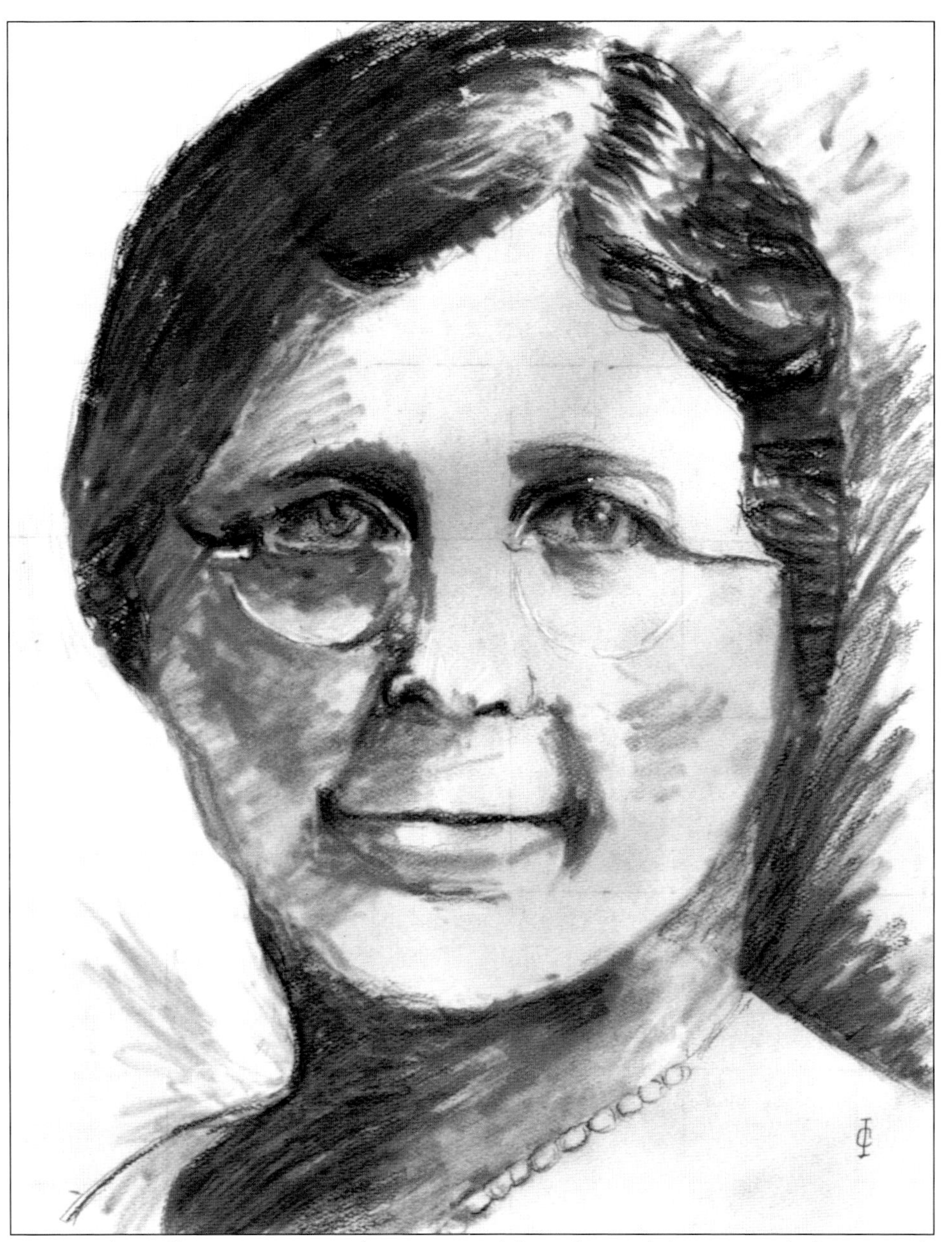

Strategic to the suffrage movement, the woman's club work paved the way, and when a need was recognized, they rallied to action. Willie Beth Miller Lowry was a "mover and shaker in Tampa Civic life," according to reporter Leland Hawes. She dedicated her life to the opening of the YWCA, Red Cross, and Colonial Dames. In March 1900, seeing a dire need for a library, Lowry wrote to Andrew Carnegie about building a free lending library in Tampa and after some time, Carnegie eventually provided $50,000. After success with a girl's club she started with her daughter known as Would Be Good, she contacted Girl Scouts founder Juliet Low to learn details of the new organization and then partnered with Jessamine Flowers Link to organize a troop in 1912. She was active in the Florida Equal Franchise League and worked on the suffrage crusade. Her husband, Sumpter de Leon Lowry, was said to address letters to her as "My Dear Suffragette." In contemporary Tampa, their name graces Lowry Park. (Sketch by Clinton Inman.)

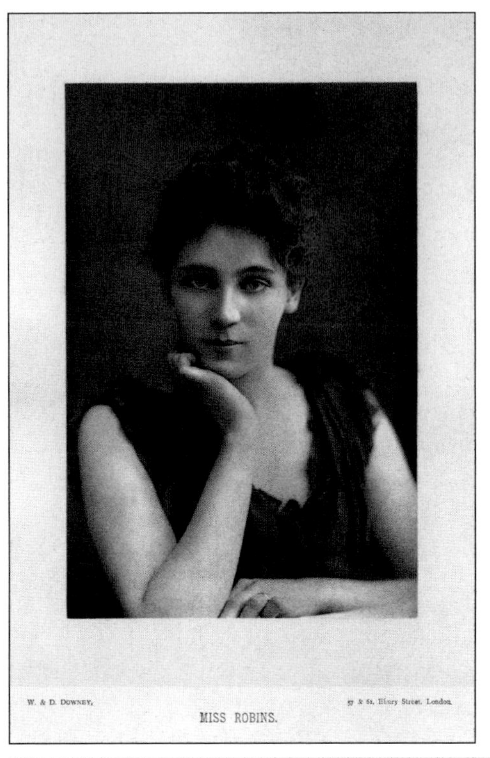

Actress and writer Elizabeth Robins was a woman of the new age who traveled the Atlantic between her home in London and her residences at Chinsegut Hill in Hernando County, Florida, and Chicago. She worked diligently with Jane Addams on the Child Labor Bill of 1902–1903, and was in the thick of women's suffrage in London with Emmeline Pankhurst, and later in the United States. Critical of a violent approach to suffrage in London, Pankhurst advised Robins to use her skills as a writer to support suffragettes. This is a W. & D. Downey portrait from the Cabinet Portrait Gallery. (Robert Gorden Henfield Museum, London.)

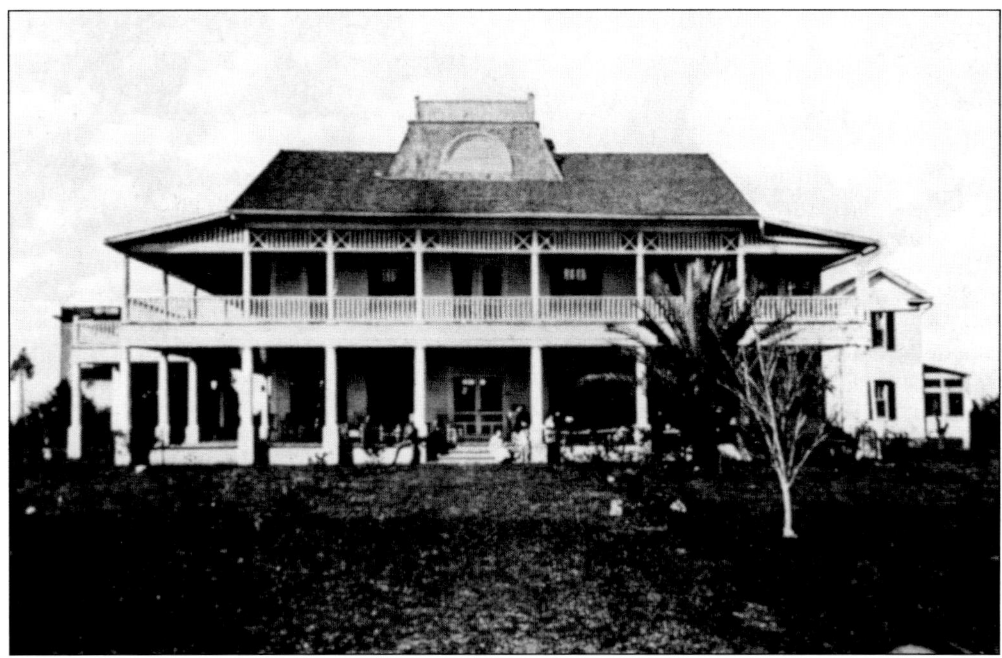

Chinsegut in Hernando County (shown in this photograph in 1940) was purchased by Elizabeth Robins and included acres of pine and hammock. An actress and author of international fame, among her best works was "My Little Sister," which appeared in serial form in *McClure's*. Later, she enjoyed wide fame in book form; her novel *The Convert* was adapted as a play entitled *Votes for Women*, which was the first play to celebrate women's suffrage. (Florida Memory.)

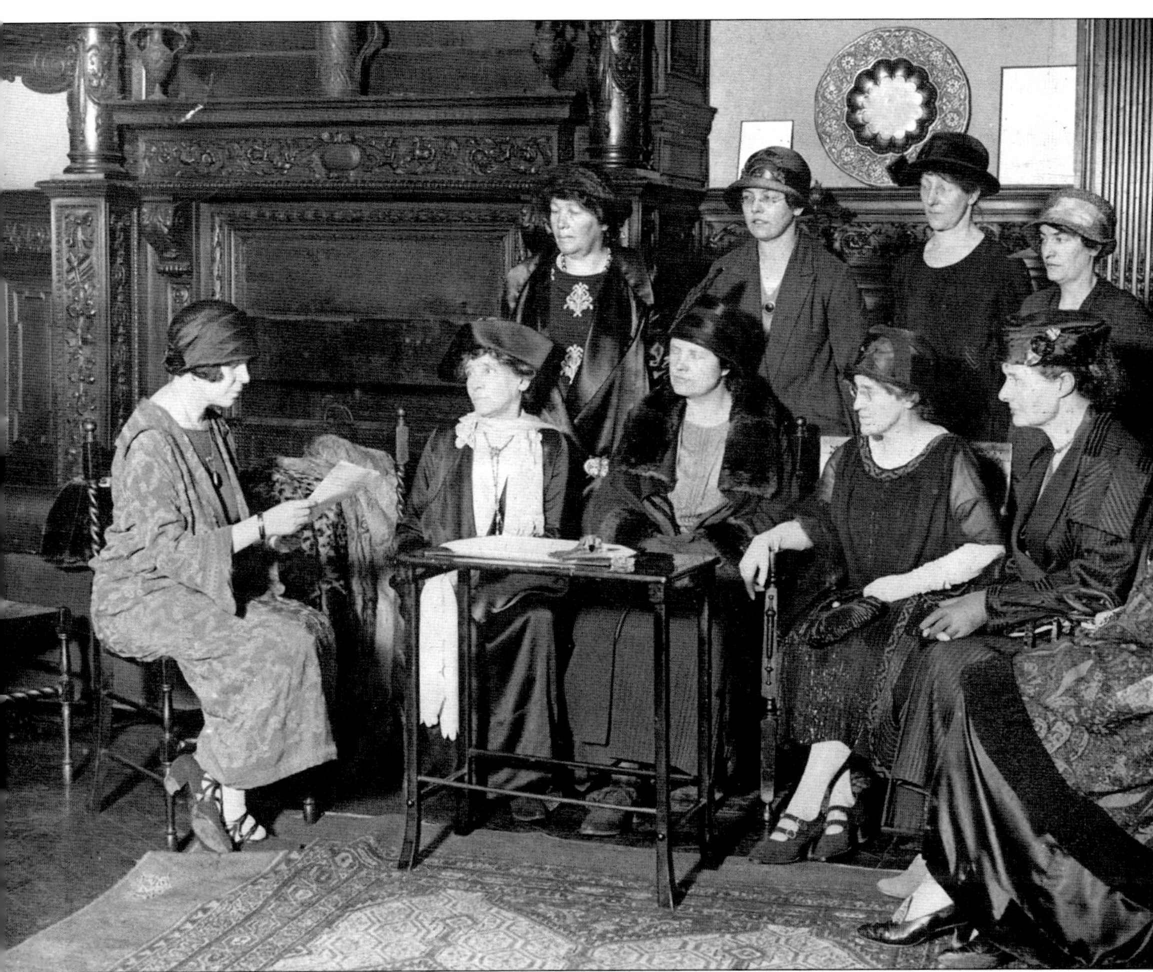

Alice Paul, American feminist and vice president of the National Woman's Party in the United States, confers with English members of the newly formed International Advisory Committee of the National Woman's Party at American's Woman's Club in June 1925. Among those pictured are Elizabeth Robins of Chinsegut/Brooksville, Viscountess Rhondda, Dr. Louisa Martindale, Virginia Crawford, and Dorothy Evans. Paul was advocating for an amendment in which "men and women shall have equal rights throughout the United States and every place subject to its jurisdiction," known as the Lucretia Mott Amendment. Her goal was to address blatant issues such as requiring women to cancel their teacher contracts upon marriage or not possessing rights to sign legal contracts despite suffrage. (London News Agency Photos, Library of Congress.)

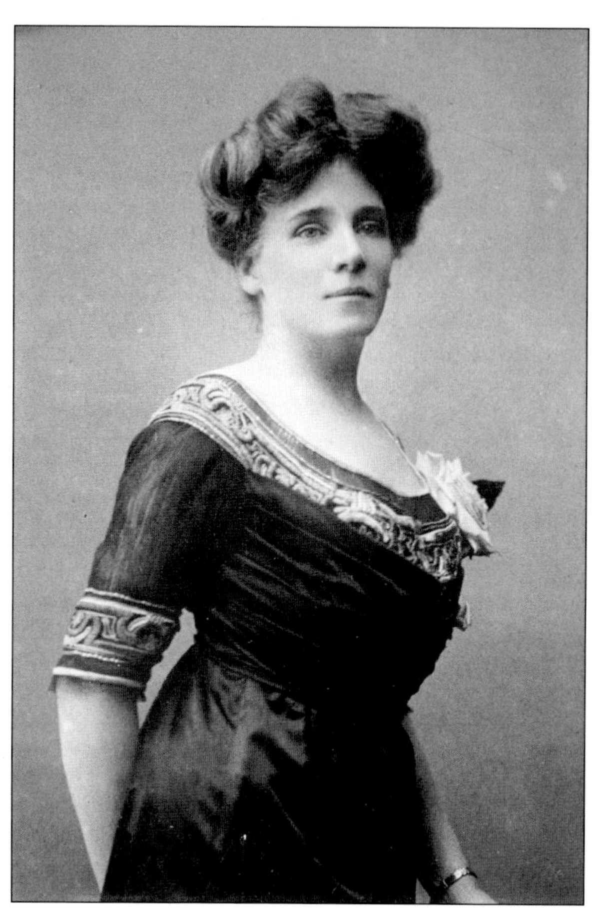

Elizabeth Robins was a woman champion in many areas. As an actress, she was a proponent of Norwegian playwright Henrik Ibsen's approach to modernism or realism in theater. She credited this philosophical approach to fueling her support of women's right to vote. She also fostered improved medical care services. (Library of Congress.)

Elizabeth Robins penned a note to Chinsegut staff about a collection of books she was donating in 1913. In the message, both a photograph and a letter are attached. The books placed at Chinsegut were later donated to the Brooksville YWCA library. (Library of Congress.)

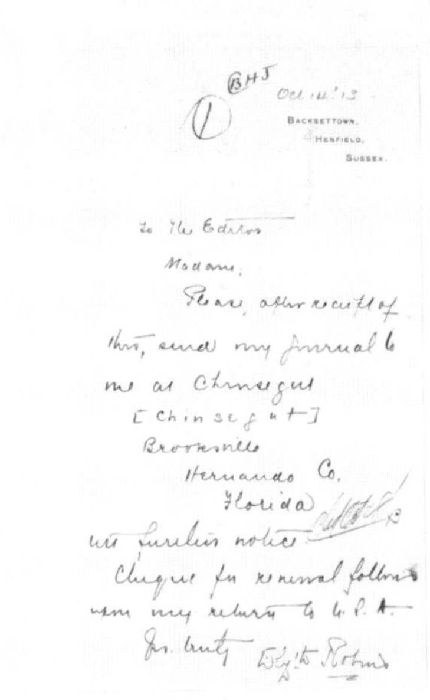

BHJ
(1)
Oct. 14. '13
BACKSETTOWN,
HENFIELD,
SUSSEX.

To the Editor

Madam,

Please, after receipt of this, send my Journal to me at Chinsegut
[Chinsegut]
Brooksville
Hernando Co.
Florida
until further notice.
Cheque for renewal follows upon my return to U.S.A.

Yrs. truly
Elizabeth Robins

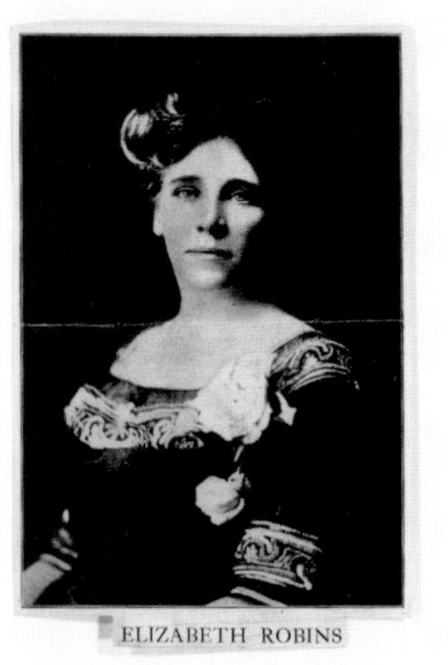

Sister-in-law of Elizabeth Robins, Margaret Drier Robins was very involved in Women's Suffrage. She and her husband, Raymond Robins, lived in Chinsegut in Brooksville, Florida, and were considered the owners although the home was purchased by Elizabeth Robins. Margaret worked in the renowned Hull House in Chicago and served as president of the National Women's Trade Union; she was also a friend of Eleanor Roosevelt. Her signature in the Backsettown guestbook at the Elizabeth Robins home in Henfield in Sussex, England, is seen here. (Robert Gorden, Henfield Museum, London.)

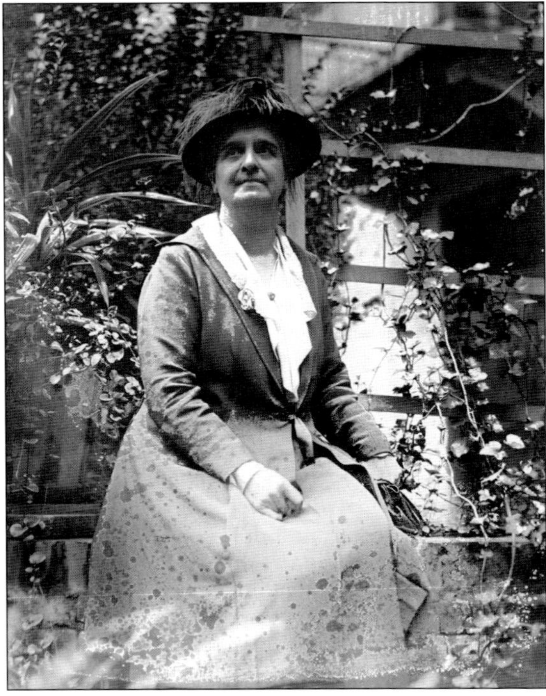

Margaret Drier Robins is shown in the garden of her family's home in Chinsegut. She received an honorary doctorate of humanities from Rollins College in 1931, at which time the presenter stated that "no woman has done more to help women themselves." Born in Brooklyn, New York, she founded the Woman's Municipal League and was president of the National Woman's Trade Union League and the International Congress of Working Women. (Library of Congress.)

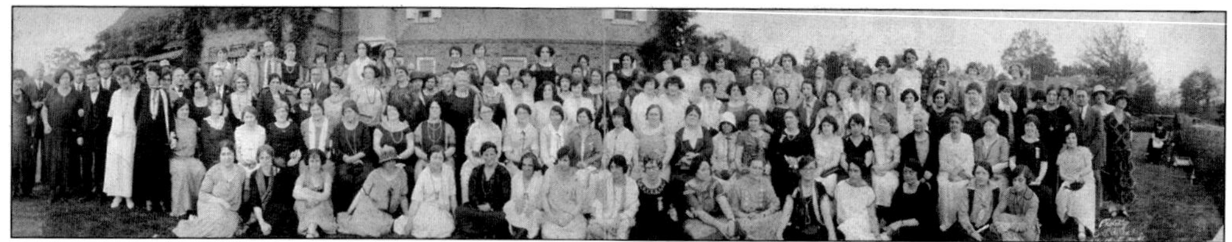

Photographer Charles F. Allen took this panoramic photograph in 1924 at the National Women's Trade Union Convention at the home of Mary Page O'Day and her husband, Daniel O'Day of Standard Oil. Margaret Dreier Robins was the national president for 15 years. She worked to organize women in unions, increase education, limit working hours, and improve conditions. (Library of Congress.)

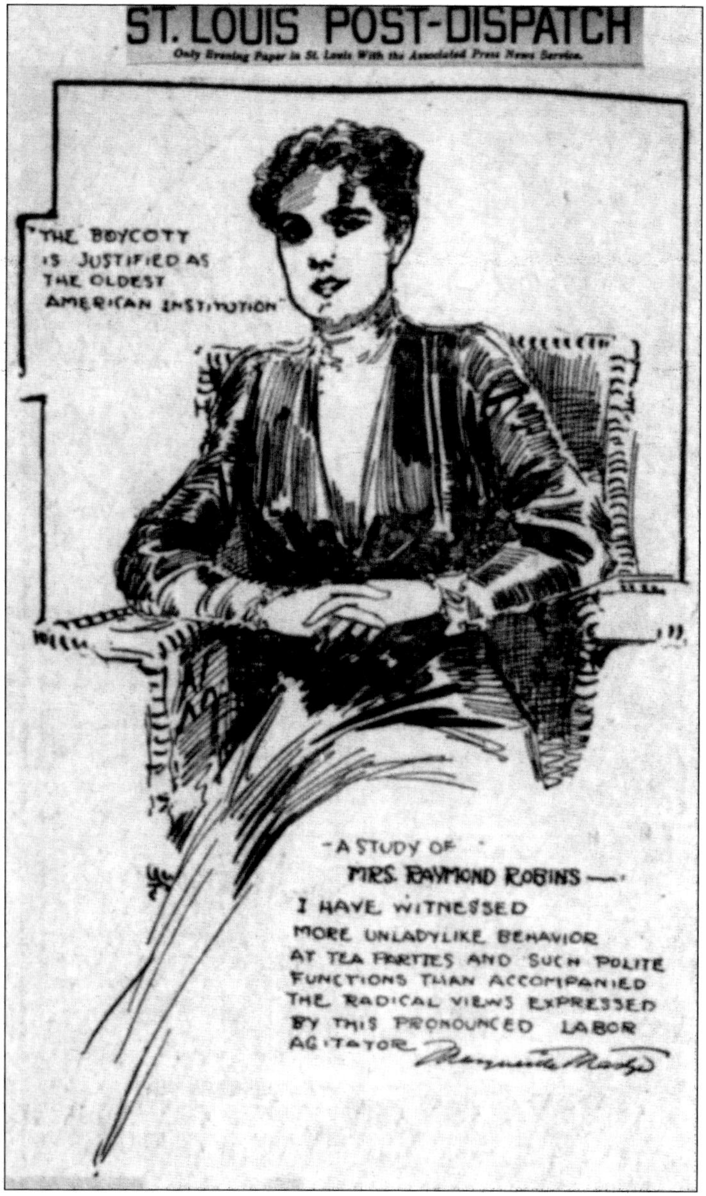

ST. LOUIS POST-DISPATCH

Only Evening Paper in St. Louis With the Associated Press News Service.

"THE BOYCOTT IS JUSTIFIED AS THE OLDEST AMERICAN INSTITUTION"

—A STUDY OF MRS. RAYMOND ROBINS—

I HAVE WITNESSED MORE UNLADYLIKE BEHAVIOR AT TEA PARTIES AND SUCH POLITE FUNCTIONS THAN ACCOMPANIED THE RADICAL VIEWS EXPRESSED BY THIS PRONOUNCED LABOR AGITATOR

Marguerite Martyn

On a speaking tour in 1910 to St. Louis, journalist Marguerite Martyn penned a review and drew a political caricature of Margaret Dreier Robins. Robins said that "the woman's trade union league is designed to give women independence." She was accompanied by Stella Franklin from Australia, who said she came to America to join Carrie Chapman Catt with expert advice, and she found the labor cause a much more live issue that embodied the suffrage cause and went a step further. This sketch by Marguerite Martyn appeared in the *St. Louis Post-Dispatch* on May 19, 1910. (Author's collection.)

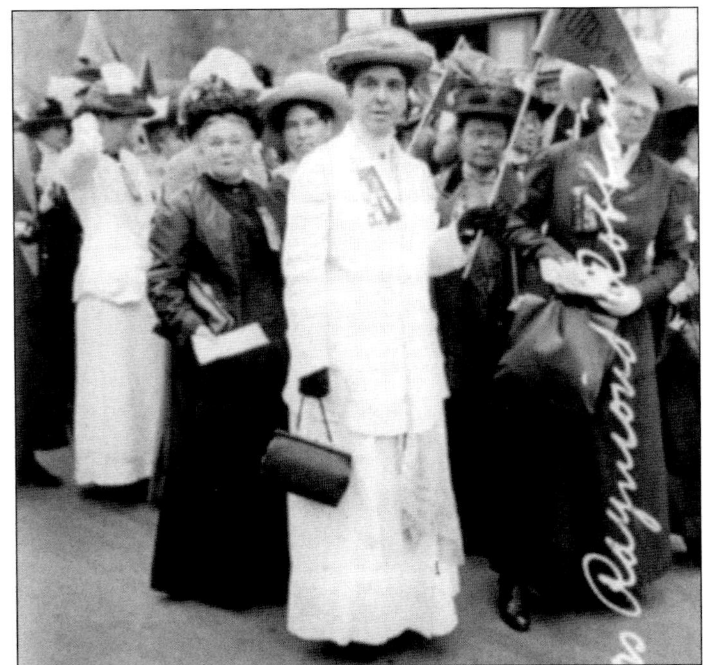

Margaret Drier Robins was a progressive who was greatly influenced by the writings of Ralph Waldo Emerson. One of her sisters, Mary Elisabeth Dreier, was also a social reformer and highly active in New York. Margaret is shown marching for women's suffrage as a tireless activist of women gaining the right to vote. (Brooksville Main Street.)

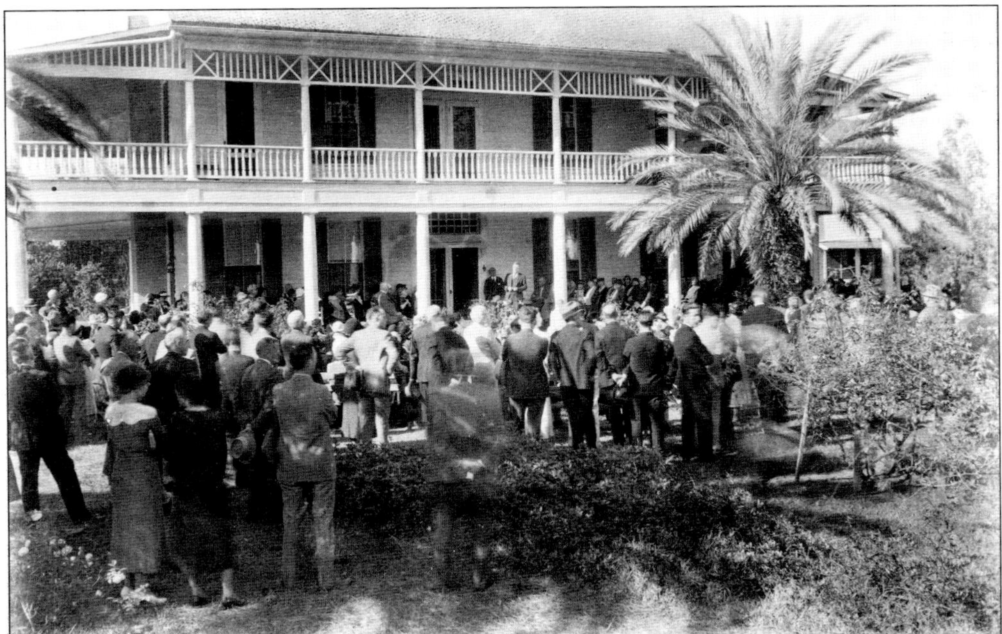

Jane Addams was hosted on the porch of Chinsegut in Brooksville on March 6, 1932; the *Tampa Daily Times* reported that hundreds attended the address by Addams and her companion Mary Rozet Smith, also considered a founder of Hull House. Host Margaret Robins stated, "Always during the time of tragedy, unemployment and suffering we have had Addams . . . we do not think of the Nobel prize or her awards, we think of her great heart." Most were familiar with Addams and her tireless years of struggle advocating for Hull House, world peace, freedom, and industrial legislation that became synonymous with the story of the little girl who witnessed suffering and poverty and was determined to make a difference. (Florida Memory.)

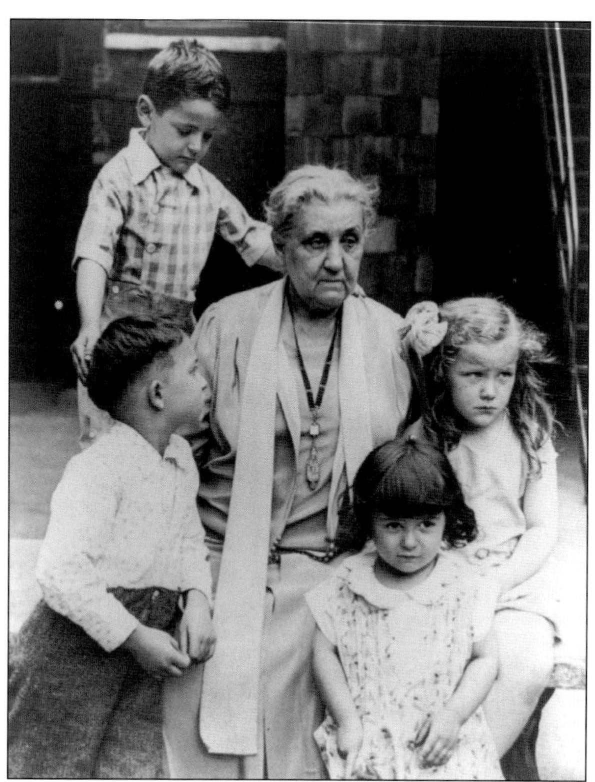

Jane Addams founded Hull House and is shown in 1930 with four children (from left to right), Paul Desalvio, Jerny Seapone, Barbara Navagoto, and Barbara Thicks. Addams was an officer of the National American Woman's Suffrage Association. A Nobel Peace Prize recipient, she was a founding member of the National Association for the Advancement of Colored People, held membership in the National Child Labor Committee, and played a pivotal role in the passage of a federal child labor law in 1916. (Library of Congress.)

1437 WEST OHIO STREET
CHICAGO

Dearest Dad:-

Just a line to send you a thousand thanks for your Easter telegram. I am sorry that I was still so caught in the Chinsegut dreamland that I forgot to send any message over the wires to you. Some day you will have to see our land of wonder and then you will understand.

I hope you received my letter with one introducing you to Mr. de Forest. Have you this extraordinarily hot weather? It was 81 degrees yesterday and seems most unrea

With a great great deal of love,

Your devoted sister,

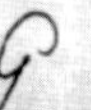

Margaret Dreier Robins was affectionately called "Gretchen" by her family and childhood friends. A 1910 telegram to her father and sister described the beloved home in Brooksville that captured her affection for the Tampa Bay area, which she referred to as "dreamland" to her father and sister. Although much of her suffrage efforts took place in other states, her research and preparation were often completed at Chinsegut. (Archives of American Art, the Smithsonian.)

This 1913 letter from Margaret Robins discussed her in-depth involvement in the suffrage movement. She informed her father that Emmeline Pankhurst had been detained at Ellis Island while traveling from London into the United States for an address in Chicago and a lecture tour. The letter detailed Robins's lobby to Pres. Woodrow Wilson along with others such as Jane Addams, and the ultimate decision that Pankhurst could indeed address the masses in Chicago but must immediately return to London thereafter. Robins declared the action to be "stupid." (Smithsonian.)

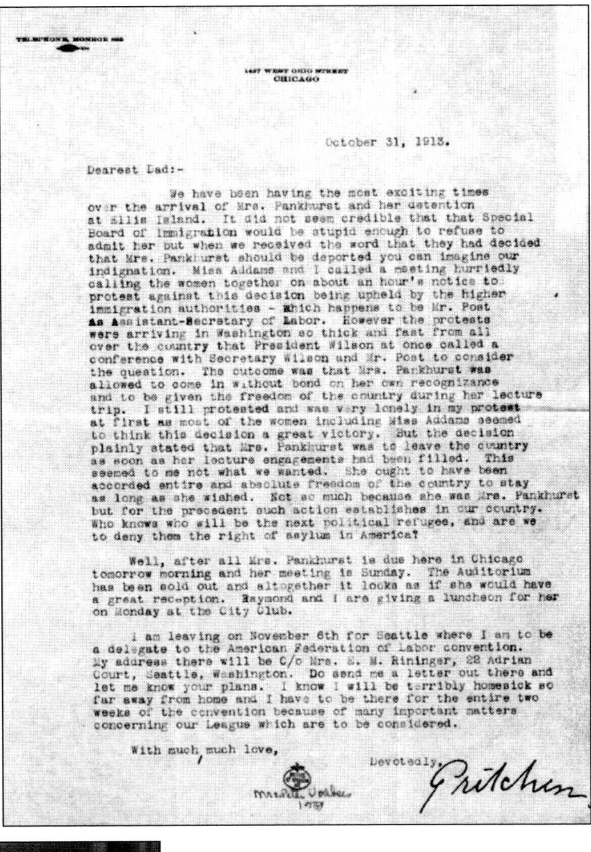

1437 WEST OHIO STREET
CHICAGO

October 31, 1913.

Dearest Dad:-

We have been having the most exciting times over the arrival of Mrs. Pankhurst and her detention at Ellis Island. It did not seem credible that that Special Board of Immigration would be stupid enough to refuse to admit her but when we received the word that they had decided that Mrs. Pankhurst should be deported you can imagine our indignation. Miss Addams and I called a meeting hurriedly calling the women together on about an hour's notice to protest against this decision being upheld by the higher immigration authorities - which happens to be Mr. Post as Assistant-Secretary of Labor. However the protests were arriving in Washington so thick and fast from all over the country that President Wilson at once called a conference with Secretary Wilson and Mr. Post to consider the question. The outcome was that Mrs. Pankhurst was allowed to come in without bond on her own recognizance and to be given the freedom of the country during her lecture trip. I still protested and was very lonely in my protest at first as most of the women including Miss Addams seemed to think this decision a great victory. But the decision plainly stated that Mrs. Pankhurst was to leave the country as soon as her lecture engagements had been filled. This seemed to me not what we wanted. She ought to have been accorded entire and absolute freedom of the country to stay as long as she wished. Not so much because she was Mrs. Pankhurst but for the precedent such action establishes in our country. Who knows who will be the next political refugee, and are we to deny them the right of asylum in America?

Well, after all Mrs. Pankhurst is due here in Chicago tomorrow morning and her meeting is Sunday. The Auditorium has been sold out and altogether it looks as if she would have a great reception. Raymond and I are giving a luncheon for her on Monday at the City Club.

I am leaving on November 6th for Seattle where I am to be a delegate to the American Federation of Labor convention. My address there will be C/o Mrs. E. M. Rininger, 22 Adrian Court, Seattle, Washington. Do send me a letter out there and let me know your plans. I know I will be terribly homesick so far away from home and I have to be there for the entire two weeks of the convention because of many important matters concerning our League which are to be considered.

With much, much love,

Devotedly,

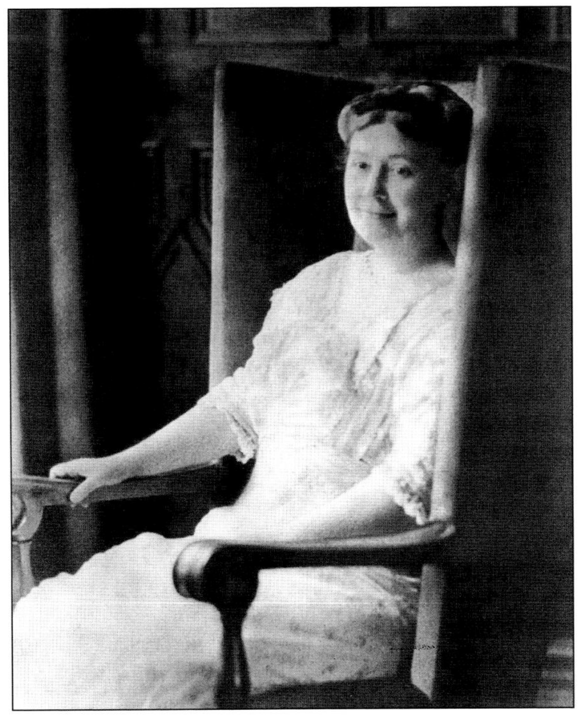

May Mann Jennings, born in 1873, the daughter of a wealthy Hernando businessman, became the wife of William Sherman Jennings, governor of Florida; her husband, who practiced law in Brooksville, was able to return to Brooksville for his law practice between legislative sessions. She was president of the Florida Federation of Women's Clubs. A 1985 biography referred to her as "Florida's genteel activist." Already a tireless suffragette, after her husband's untimely death in 1920, she advocated for child welfare reform, mental health, conservation, and prison reform, traveling the state. Many consider her greatest contribution to be in conservation as she led the drive to create Royal Palm Park in South Florida; when it was dedicated in 1947, she was on the platform with Pres. Harry Truman. (Florida Memory.)

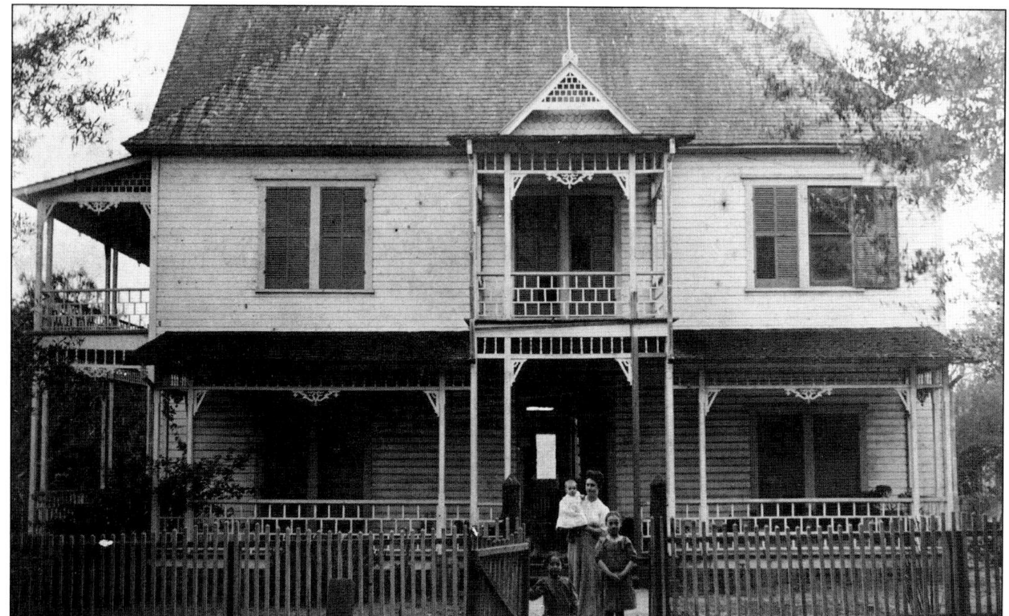

William and May Jennings's beautiful Queen Anne/Colonial Revival home at 48 Olive Street in Brooksville, Florida, is pictured in 1890. The Jenningses were married on May 12, 1891. A native of New York, May was the daughter of Austin S. Mann and attended St. Joseph's Academy in St. Augustine, where she graduated first in her class. "Mrs. Jennings takes a very keen and intelligent interest in political affairs," wrote the *Ocala Banner* in 1901. (Florida Memory.)

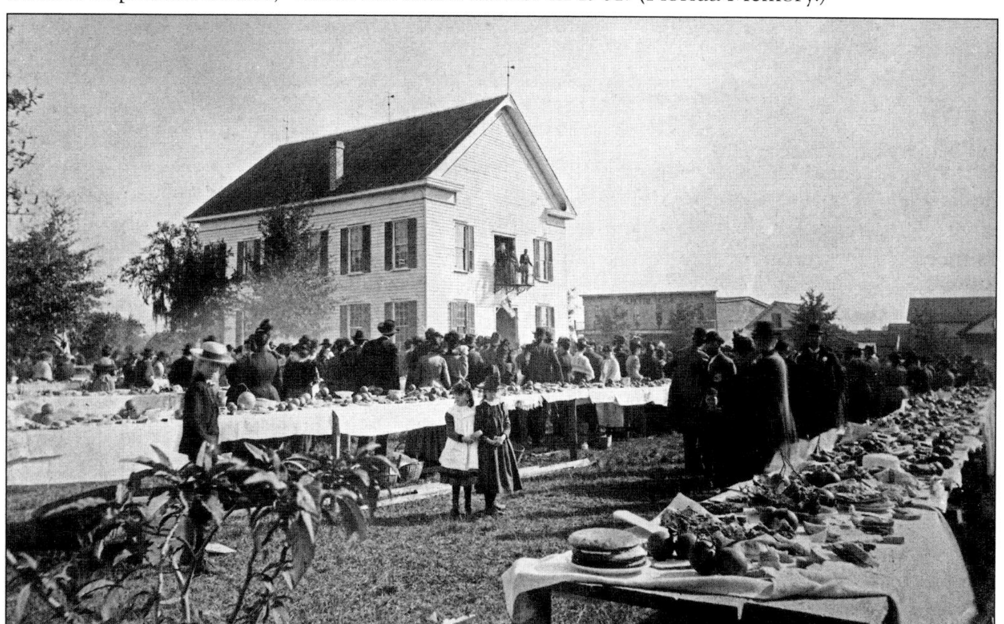

This celebration at the Jennings house in Brooksville was well attended. William Jennings served as the 18th governor of Florida from 1901 to 1905. In a speech for the candidacy for officer of the Federation of Women's Club and dressed in the signature black of her recent widowhood in May 1920, May Jennings said to the woman's club audience, "Do not underestimate your value in any movement." (Florida Memory.)

Three

On the Shoulders of Movers and Shakers

On the shoulders of the brave suffragettes, a new generation of women emerged. They were ready to tackle reform that had not previously been formally recorded nor often undertaken by women. Although barriers remained, women sought professional training and ran for governmental office while exploring new arenas in Tampa Bay. Trailblazing involved risk-taking, and the examples in this chapter were gutsy in many spheres—endangerment, physical labor, entrepreneurship, professions such as medicine and law, and leadership at the local, state, and national levels.

Space limits the women who could be chronicled as trailblazers. Undoubtedly, the reader will reflect upon role models—perhaps a scientist such as Lena Smithers Hughes, who worked on the development of the Valencia orange budwood strain, which accounted for a large percentage of the state's citrus crop prior to the plight of citrus greening disease. Or is it valor, such as that of Dorcas Bryant, who persevered through Reconstruction and tended the ill in need? One may ponder the trailblazer who was a first, such as Gwendolyn Miller, the earliest Black woman elected to the Tampa City Council, or Lillyan Dee Neusner, the first female president of Temple Schaarai Zedek Congregation. Four rabbis spoke at Neusner's memorial, and the *Tribune* proclaimed in its headline, "Lillyan Neusner Blazed Trails with Devotion and Outspokenness."

These trailblazers highlighted and the extraordinary torchbearers share raw courage, mental fortitude, tenacity, and love of all nature of learning.

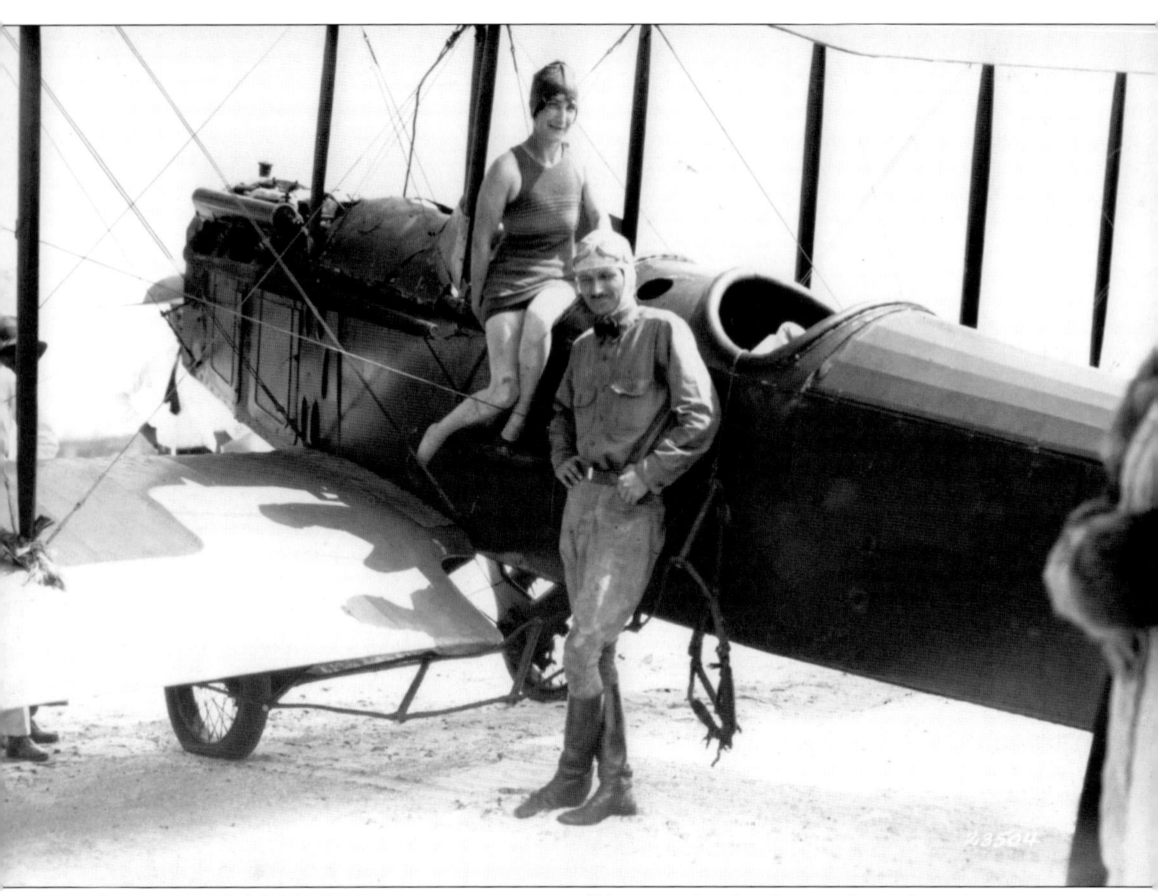

Born in 1886, Mable Cody spent years as a trailblazer and risk-taker as she did acrobatic stunts that included wing-walking and daredevil parachuting in a world-renowned air circus. She became known for her signature move in which she leaped from various vehicles (automobiles, trains, motorcycles, boats, and surfboard) at high speed and was propelled into an airplane. The move was first perfected in late 1921, just a year after women won the right to vote. As a metaphorical symbol of the courage of women emerging into the world of work, Cody epitomized unimaginable grit and relentless adventure. In the 1920s, a visit to her show was a transforming experience, as most spectators had not set eyes on an airplane. (Florida Memory.)

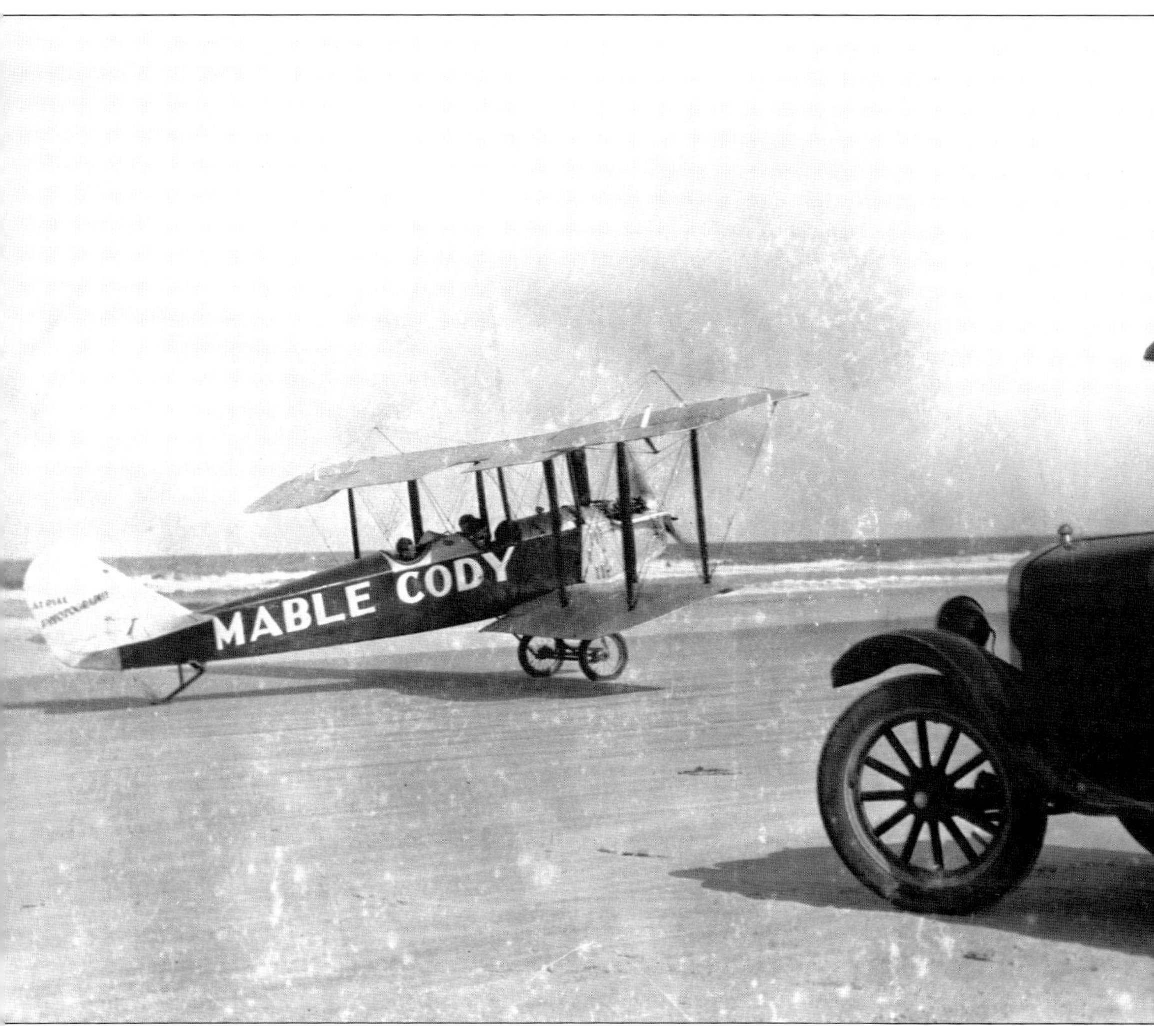

In 1927, Mable Cody was the rage in Tampa Bay as she made 113 attempts at Davis Islands to seize a rope from a moving surfboard and propel herself into an airplane. Jerry McLeod, a publicist for the Davis Islands organization, said, "Cody was black and blue from the relentless attempts." Describing her incredible fortitude, he explained, "Cody walked along the wings of the Flying Jennies, then would slide down the side of the fuselage. After she worked her way down to the spreader bar between the landing wheels, she would hang by her fingers from the bar while the biplane zoomed close to the crowd." Unapologetically a feminist, she donned pants, boots, and goggles for her array of stunts and overlooked the backlash and naysayers from her own gender while she persevered with sheer joy. This photograph shows Cody with her pilot Don C. McMullen. (Burgert Brothers Collection, Tampa–Hillsborough County Public Library.)

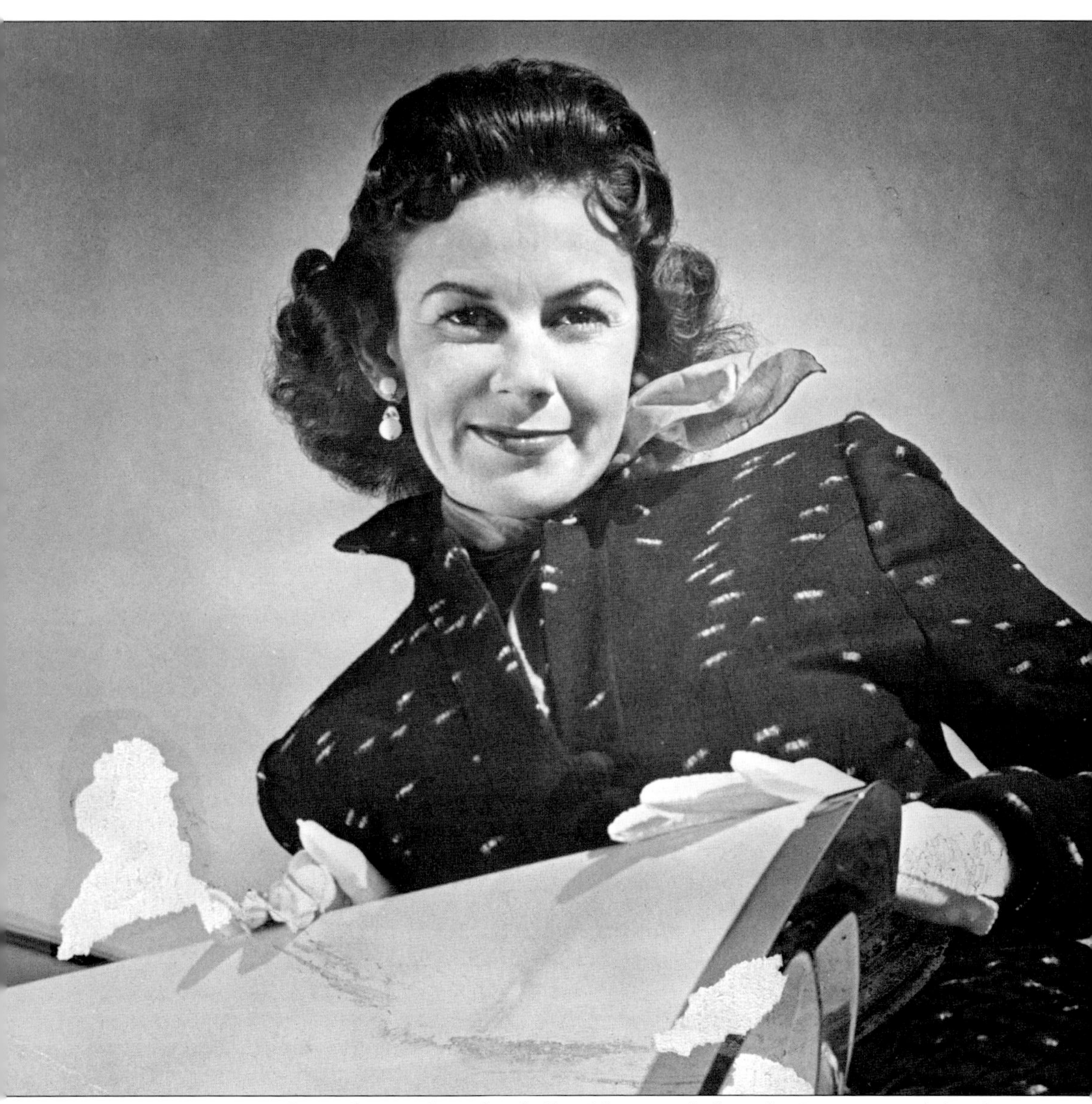

As a competitive pilot and a member of 10 halls of fame, including the International Aerobatic Hall of Fame, Betty Skelton set a series of women's records for light planes, among them reaching 29,050 feet in a Piper Cub at an airfield in Tampa in 1951. Holding the aerobatic flight championship in 1948, 1949, and 1950, Skelton's plane *Little Stinker* remains on display at the Smithsonian Institution. Active in air shows, Skelton toured the country doing stunts. "I considered it an art," she said, "and I spent a great deal of time trying to convince people that it was not simply diving to thrill a crowd, to make a lot of noise and to put out a lot of smoke. It was an art that took many thousands of hours to perfect." Later, she worked with Bill France Sr., a founder of NASCAR, testing and racing stock cars. As a test pilot for vehicles, she also served as a national spokesperson for Chevrolet. (Florida Memory.)

ANNIE JOE LAW, LL.B.,
BROOKSVILLE, FLORIDA.
"JOE."

Secretary-Treasurer Law Class, Junior and Senior Years; Secretary-Treasurer Kent Club, Spring, '15. Two years at Stetson.

"She began alone—a woman of the law is she."

The only lady member of our class, the fourth to graduate from Stetson. Joe, we all love and adore you.

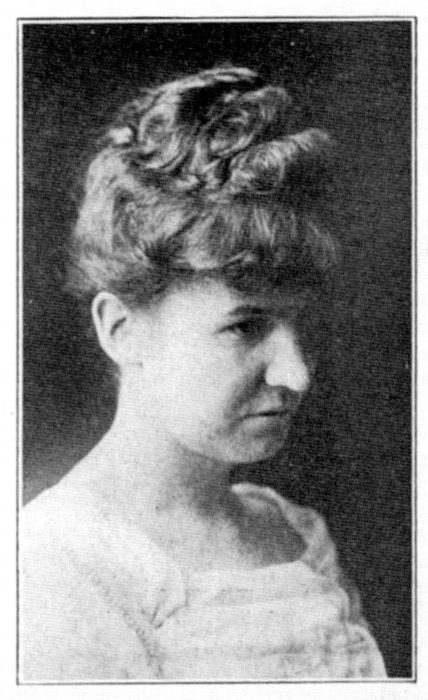

Annie Joe Law was the first female county attorney in Hernando in the 1920s. She was a 1915 graduate of Stetson Law School, the only woman in her class, and the fourth woman to graduate from the institution. Secretary-treasurer of her graduating class, her fellow class members wrote, "we all love and adore you." To have earned the respect of her male colleagues in this early era says much about her ability to navigate paths rarely trod previously. (Author's collection.)

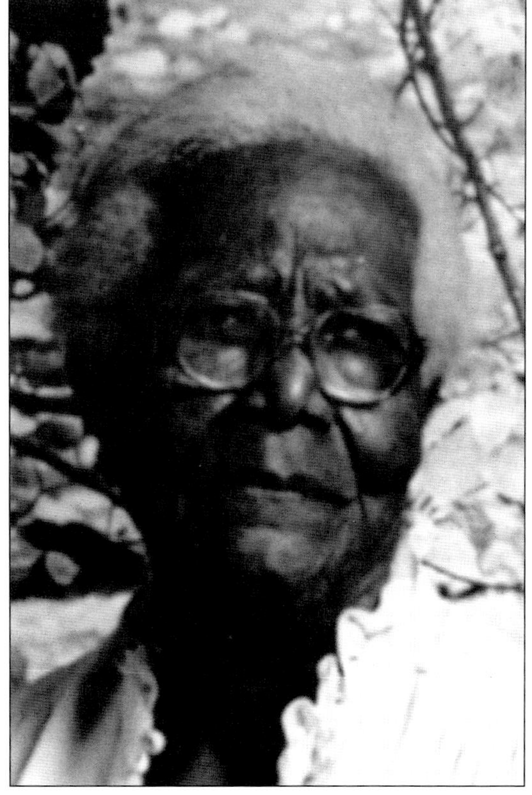

Mary T. Brown Cash, Florida's first African American registered nurse, worked in the office of Dr. Mack Ramsey Winton in Tampa. He noticed her quick wit and intelligence and assisted her with her application to St. Agnes College of Nursing in Raleigh. Later, Cash worked at the Clara Frye Hospital and Tampa General. She also served as a nurse and midwife for the Barnum & Bailey Circus. (Hillsborough County.)

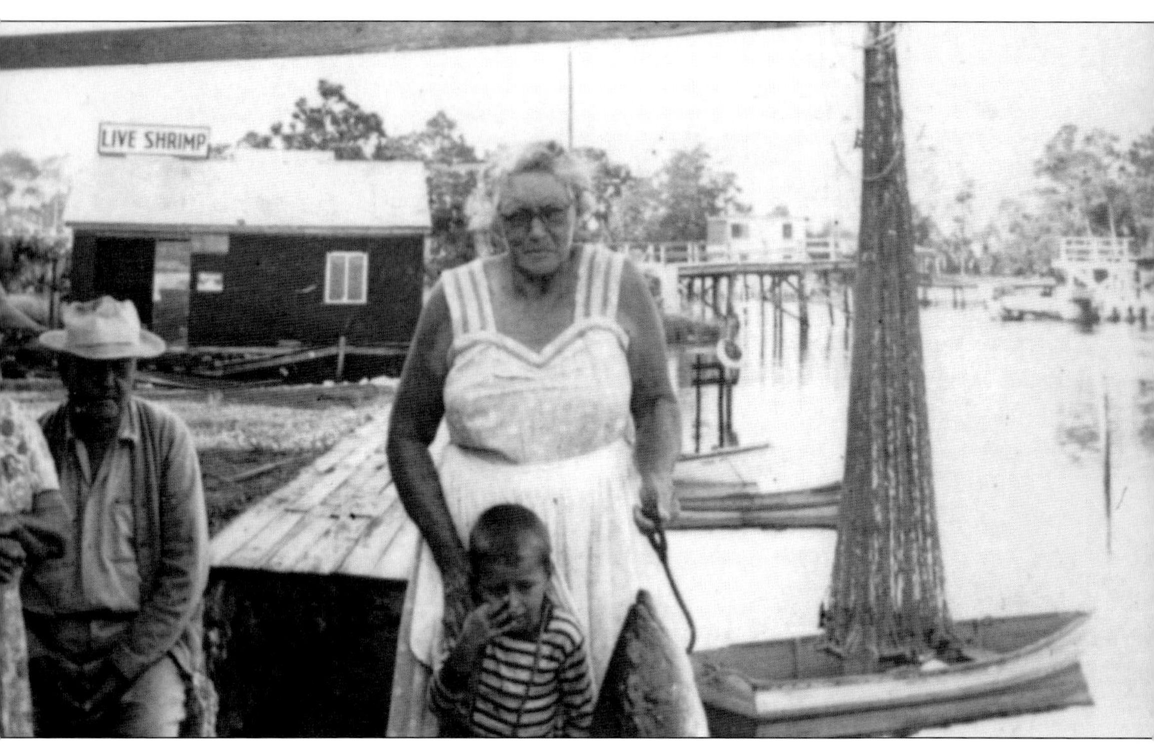

Susan M. Page Clark served on Port Richey's city council in the 1920s, and according to her grandniece Susan Ecksein, who portrayed her in a historical reenactment at a 2005 Founder's Day event, she was the first woman president of the council. As her son David "Hap" Clark gathered his family at his home in 1973 in New Port Richey for the christening of his three-month-old daughter, her namesake, he proudly proclaimed that Susan Page Clark was among the pioneer residents who first settled in Brooksville but then discovered the beauty of Port Richey, built on the banks of the Pithlachascotee River. (Jeff Miller.)

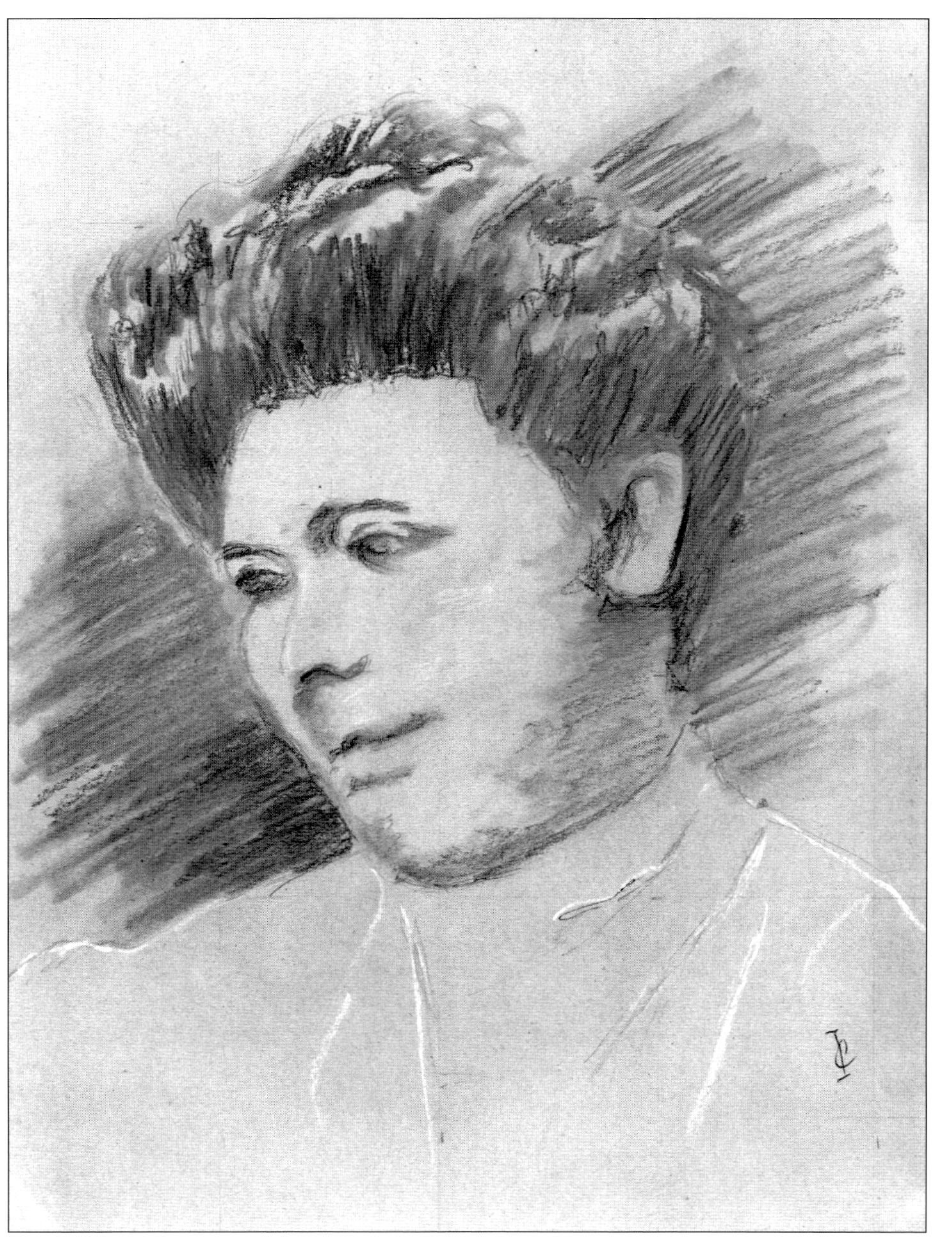

Clara C. Frye, honored at Tampa's Riverwalk Hall of Fame, was of Native American descent and trained as a nurse in Chicago and Montgomery. When she moved to Tampa in 1901, she was concerned that the medical facilities posted "whites only," and that medical treatment for patients of color was deficient and challenging to obtain. She began treating patients at her own home at 1615 Lamar Avenue in Tampa Heights, even performing operations on her dining room table. In 1923, Frye purchased a building on her street and turned it into a hospital that served patients regardless of their race or income level. The City of Tampa purchased Frye's hospital just five years later and it was renamed the *Tampa Negro Hospital*. After Frye's death in 1936, a new hospital for people of color was built on Union Street and named Clara Frye Memorial Hospital. This drawing is from an interpretation of a photograph that appeared in the *Colored American Magazine* in 1907. (Sketch by Clinton Inman.)

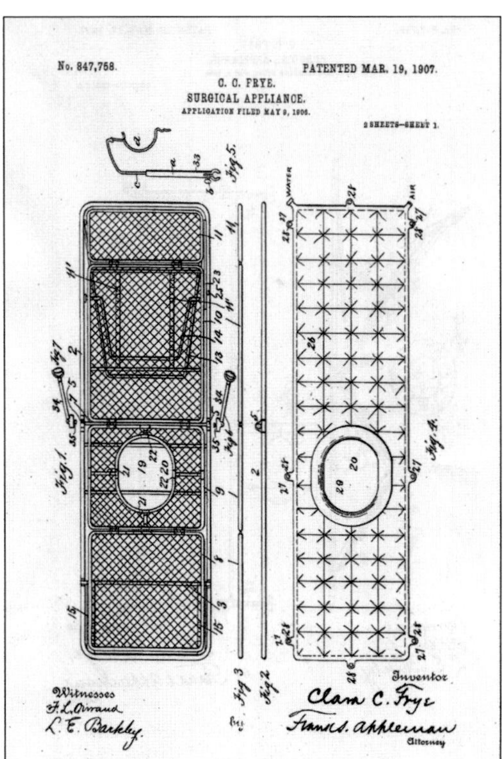

Little known, Frye was also an industrious inventor and perfected a sophisticated hospital bed. Patent No. 847, 758, issued on March 19, 1907, states, "Be it known that I, Clara C. Frye . . . have invented certain new and useful improvements in Surgical Appliances . . . a combination chair and bed." (USF.)

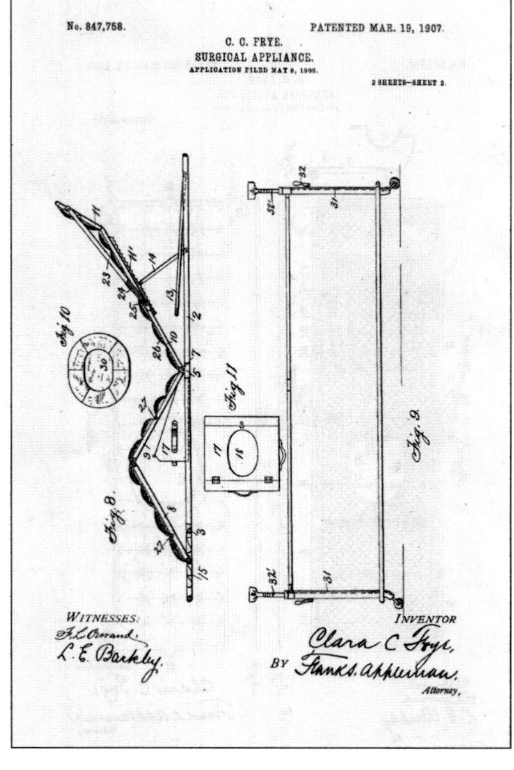

At a time when women of color were not allowed to participate in business or mainstream society, Frye courageously opened a hospital bed factory that operated for nearly 30 years in Tampa. Her sophisticated hospital bed was particularly perfected for obstetrical care. (USF.)

Mary Lou Baker, the second woman to run for the Florida House of Representatives, was most known for the Woman's Emancipation Act. While at Stetson Law, as the only female student in the class of 1938, she won a prize for her essay on civil rights. With the Married Women's Rights Law, married women were given the right to manage their separate property, enter contracts, and sue. Conveying property and executing documents had previously been the domain of their husbands or fathers, and this allowed women to enter partnerships. (Florida Memory.)

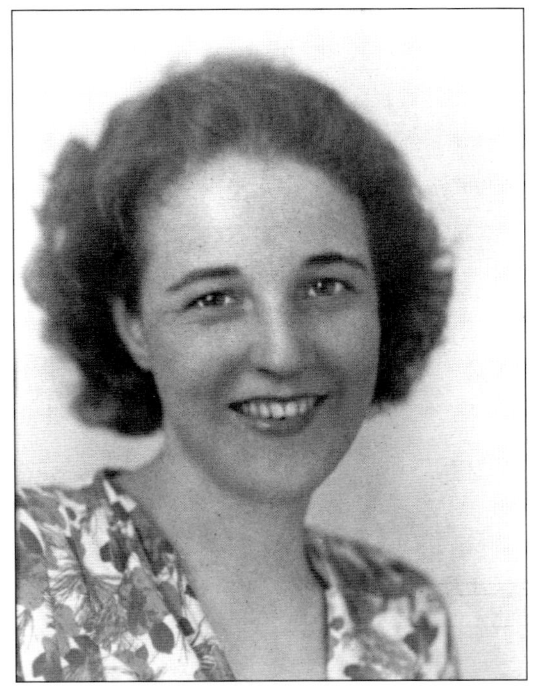

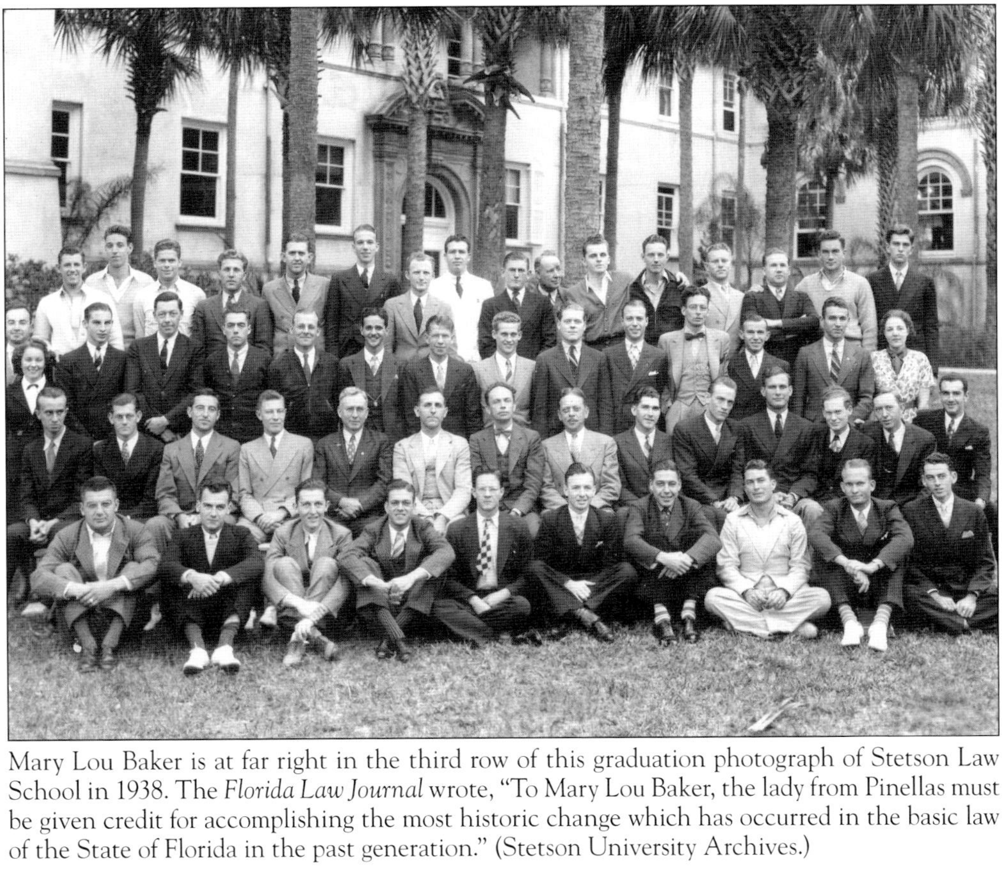

Mary Lou Baker is at far right in the third row of this graduation photograph of Stetson Law School in 1938. The *Florida Law Journal* wrote, "To Mary Lou Baker, the lady from Pinellas must be given credit for accomplishing the most historic change which has occurred in the basic law of the State of Florida in the past generation." (Stetson University Archives.)

St. Petersburg Times

Mary Lou Baker Defends Use Of Maiden Name

Campaign technicalizing, first noted in the senate race, spread yesterday to the Group 3 house race, with word that Rep. Mary Lou Baker might face challenge of the use of her maiden name in qualifying for re-election and hence on the ballot. She registered and qualified at Clearwater as Mary Lou Baker. It was commented in political discussion that her name now is Mary Lou Matthews.

"This was brought up when I was elected two years ago," said Miss Baker yesterday, "but I was not challenged on it. I did, however, seek opinions from high authorities and have no doubt that in case of challenge the courts would uphold me.

"Mary Lou Baker is the name under which I am best known. That is the main principle involved. If I use that name on the ballot, there can be no confusion of identity. People cannot be under any misapprehension as to whom they are voting for."

In legal practice and public life Miss Baker has generally gone under her maiden name. She is so listed in the St. Petersburg city and telephone directories, but has appeared in the Clearwater city directory as Mary Lou Matthews. She is the wife of Capt. Seale H. Matthews.

A trailblazer, at reelection in 1944, Mary Lou Baker was criticized for keeping her maiden name. She replied, "The purpose of a name is to designate an individual and it may even be considered unsportsmanlike for me to use the name of my husband upon the ballot and thereby borrow from the goodwill established by the name of Captain Seale H. Mathews." (*Tampa Bay Times*.)

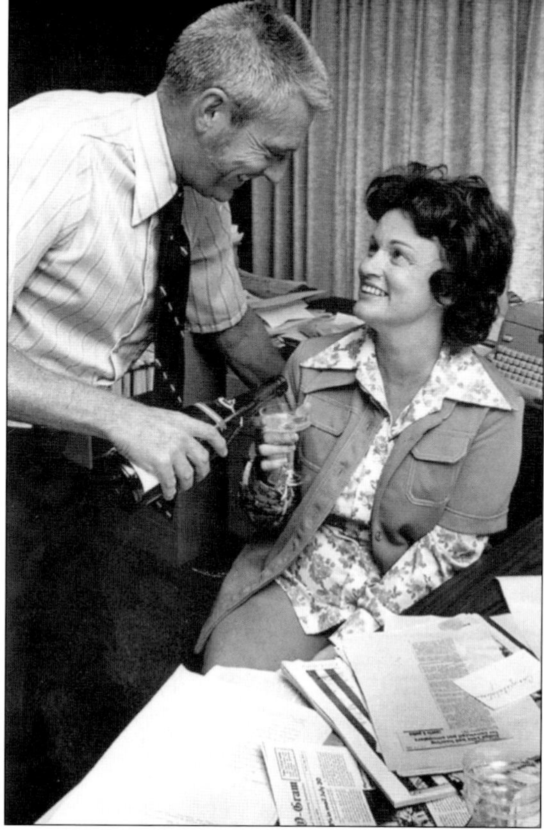

A trailblazer journalist who acted heroically to protect the ethics of her profession, *Times* reporter Lucy Morgan refused to divulge confidential sources in a local government corruption case and was held in contempt of court. Morgan relentlessly appealed the case, and during three excruciating years, she held fast that she would face the consequences to stand by her ethical convictions. She even remembered that her children worried about whether their mother would be going to jail. On July 30, 1976, however, Judge Joseph Hatchett of the Florida Supreme Court wrote that the First Amendment shields reporters from government coercion. Morgan said it left her "with a renewed faith in the people around us and in the courts of Florida." (Florida Memory.)

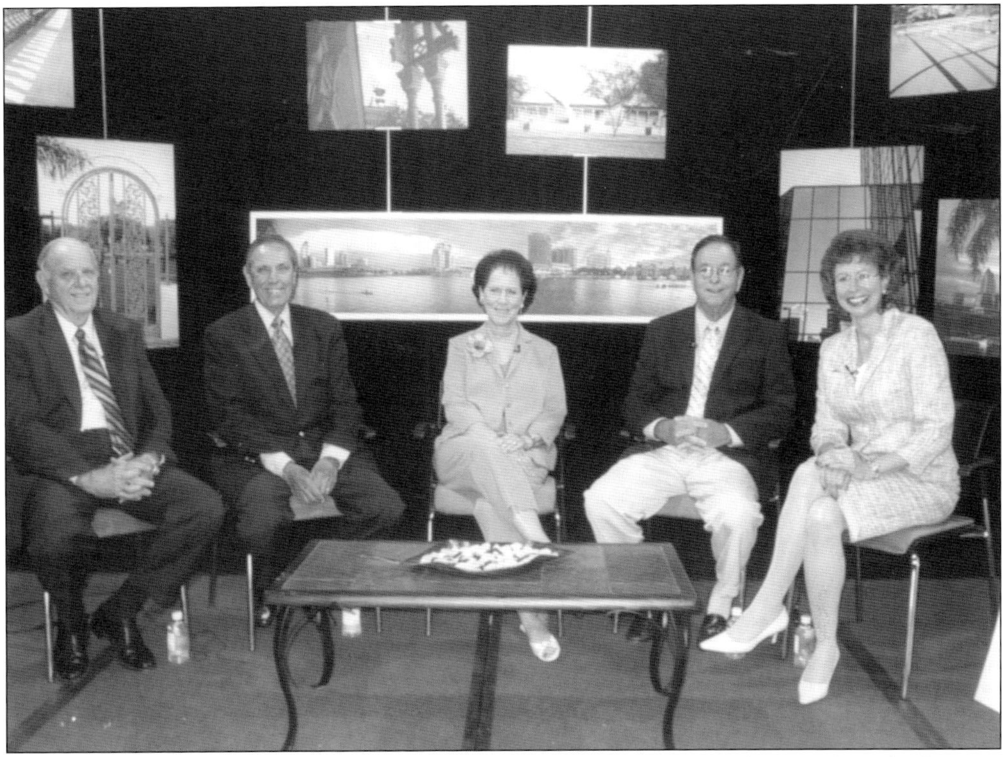

Pamela Dorothy Iorio was the mayor of Tampa from 2003 to 2011. At the age of 26, she became the youngest person elected to the Hillsborough County Commission. She worked tirelessly for her community and was credited with enthusiastically tackling issues head-on, successfully battling drug trafficking and improving mass transit. *People* magazine named her one of 25 women "changing the world" in 2018. Five of Tampa's mayors are shown here. From left to right are William Poe, Robert Martinez, Sandra Freedman, Dick Greco, and Pam Iorio. (Tampa Bay History Center.)

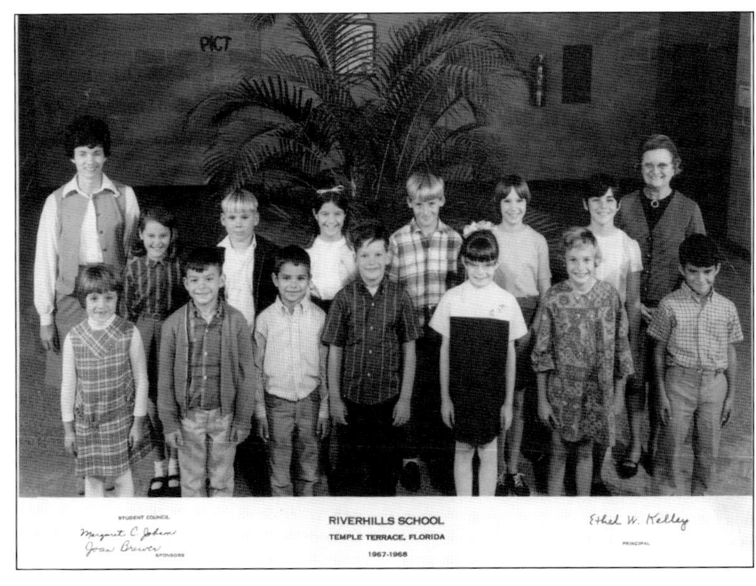

Future mayor Pam Iorio is shown in her Riverhills School class at Temple Terrace in 1967. While mayor, she orchestrated events for the city's hosting of the 2012 Republican National Convention. A big supporter of the arts, she led efforts for Curtis Hixon Park, Riverwalk, and the Tampa Bay History Center. (Tampa Bay History Center.)

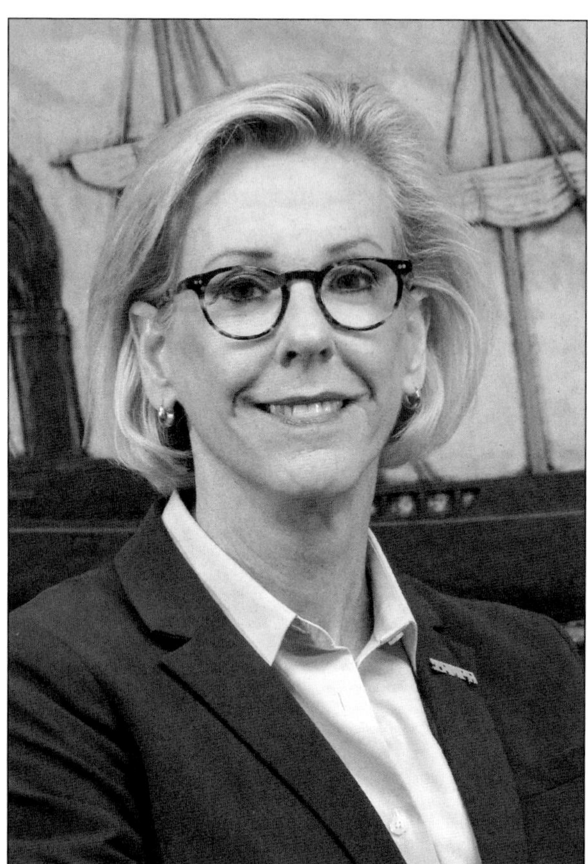

Courageous and innovative, Jane Castor served as the 59th mayor of Tampa. A lifelong community servant, she was a member of the Tampa Police Department for 31 years and became the first female chief of police for the city of Tampa. (City of Tampa.)

Mayor Castor appointed Tampa Bay native Barbara Tripp as the first female Tampa fire chief. A veteran, Tripp served 33 years in fire and rescue and was the 13th Black female fire chief in the country. Cuban immigrant Mechy Fernandez Wright was the first woman firefighter in Tampa, serving as a paramedic and investigator for 20 years. Josephine Rinaldi was the first female volunteer fire fighter in Pasco County. (City of Tampa.)

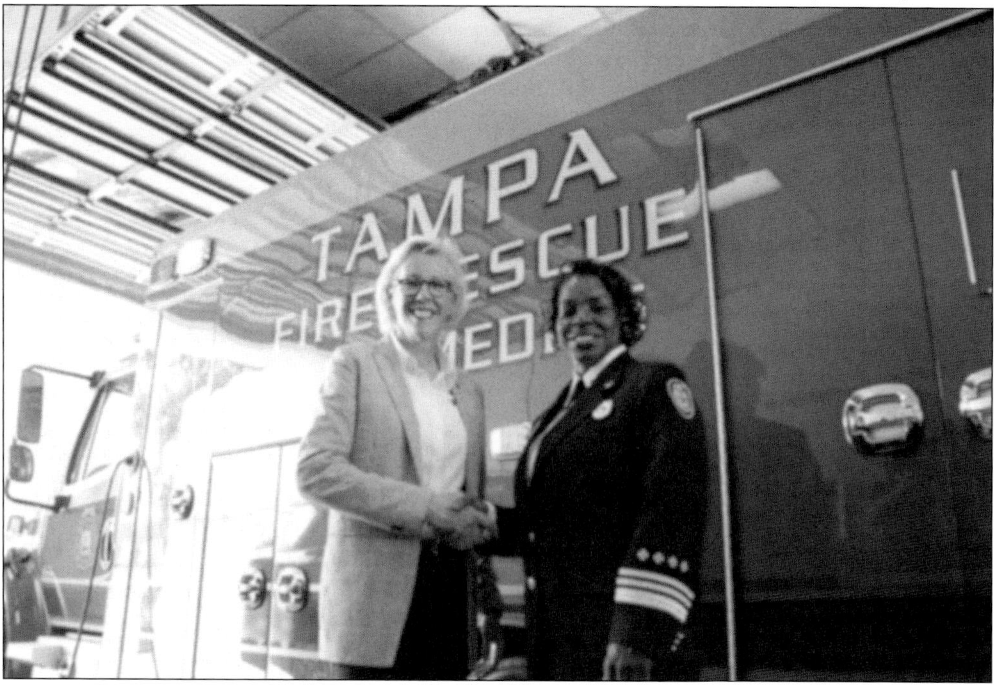

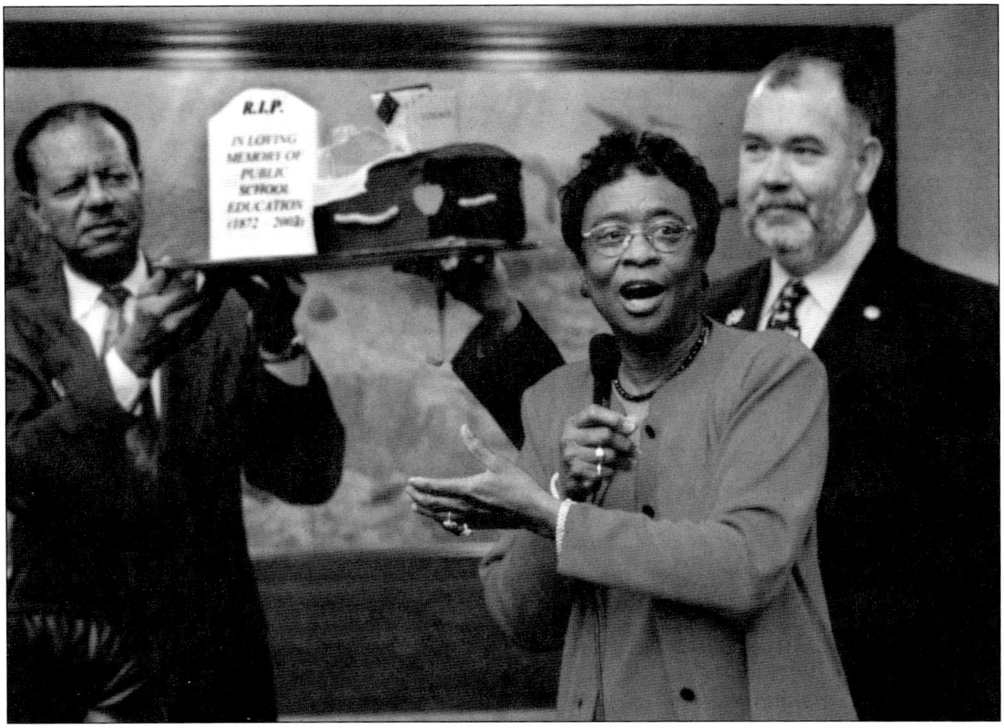

Arthenia L. Joyner from Tampa debated in opposition to inadequate educational funding in 2003 on the Florida House of Representatives floor. Assisting Representative Joyner were Representatives Matt Meadows (left) and Will Kendrick. An attorney and civil rights activist, she was a Florida senator from Tampa Bay for 10 years. She served as Senate minority leader for two of those years. Joyner courageously broke many racial barriers, including being elected president of the National Bar Association. (Mark Foley collection, Florida Memory.)

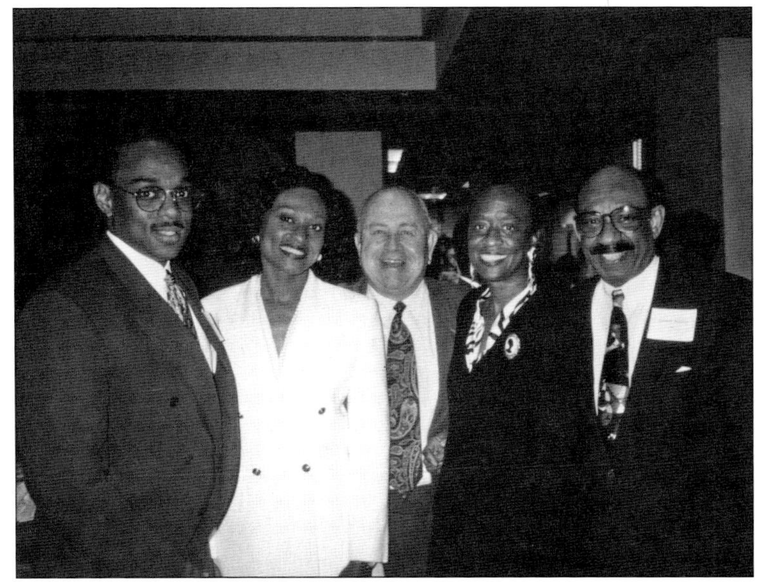

Michael Russell of Atlanta's H.J. Russell Company, Sherlyn Richardson of Tampa's Barnett Bank, Gen. John Paulk, Arthenia L. Joyner of Hillsborough Aviation Authority, and Herman J. Russell, founder and chairman of H.J. Russell, were in discussion and political debate. (Tampa Bay History Center.)

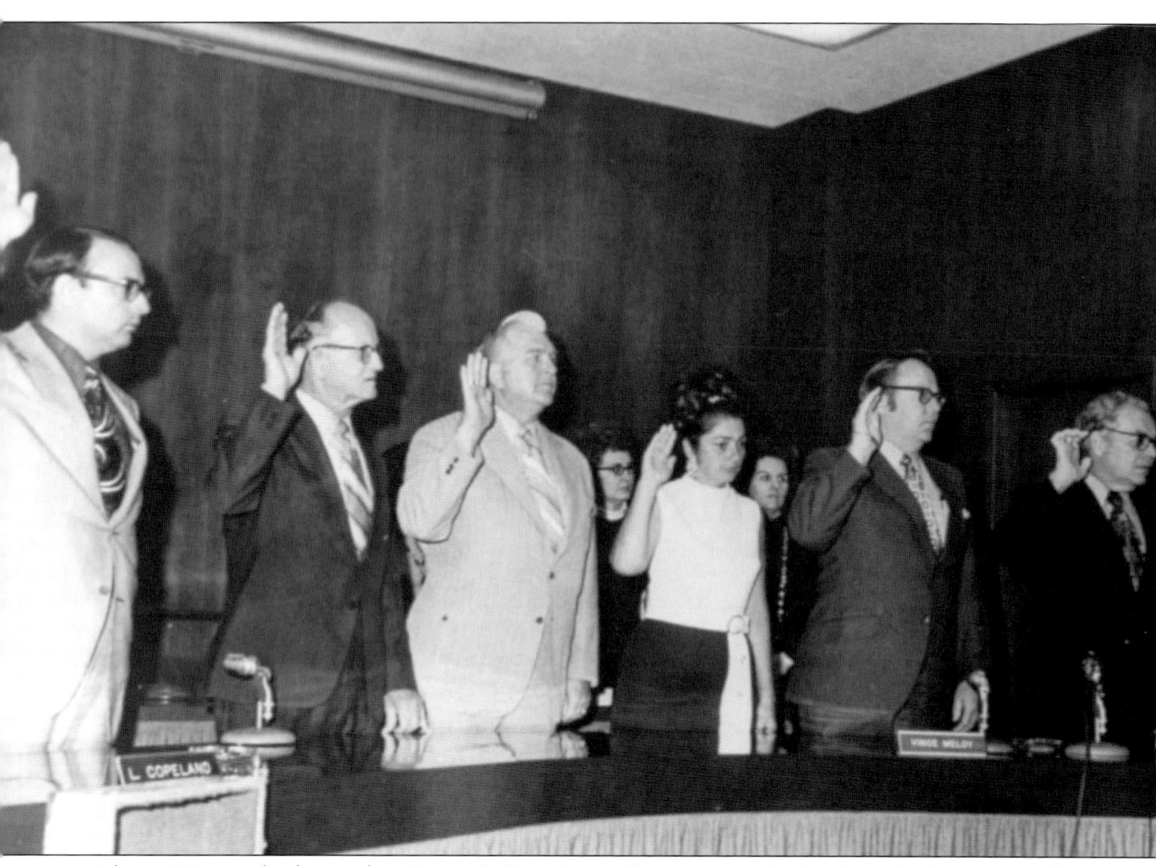

About 280 men had served on Tampa's City Council prior to Catherine Barja's election in 1971. Barja had sought election in 1967 and lost, but persevered. She served as the first woman acting chair pro-tempore. Legally blind, Barja was active in the Hillsborough County Citizens for Disabilities and the Tampa chapter of the National Federation of the Blind. "It was like living in a fishbowl," she recalled in an interview with Tampa city clerk Shirley Foxx-Knowles. "Everybody is watching: 'Is she going to mess up somewhere?' They were just looking for a woman to make a big mistake." She did not have any reluctance to speak her mind, commissioner Joe Chillura said; she identified with the rank and file and was always for the underdog. She also owned a wig shop and showed up at council meetings modeling them—one color at one meeting and another color at the next. "I think she did it just for shock value," Chillura said. (City of Tampa.)

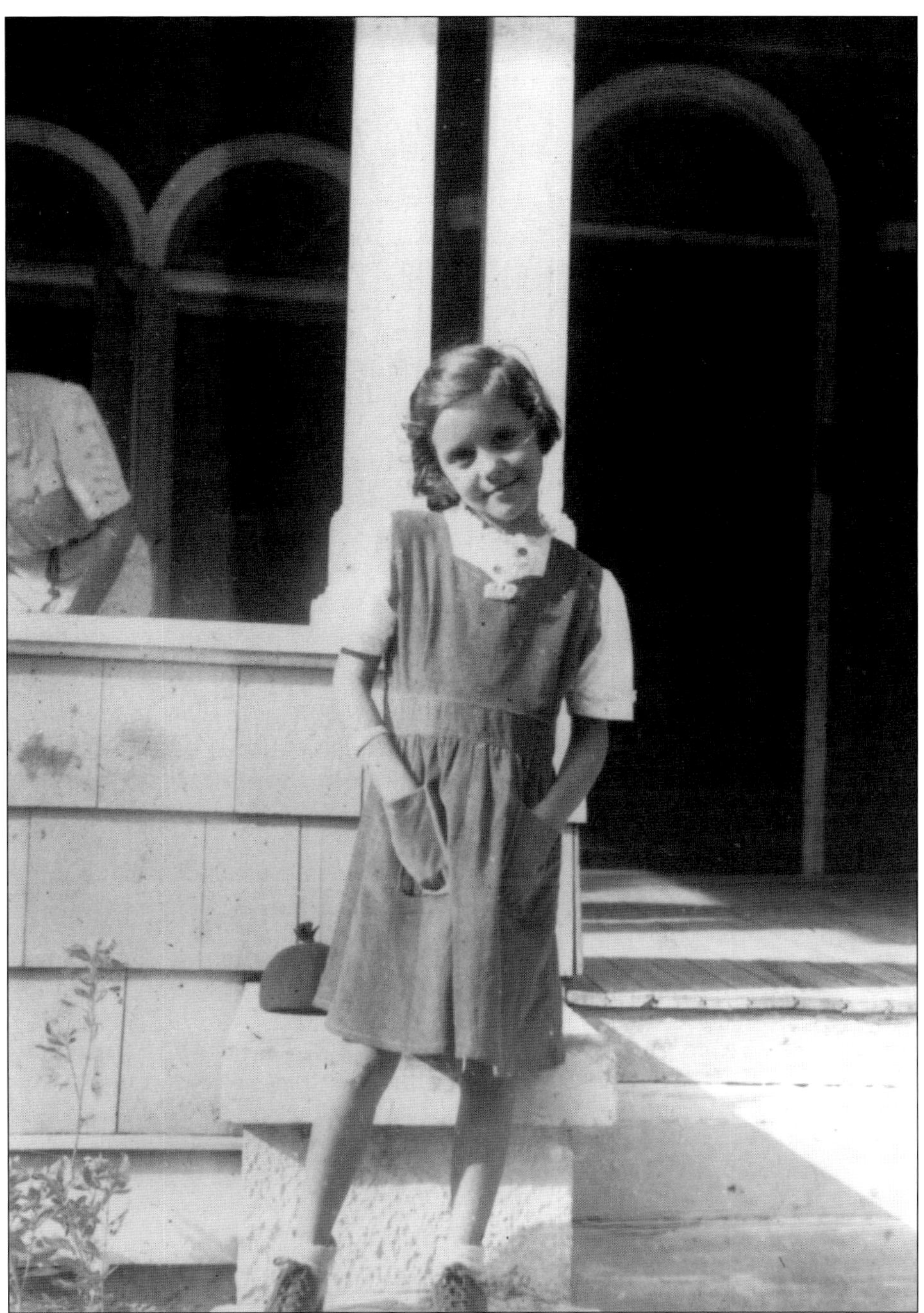

Jan Kaminis Platt is pictured in 1943 at age seven in her native Lakeland, Florida. Platt served as a county commissioner in Hillsborough County and its first woman chair. Over 40 years of public service, she was informally known as "Commissioner No" for her courage to vote no on poorly planned or harmful development. Former mayor Iorio said at her memorial in 2017, "She could always be counted on to be a voice for honest and open government . . . who never wavered from her convictions." Platt said, "Growing up in the 1950s, women weren't supposed to do this sort of thing . . . it was far-fetched to think that a woman could be in public office." After working as a teacher, Platt took the plunge and ran for city council in 1974. (Tampa Bay History Center.)

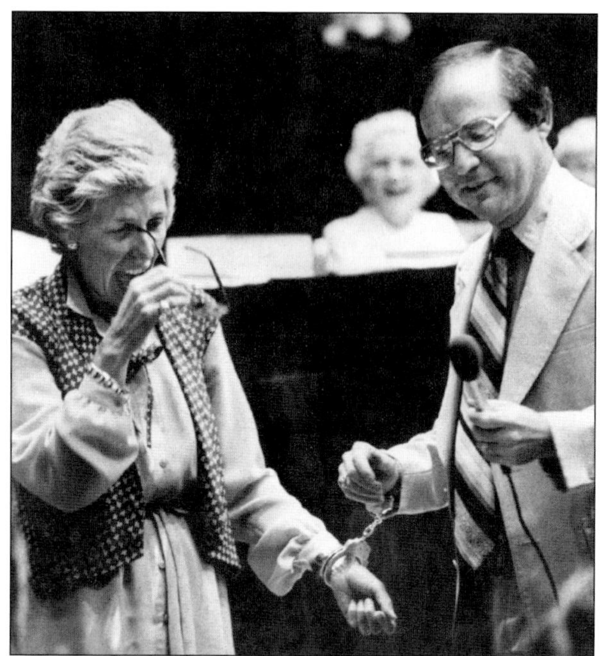

Sen. Pat Collier Frank was handcuffed to Sen. Guy Spicola, both of Tampa, on June 1, 1979, in the Florida legislature. An accompanying note quipped that "until someone finds a key to the handcuffs, Equal Rights Amendment proponents will stand their ground." Frank was the only woman in her Georgetown law class and the first woman in the school. She served on the school board and county commission as well as clerk of the city council. Pat Frank was active with her husband in advocating for Cuban workers in the cigar industry and started Sociedad MartiMaceo for race relations. (Don Dughi Collection, Florida Memory.)

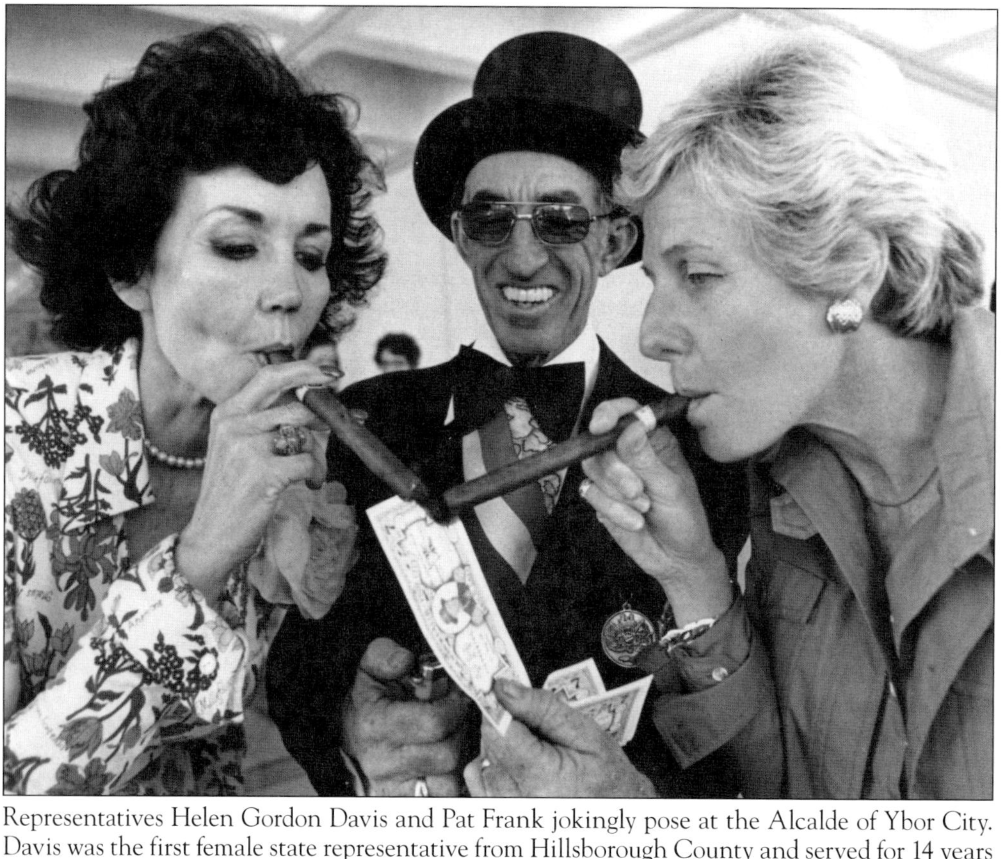

Representatives Helen Gordon Davis and Pat Frank jokingly pose at the Alcalde of Ybor City. Davis was the first female state representative from Hillsborough County and served for 14 years in the House, followed by four years in the Senate. (Don Dughi Collection, Florida Memory.)

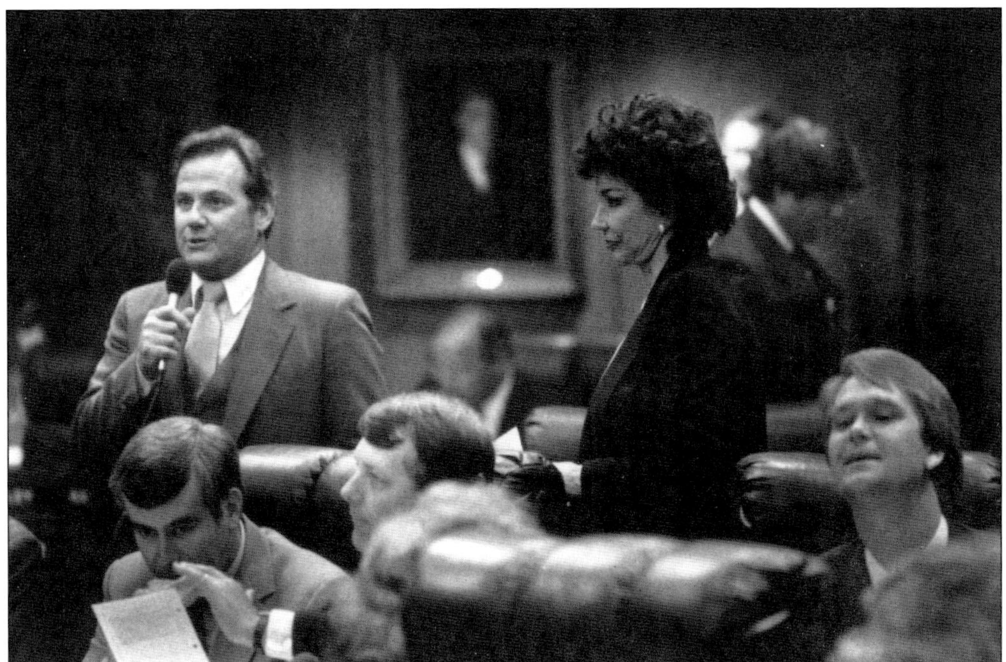

Florida representative Elvin Martinez of District 65 discussed proposed actions regarding the Sunshine Skyway Bridge disaster during a Florida house session, alongside Representative Helen Gordon Davis of District 64, in 1987. Also identified seated in the foreground are Representatives John Morgan (left), John Costgrove (center), and Tom Guston, while Tom Gallagher is standing in the background. Helen Gordon Davis was a tireless advocate of women and minorities in the Florida legislature for 18 years. Raised in Brooklyn and trained as an actress, she was a poised and articulate advocate for equal pay for women and sponsored legislation for displaced homemakers, spouse abuse centers, and much more. (Above, Tampa Bay History Center; below, Florida Memory.)

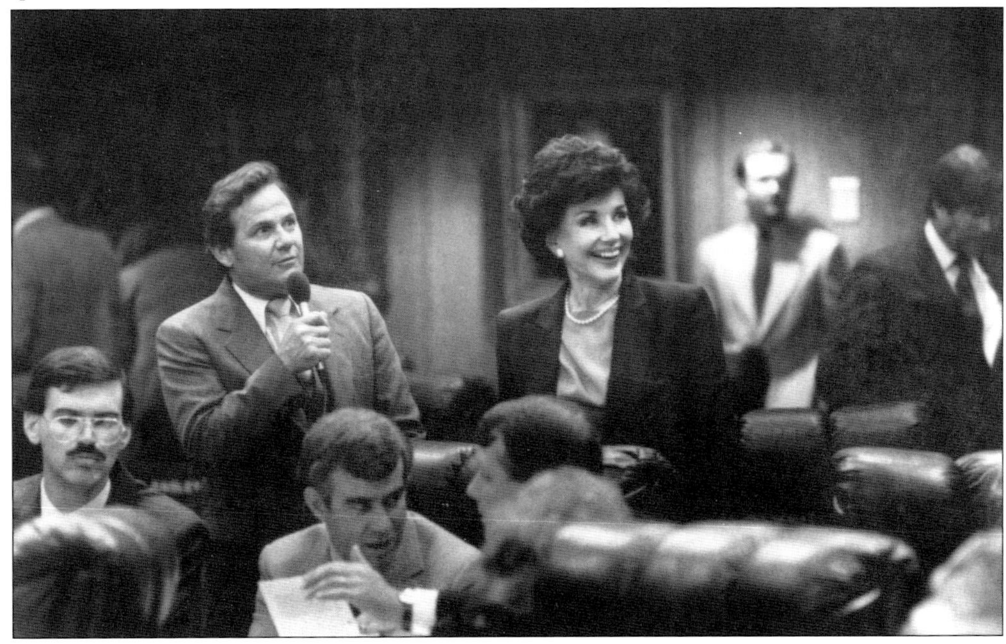

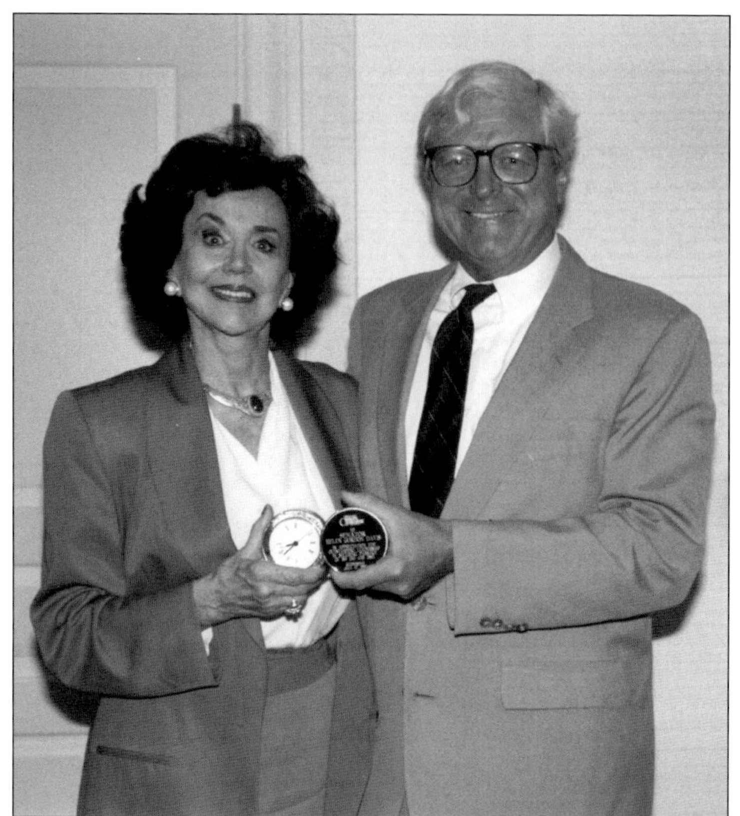

Sen. Helen Gordon Davis and James W. Apthorp are pictured at a Greater Tampa Chamber of Commerce event. (Tampa Bay History Center.)

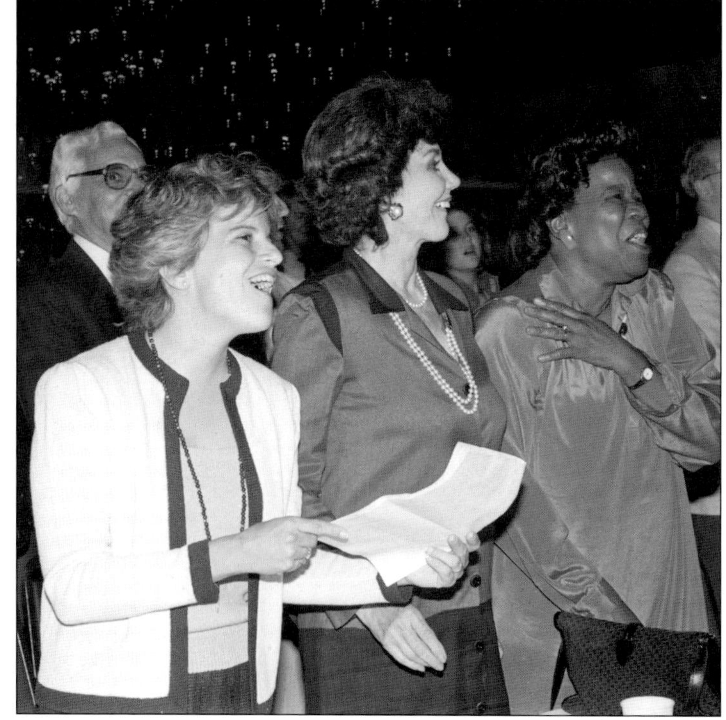

Senator Davis (center), Carrie Pittman Meek (right) and Allen Covington Morris (background) cheer at the Legislative Talent Show in Tallahassee in 1985. Meek won election to the US House of Representatives in 1992, one of the first African Americans to represent Florida in Congress since Reconstruction. Davis was on the House Appropriations Committee, a coveted position, as a first-term lawmaker. (Florida Memory.)

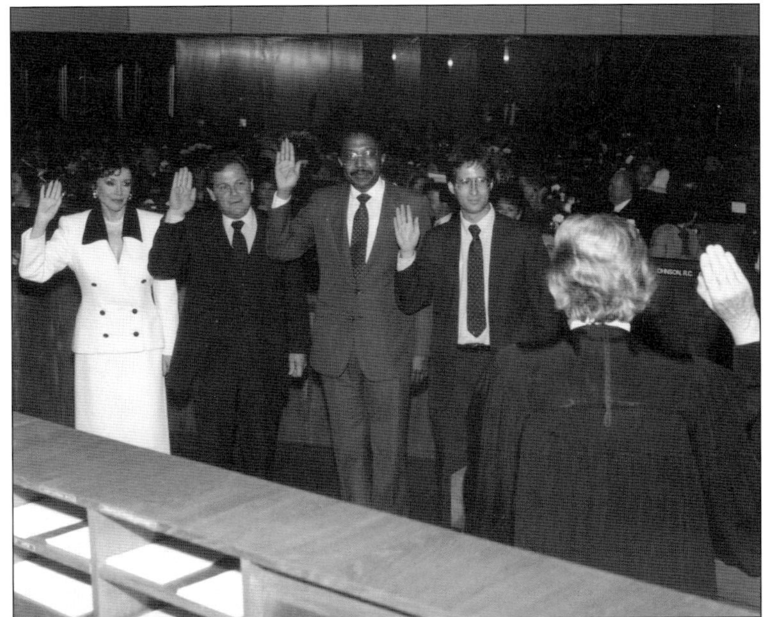

Florida House of Representative members from Hillsborough County are being sworn in for the 1986–1988 term. From left to right are Helen Gordon Davis, Elvin L. Martinez, James T. Hargrett Jr., and Ronald Carl Glickman. (Tampa Bay History Center.)

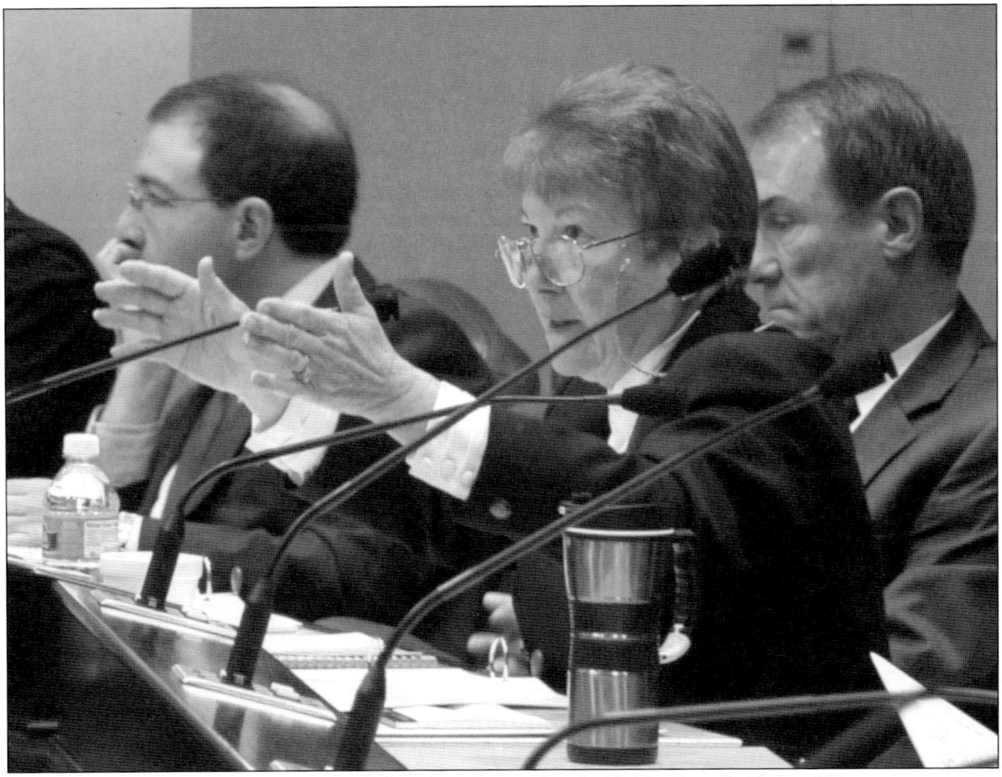

Chair of the Government Accountability Act Council in 2010, Dr. Faye B. Culp of Tampa comments on an issue during the policy council at the state legislature. Culp served on the school board before being elected to the legislature for three terms, serving as majority whip and chair of the joint house and senate committees on technology and as president of the National Organization of Women Legislators. (Photograph by Meredith Hill Geddings, courtesy of Florida Memory.)

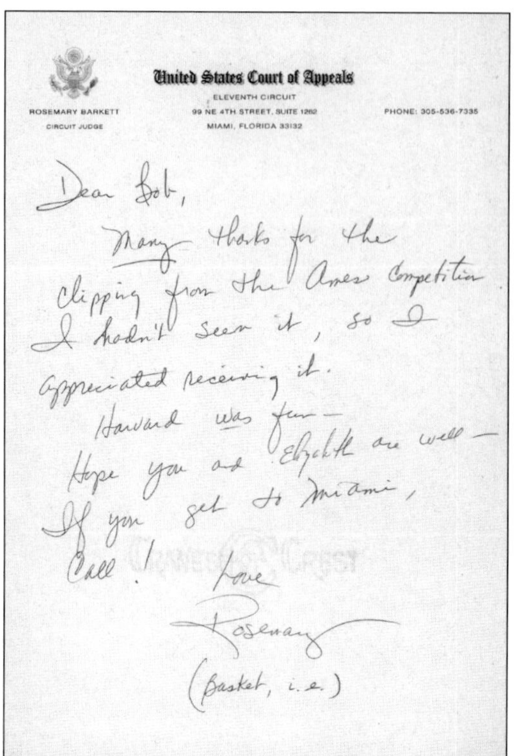

United States Court of Appeals
ELEVENTH CIRCUIT

ROSEMARY BARKETT
CIRCUIT JUDGE

99 NE 4TH STREET, SUITE 1262
MIAMI, FLORIDA 33132

PHONE: 305-536-7335

Dear Bob,

Many thanks for the clipping from the Ames Competition. I hadn't seen it, so I appreciated receiving it.

Harvard was fun—

Hope you and Elizabeth are well—

If you get to Miami, Call!

Love
Rosemary
(Barkett, i.e.)

On the letterhead of the US Court of Appeals, 11th Circuit, Rosemary Barkett, then circuit judge, wrote a thank-you note to the governor, Bob Graham. She later received a nomination to the Florida Supreme Court. (Tampa Bay History Center.)

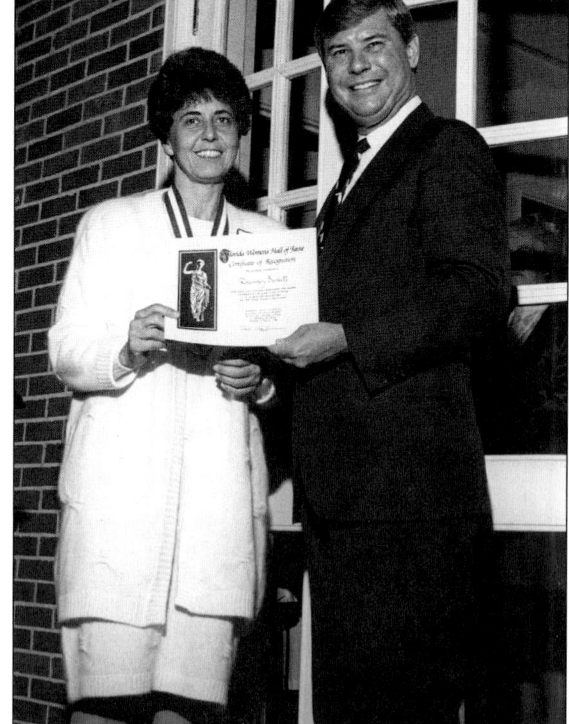

Gov. Bob Graham presented the first woman to serve on the Florida Supreme Court, Rosemary Barkett, with entry into the Florida Women's Hall of Fame at the governor's mansion in Tallahassee in March 1986. (Florida Memory.)

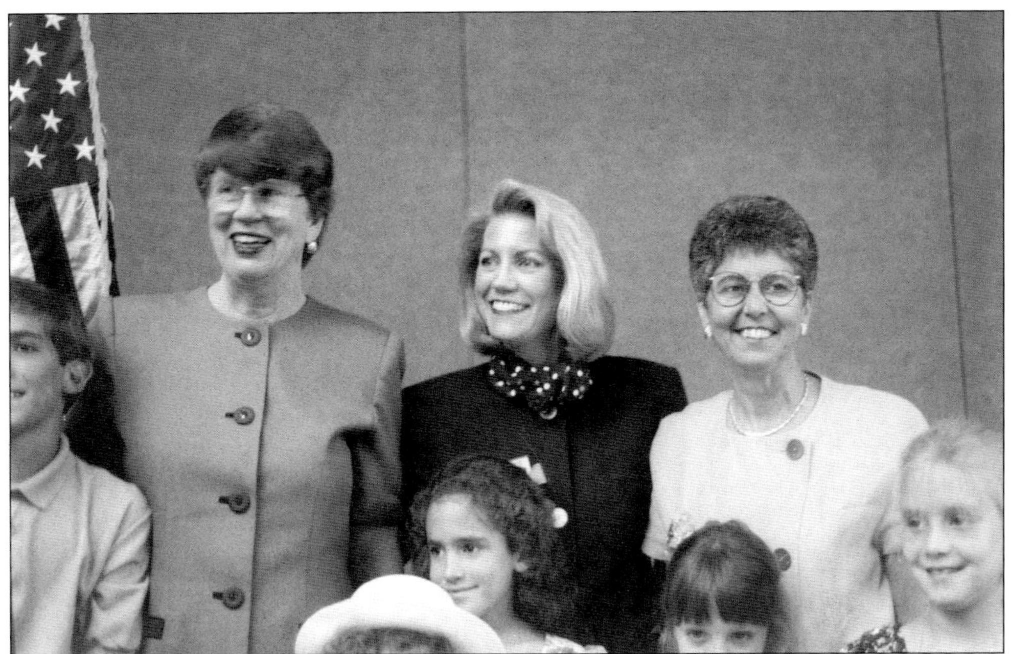

On June 5, 1993, from left to right, Janet Reno, Patricia A Seitz, and Rosemary Barkett attended Seitz's installation as the first woman president of the Florida Bar Association. Reno, a Floridian, was the first woman to serve as attorney general of the United States. Barkett was chief justice and the first woman member of the Florida Supreme Court. Seitz and Reno had been partners at the same law firm. Seitz said, "I remember looking at all the blue suits around the table and being the only woman there." (Florida Memory.)

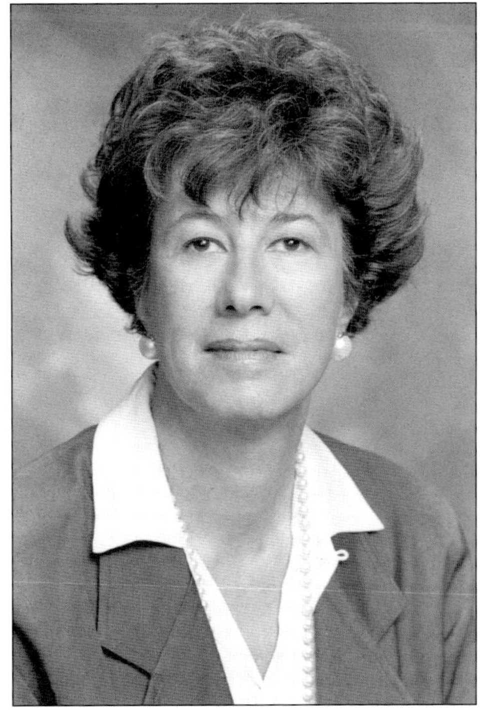

As she zipped around town, Phyllis Henler Busansky was a sight, with her tall frame squeezed into a red Mustang convertible. Busansky was the Hillsborough supervisor of election when she passed away suddenly in June 2009. She had been elected to the commission against great odds in 1988, and was renowned for her work in addressing indigent health care. Collaborating with Jay Wolfson from USF Public Health, they produced a health plan for Hillsborough as the county was losing millions on indigent health care. She later served as the director of the Florida welfare system. "She inspired a generation of people to believe they had a voice in government," said her husband, Sheldon, at the memorial service at her synagogue. (Shelby Bender, East Hillsborough Historical Society.)

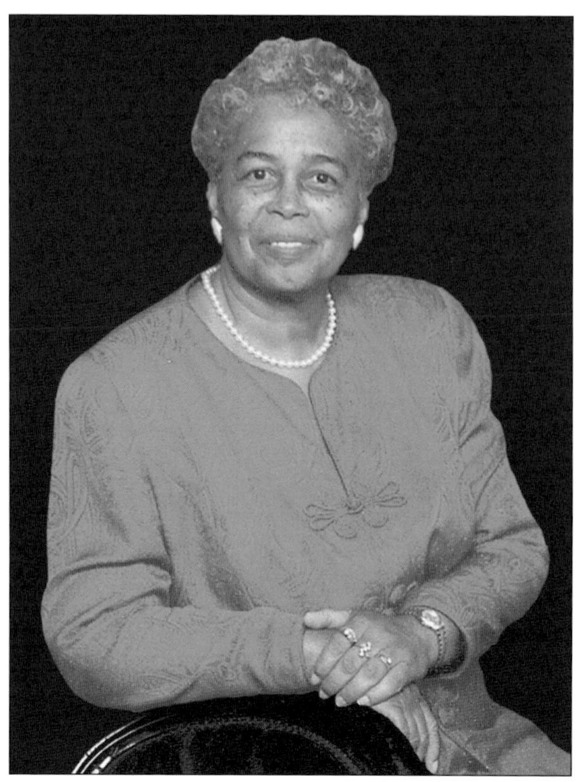

Doris Ross Reddick was the first African American woman elected to the Hillsborough County School Board. A school was named in Reddick's honor. In addition, Dorothea Wynn Edgecomb was in the Tampa school system for 52 years as she began teaching at Harlem Academy where her mother had also taught. Rep. Kathy Castor recognized her in writing in 2016: "Edgecomb was elected to the Hillsborough County School Board in 2004 and re-elected in 2008, where she served as Vice Chair in 2010 and Chair in 2011. She also shared a strong partnership with her distinguished late husband the Honorable Judge George E. Edgecomb." (Clemmie C. Perry.)

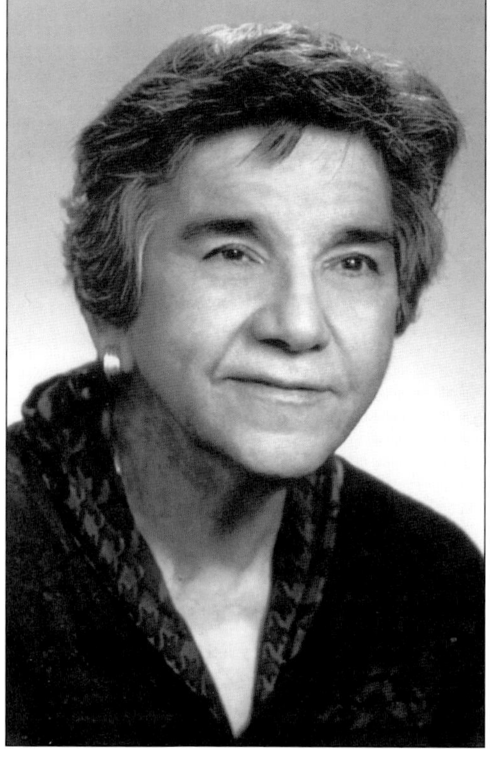

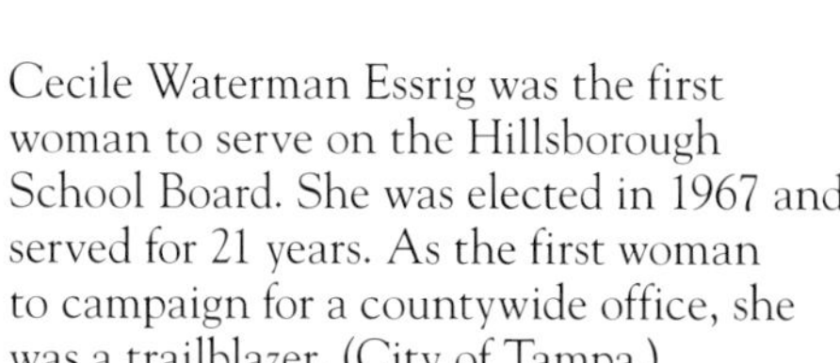

Cecile Waterman Essrig was the first woman to serve on the Hillsborough School Board. She was elected in 1967 and served for 21 years. As the first woman to campaign for a countywide office, she was a trailblazer. (City of Tampa.)

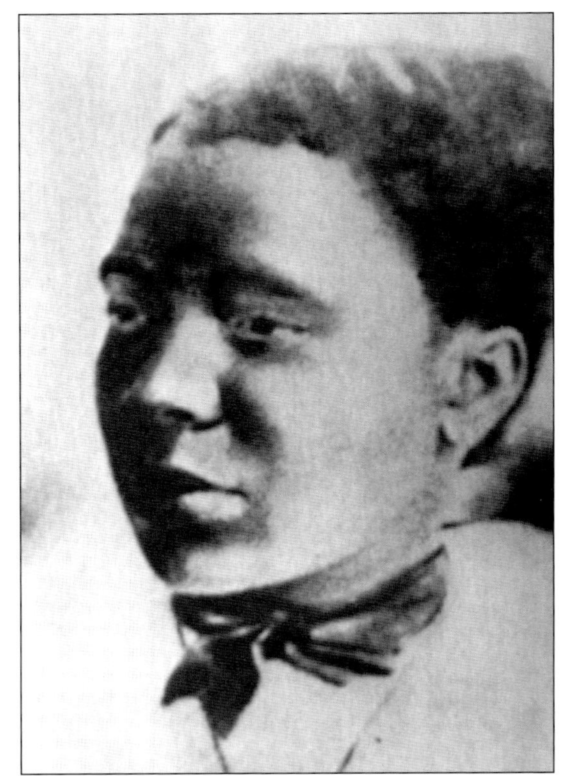

Known as "a bronze woman with a heart of gold," Pauline Pedroso was inducted into the Florida Women's Hall of Fame in 1993. She and her husband, Ruperto, ran an Ybor City boardinghouse, and during the Cuban revolution, she permitted Jose Marti to stay at the center, taking an enormous risk. Born in the Cuban province of Pinar del Rio during the Ten Years' War against Spanish rule, they moved to Havana, then Key West, and eventually Ybor City. The site of the Pedroso boardinghouse where Jose Marti stayed in the 1890s during visits to Ybor City (including his recovery from an assassination attempt in 1892) is now Marti Park. (Florida Memory.)

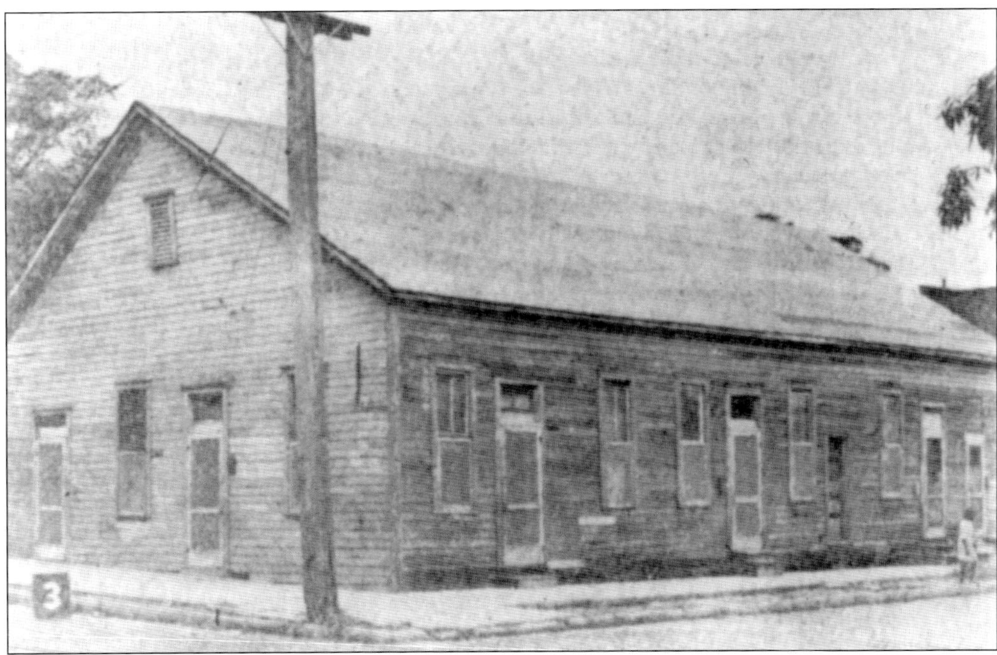

The only surviving photograph of the house and lot known as Marti Park at Thirteenth and Eighth Streets was donated to the Republic of Cuba in 1956 by Paulina Pedroso, three years before the Communist revolution. Pedroso is considered a prominent female leader of the revolution. (Tampa Bay History Center.)

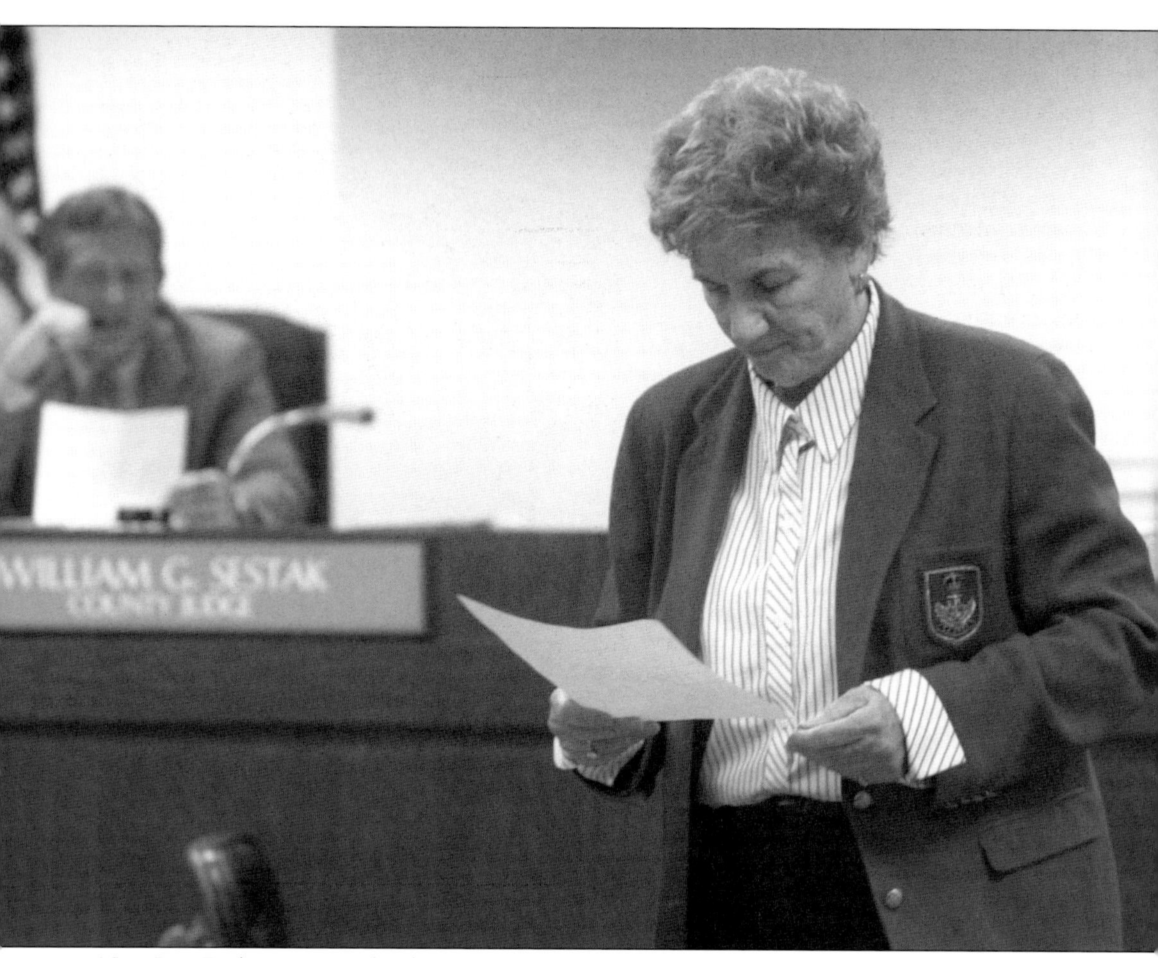

New Port Richey possessed only two female mayors in its history: Debra A. Prewitt from 1992 to 1994, and Wendy Brenner from 2000 to 2002. Nearby Port Richey had Eileen Ferdinand from 1997 to 2000 and Eloise Taylor, who served two nonconsecutive terms of 2000–2004 and 2012–2015. Taylor migrated from Ohio, had a doctorate in political science, and served as the assistant county attorney for Hernando and Pasco and also as Port Richey's city attorney. Lawyer Craig Laporte said, "Taylor was unflappable, and colleagues described her as a trustworthy public servant." Reflecting upon her career, Taylor explained she had wanted to go to law school from her earliest childhood, but in the 1960s, not many women went to law or medical school as education was the accepted field. When she taught political science at Kent State, she even remembered being one of the only female professors. Eventually, she earned a law degree from the University of Akron. A particular joy was hanging out with her two shelties, Polo and Flea Bailey. (Photograph by Fred Bellet, courtesy of the *Tampa Bay Times*.)

"A Plant City girl by birth, Sayde Pearl Gibbs-Martin's love for her community shone bright in every position she undertook," said Elizabeth Edwardson. A beautician who earned two degrees in education and became principal at Gary Elementary and, later, Knights Elementary, she then served as a Plant City commissioner for 15 years and was subsequently elected as the first woman mayor of Plant City for five terms. She was the first African American female mayor in the entire state. Special accolades included serving as president of the Florida League of Cities. "In the eyes of those who knew her, Sadye was an angel, caretaker, hero, leader, pioneer, and visionary," said Edwardson. (Shelby Bender, East Hillsborough Historical Society.)

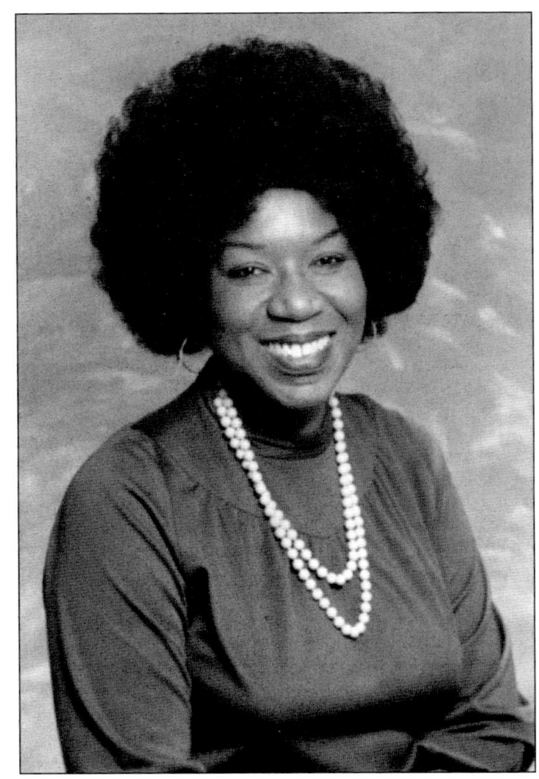

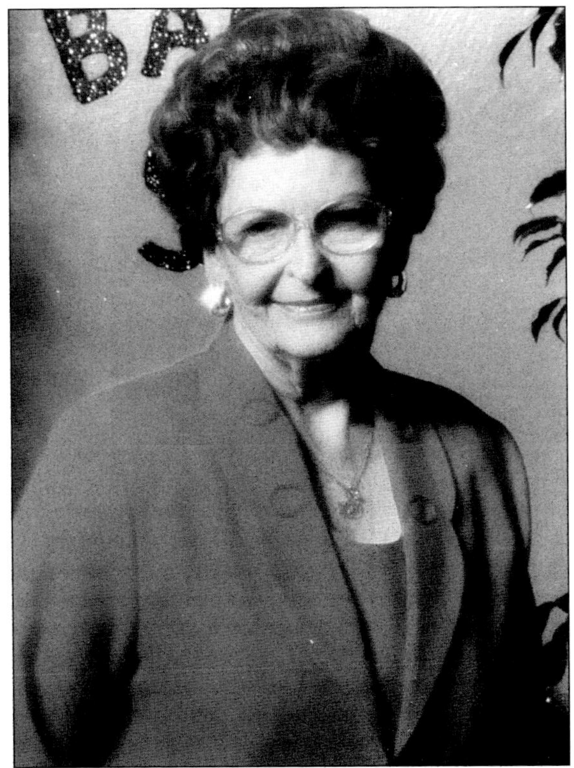

Coined the "Caretaker of Plant City," city manager Nettie Berry Draughon was one of the first women to conduct the daily operations of a municipality in Florida. She became city manager in 1974. In her 50th year of service in 1990, the town christened the city hall the Nettie Berry Draughon Municipal Building. With a sincere devotion to the Cincinnati Reds, Draughon was proud to see her beloved town become the spring training base for her team. (Shelby Bender, East Hillsborough Historical Society.)

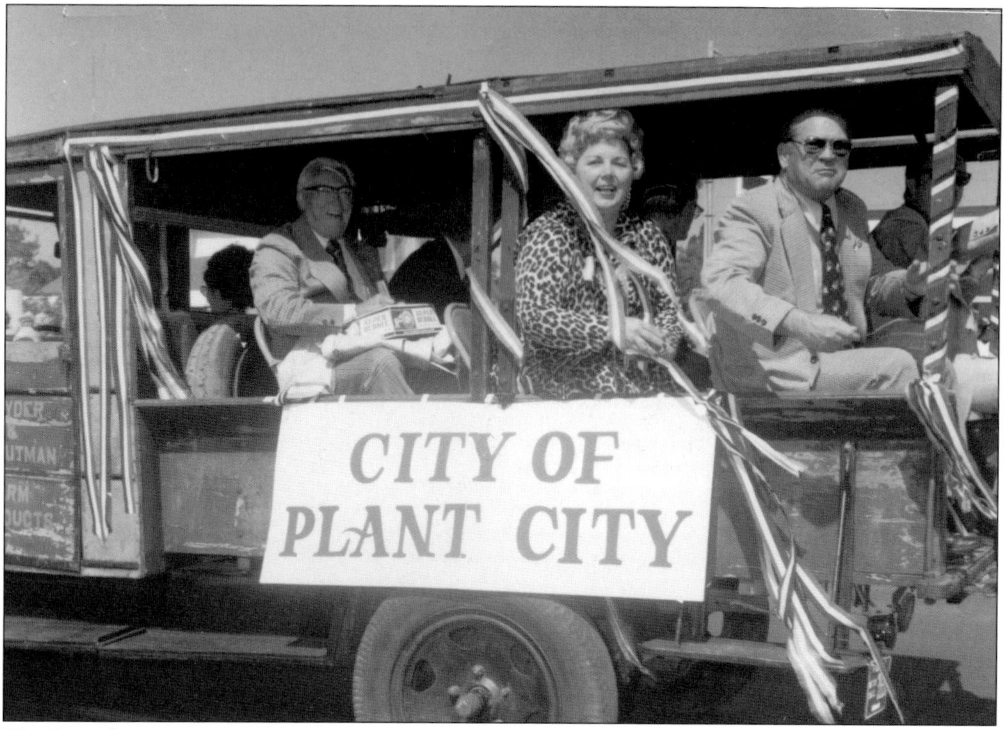

The first Plant City woman commissioner in the late 1960s, Betty Barker Watkins was also known for her ubiquitous hats and boogie-woogie piano playing. She served as a missionary to Africa and as an educator. According to Carolyn Powell, who entered Betty Barker in a talent contest in 1946, "Everybody in Plant City knew Betty was the best piano player around. She didn't just let her fingers caress the ivories . . . her big toe got into the act too. She would play barefoot and let the big toe on her right foot bang out the tempos." This photograph is of the 1975 Strawberry Festival Parade. (Shelby Bender, East Hillsborough Historical Society.)

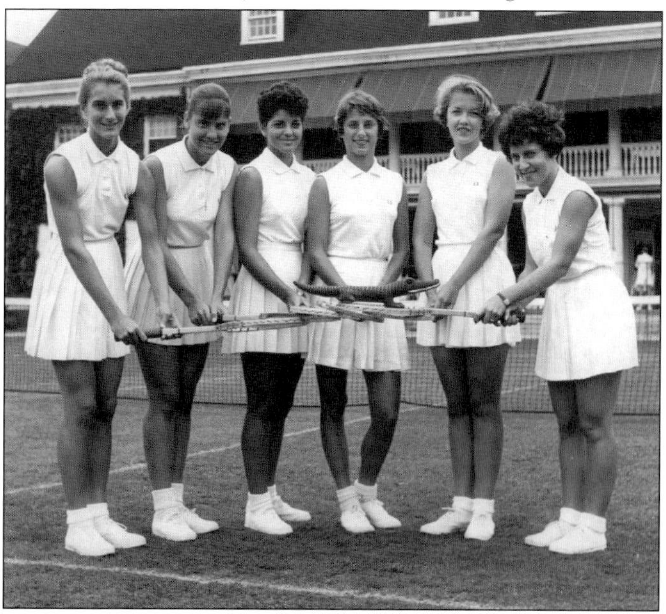

Sandy Warshaw Freedman was the first female mayor of Tampa, from June 1986 through April 1995. This photograph shows six young women tennis players with Warshaw on the far right. On their tennis rackets is a toy alligator with "Florida" written on it. The tennis center in Tampa was subsequently named the Sandra W. Freedman Tennis Complex. (Photograph by Edmund B. Gilchrist Jr., courtesy of Tampa Bay History Center.)

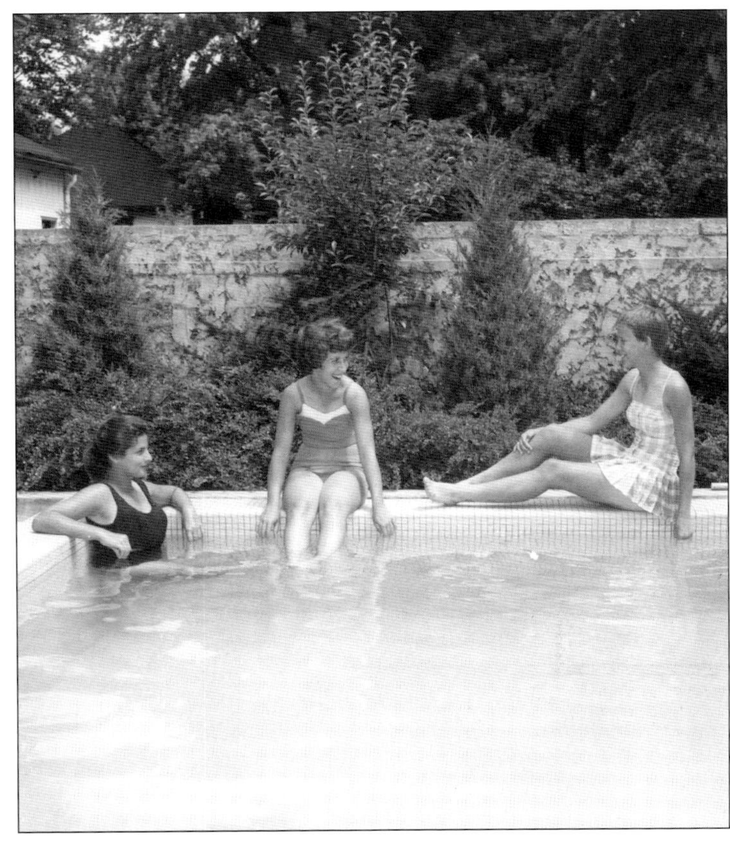

In July 1959, a newspaper society page ran this photograph of three young women lounging poolside. Sandy Warshaw Freedman is in the center, sitting on the edge of the pool. She was the second woman elected to the Tampa City Council and then ascended from city council chairperson, serving from 1974 until 1986, to the mayor of Tampa for two terms. Under her watch, Tampa launched the Bayshore Boulevard restoration efforts and opened the Florida Aquarium and the City Convention Center. (Tampa Bay History Center.)

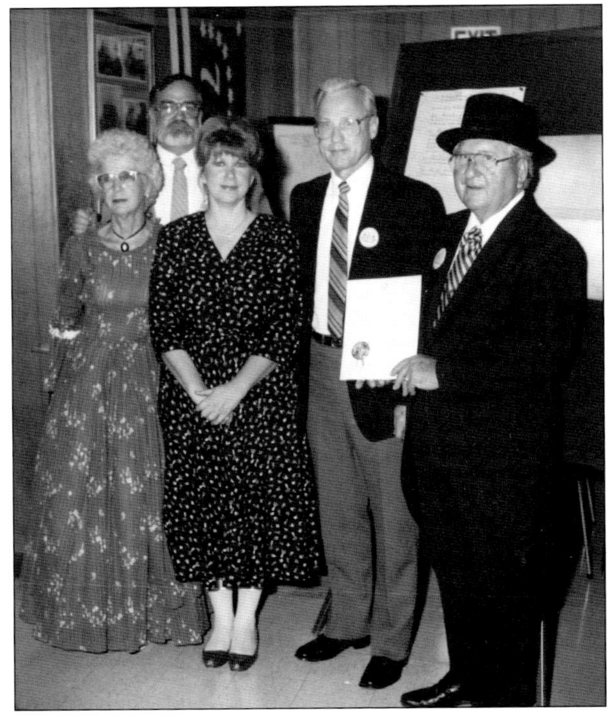

Agnes H. Lamb served on the Dade City Commission from 1970 to 1990 and was elected the first female mayor in 1974. She and her husband owned a retail egg business. Later, she worked in public relations for an area bank. Dade City commissioners are pictured at a 1989 event: Agnes Lamb, Fred Johnson, Patricia Weaver, Bill Dennis, and Col. Charles McIntosh. The town's centennial included a week of activities sponsored by the chamber of commerce. Lamb's 2008 obituary read, "Called a shining example of a public servant, she was described as an icon." (Scott Black.)

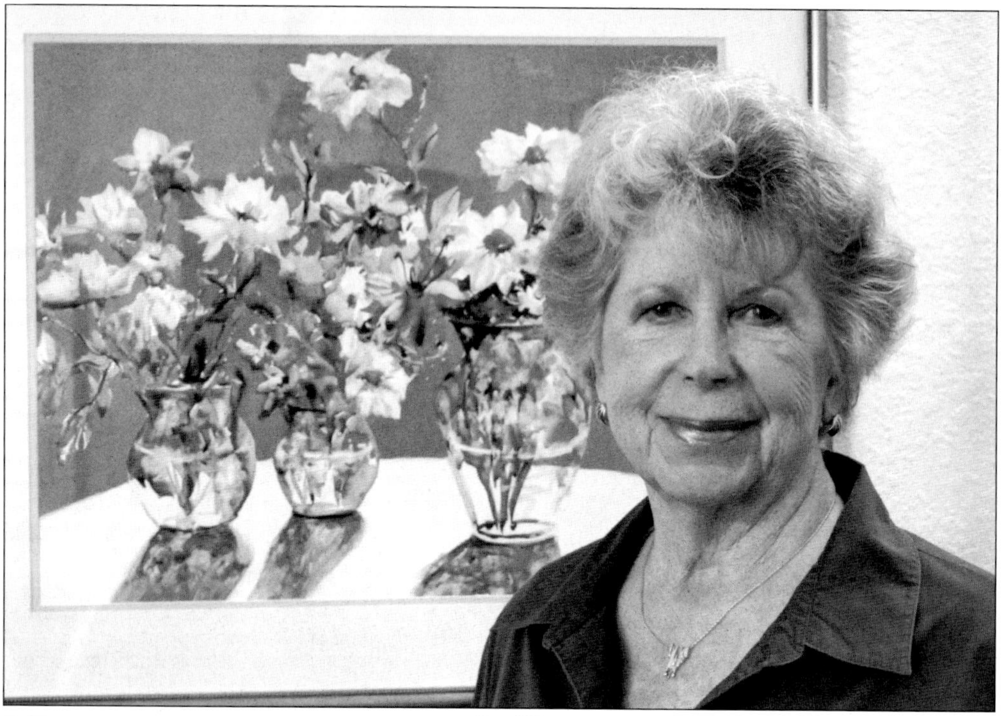

Pat Weaver was mayor of Dade City from 1990 to 1992, having previously served as a city commissioner and as president of Downtown Dade City Main Street. Also an artist, her book *Watercolor Simplified: A Fresh Approach to Painting Better and Faster with Confidence* details the fundamentals of watercolor painting. (Richard K. Riley.)

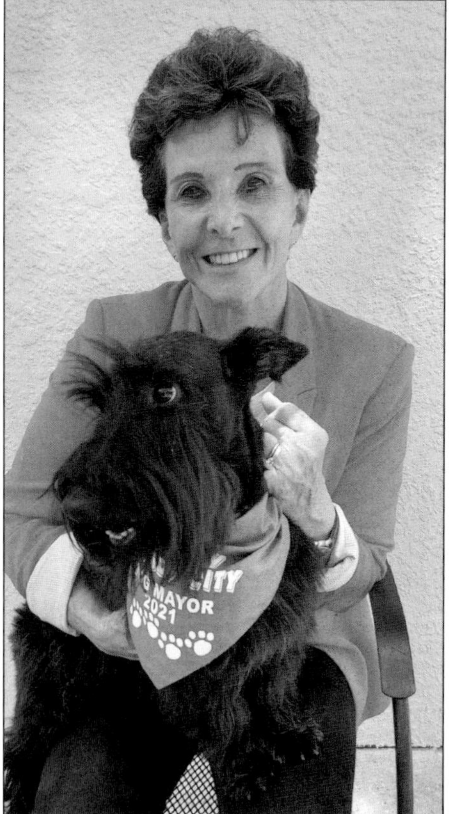

Camille Sutherland Hernandez was mayor of Dade City for over 10 years. A graduate of Brown University and Yale, she was a Rotary International Graduate Scholar. Her robust work included the Pasco Metropolitan Planning Organization, Tourist Development Council, and president of the Area Agency on Aging for Pasco and Pinellas. She is seen here holding Lucy Avilla's dog Abigail at the annual Dog Days in Dade City at Agnes Lamb Park, sponsored by the Dade City Youth Council. (Richard K. Riley.)

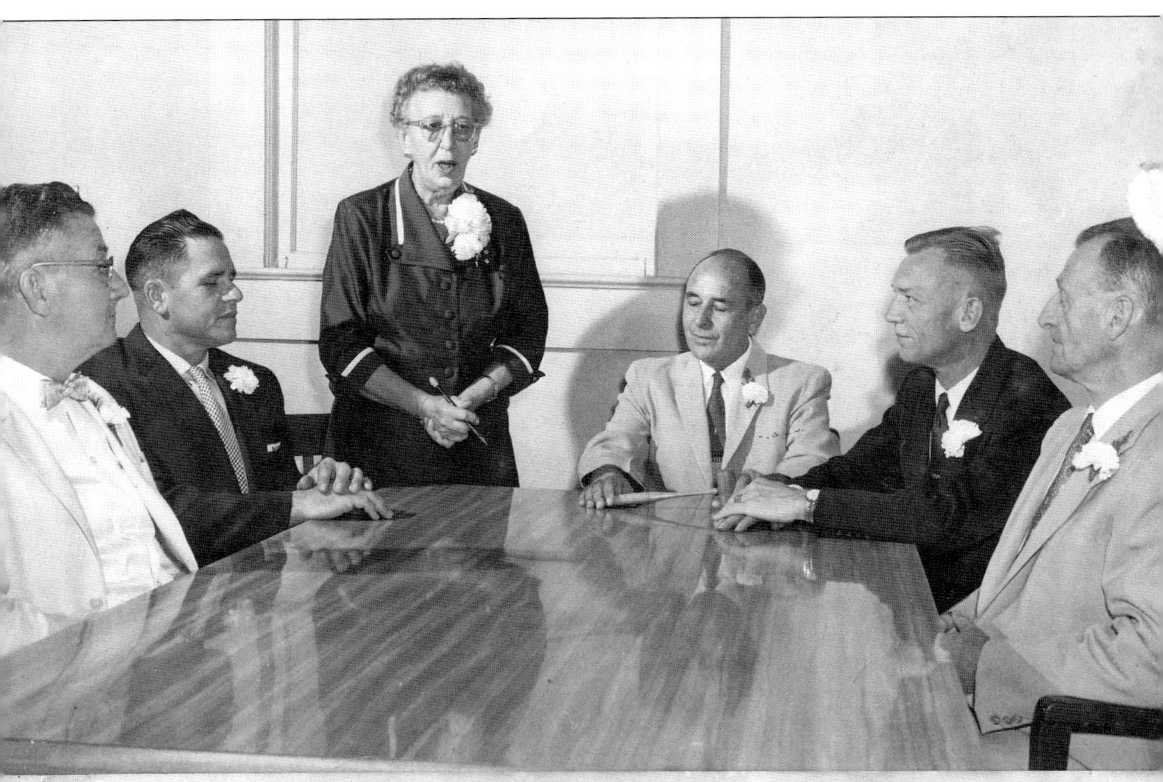

MAYOR WILLA RICE,standing, ADDRESSES CITY COUNCILMEN PAUL SCHULZ,SAM SURRATT, BERNARD E. BURNS(president), JAMES JARRETT AND ALBERT C. HOOKS(seated l to r) 17

Willa Hickock Rice was the first woman mayor of Zephyrhills. The owner/operator of a hotel in Sidney, Ohio, with her husband, Harry Rice, she moved to 1012 Fifth Avenue in 1941. She entered politics in 1953, with a desire for beautification and conservation, and was elected the first woman council member, later becoming council president. Soon after, she was elected mayor in 1957 and served three years. She attended the Cincinnati Conservatory of Music and enjoyed directing the local lady's choir. The *Fort Myers News* reported on June 15, 1957, "a seventy-two-year-old grandmother is the peppery new mayor of the central Florida city of four thousand and has started her administration with a police department shake-up." Her mission was to remove politics from public safety, and she was outspoken and attentive to public needs. Quite the novelty at the time, Rice shared her experiences in governing with surrounding civic organizations and treasured her role as a trailblazer for other women. She was the first and only female mayor of the town. (Zephyrhills Historical Association.)

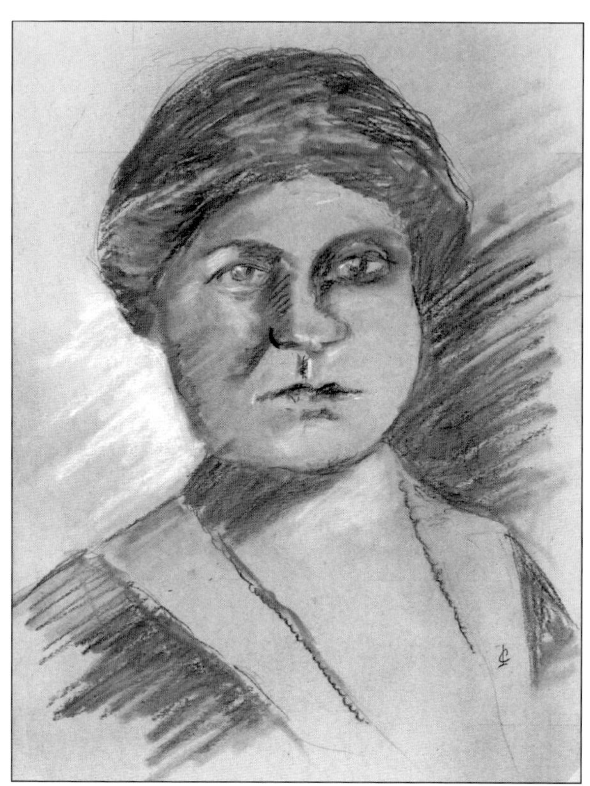

In 1928, when Amelia Earhart was working on a transatlantic flight, Lena Culver Hawkins took on leadership as Brooksville mayor. President of the Brooksville Woman's Club, Culver had to contend with traffic problems, financial crises, and a Mediterranean fruit fly emergency during her term. These are sketches of the mayor in 1928 (left) and 1949 (below). (Both sketches by Clinton Inman.)

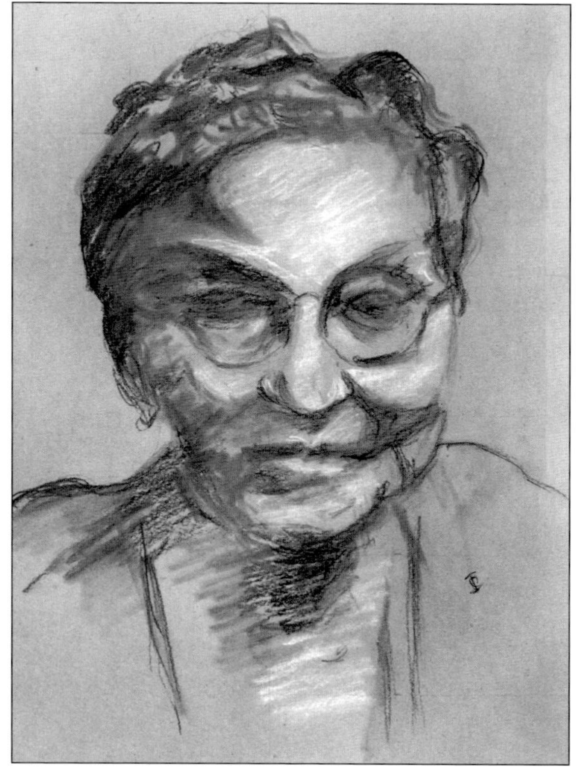

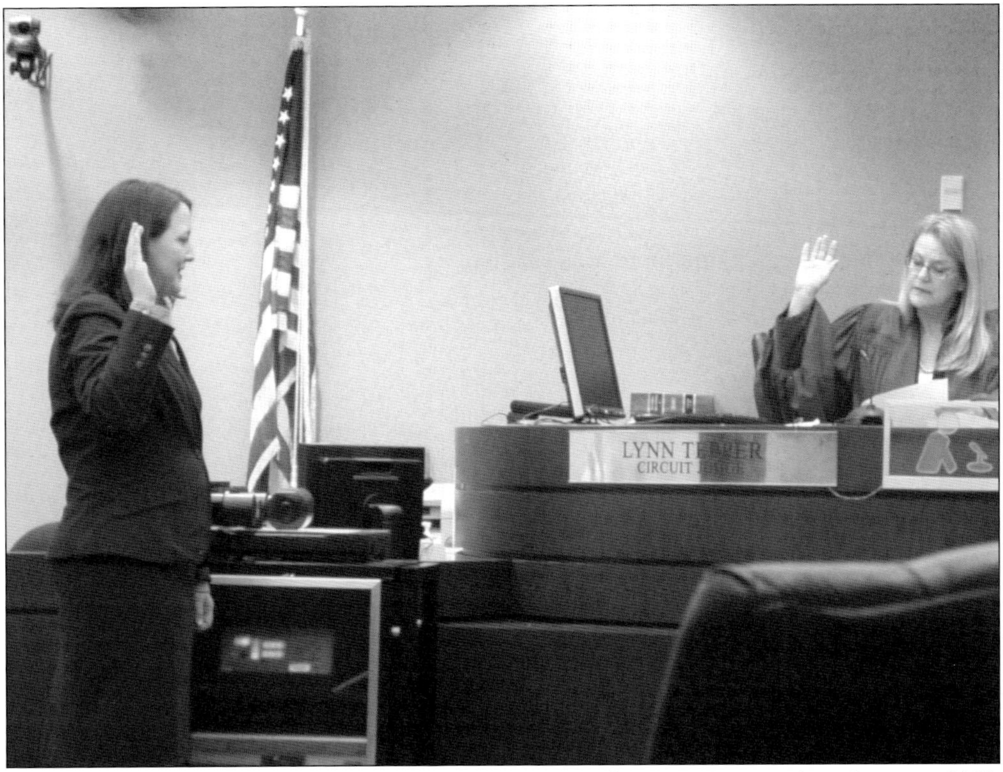

Judge Lynn Tepper swore in a new lawyer, Mamie Wise, at the Pasco County Courthouse in 2009. Tepper served as Florida's Sixth Judicial Circuit Court judge for over 37 years. A trailblazer, she incorporated Trauma-Informed-Care from the Kaiser Adverse Childhood Experiences Study in her unified family court and modified her courtroom to be safer and less threatening to defendants with a history of childhood trauma. (Ernest E. Wise.)

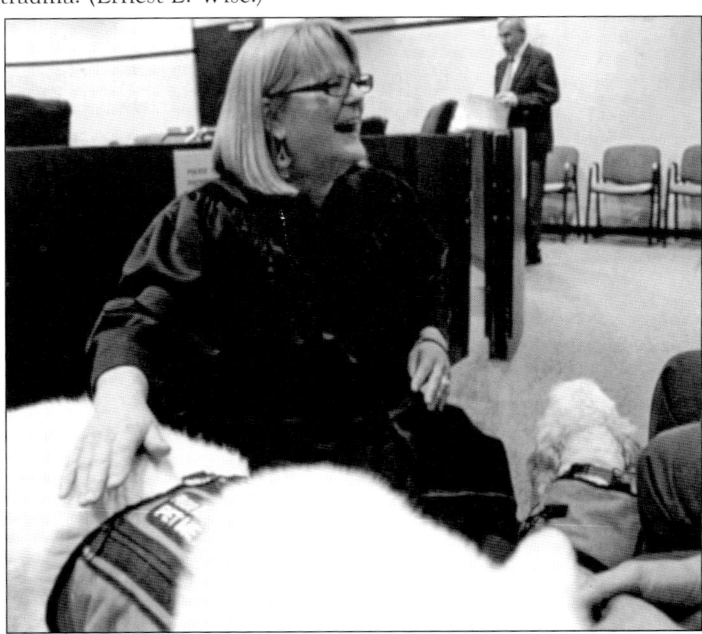

Tepper is shown with a therapy dog in her courtroom. She was elected in 1988 and retired in 2019. The Florida Association of Community Corrections honored her with a lifetime achievement award for her work with juveniles. Director John McMahon cited Tepper's work on visionary programs such as One Court/One Family, Drug Court, and Unified Family Court. (ACES Too High.)

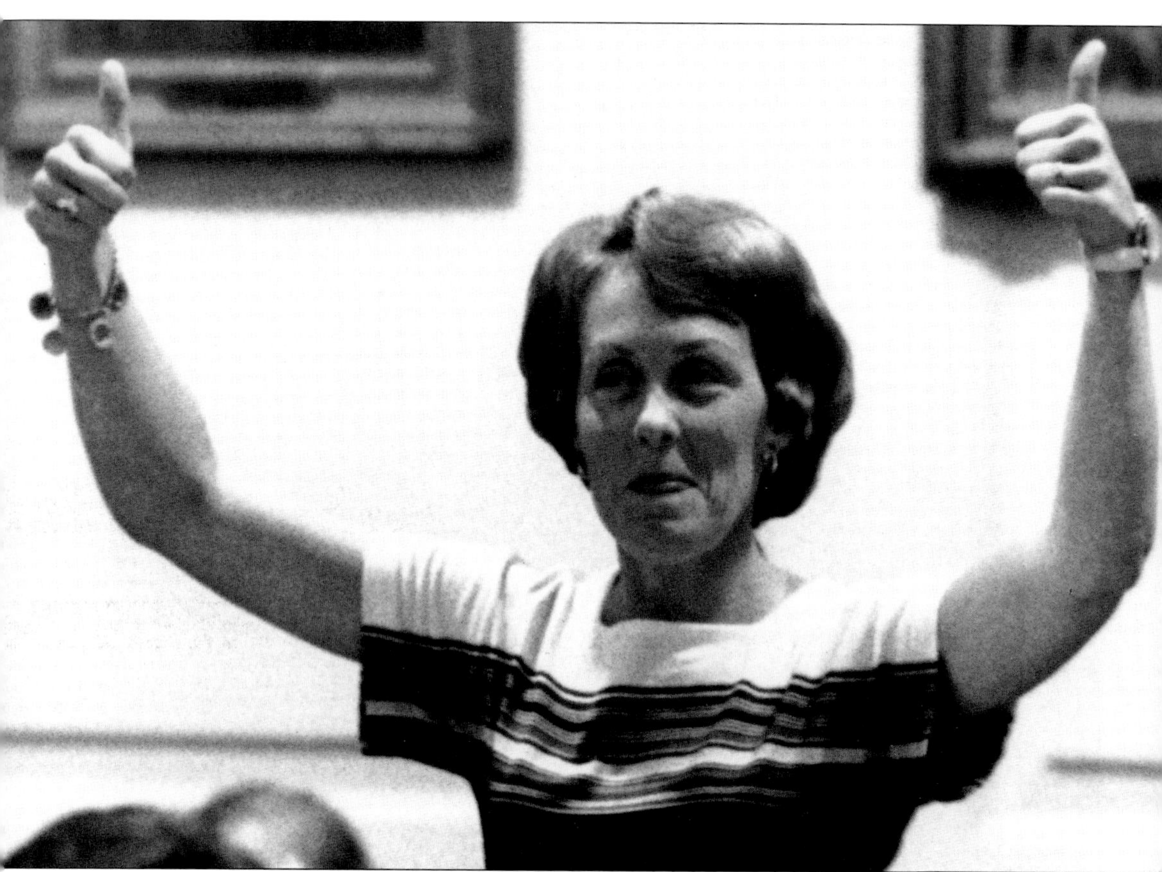

Sen. Betty Castor urged fellow senators to vote for the ERA in 1982. The Senate rejected the amendment 22-16 with only nine days left and three states short of ratification. Some 43 years later, Castor spoke in Tampa about the experience. As the passing vote was announced in 2019, Castor beamed. "Six to zero," she said, flashing two thumbs up. She had often been the first woman in each situation. The first female member of the Hillsborough County Commission, first female president pro tempore of the state senate; first female cabinet member; first female president of the University of South Florida, and others. If it was frustrating at 78 to still be fighting, she did not show it. She clapped a colleague on the back and gazed around the room, soaking in the collective power. On stage, Tampa mayor Jane Castor (no relation) said, "It is the right thing to do and should have been done a long time ago." Mayor Castor added, "The majority of people, when asked, feel like it's already been ratified." (Florida Memory.)

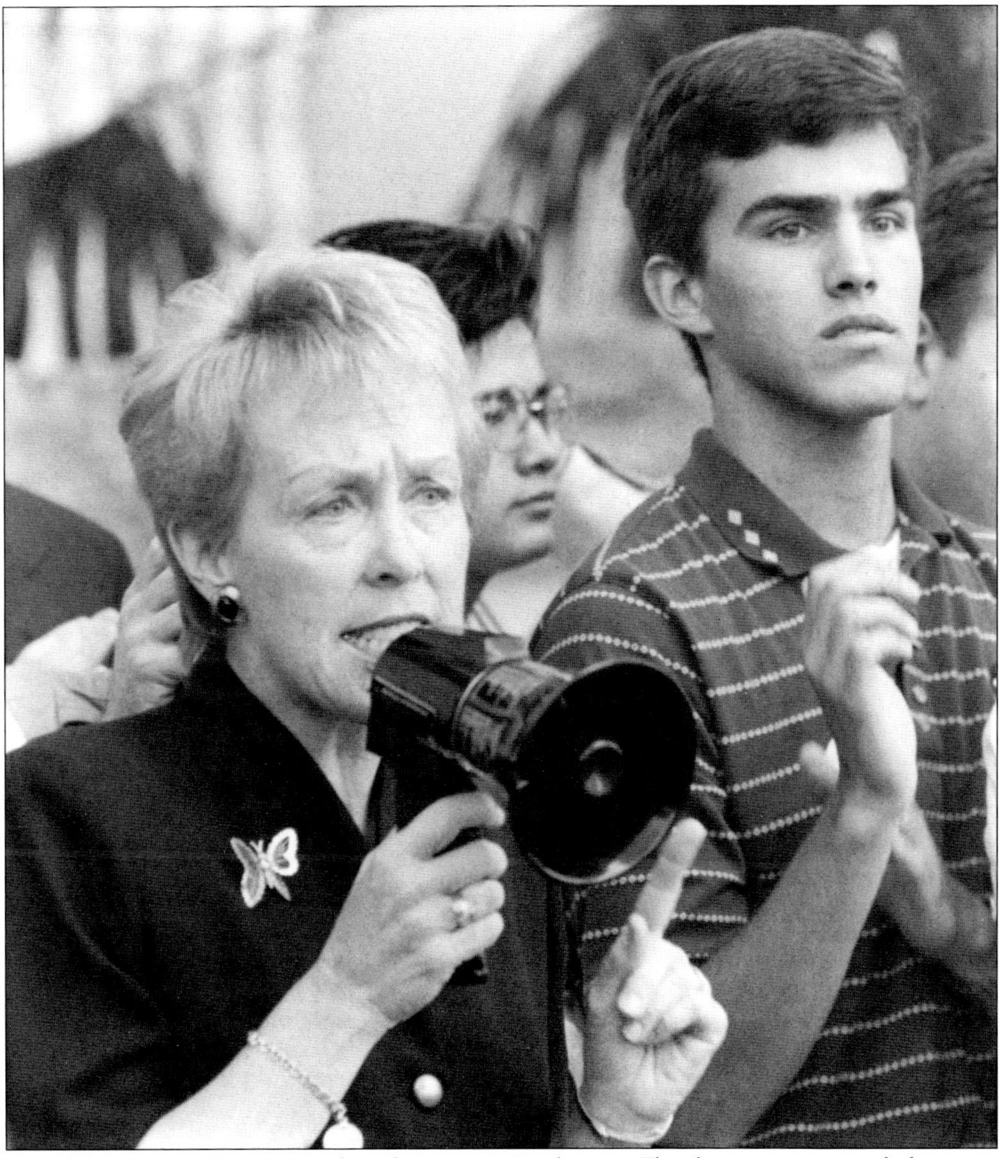

A trailblazer, Betty Castor served on the governor's cabinet as Florida commissioner of education. In this image, she is speaking to a crowd of some 1,000 college students on the steps of the old capitol as students protested educational budget cuts on September 24, 1991. As the president of the University of South Florida from 1994 to 1999, Castor oversaw several changes to USF. She also spent a few years as the executive director of USF's Patel Center for Global Solutions. Her daughter Kathy followed in her mother's footsteps as a congresswoman. (Mark Foley Collection, Florida Memory.)

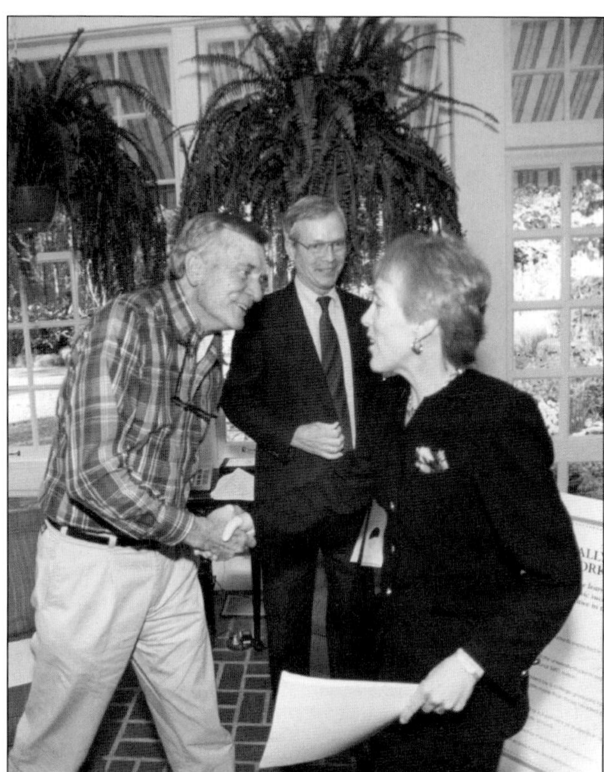

Gov. Lawton Chiles (left) and Lt. Gov. Buddy MacKay greet Betty Castor, the first woman elected to the Florida cabinet and president pro tempore of the Florida Senate. (Florida Memory.)

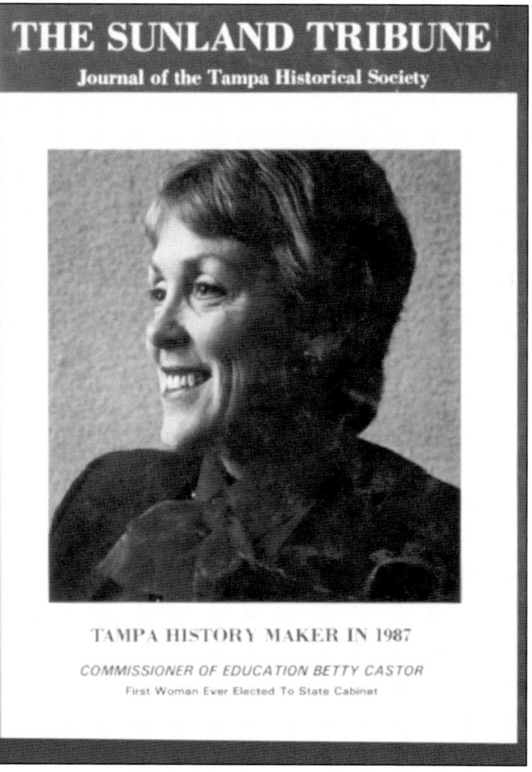

Betty Castor was the middle child with her twin brother, Tom. She appeared on *American Bandstand* in the 1960s. Inspired by Pres. John F. Kennedy, she taught English in Uganda, coached field hockey, and led 40 girls up Mount Kilimanjaro. Later, she was a teacher and housewife. When she decided to run for office, the League of Women Voters (LWV) walked door to door and hosted fundraiser dinners. "She changed the way politics was done in Hillsborough County," said Pam Iorio. (Tampa Historical Society.)

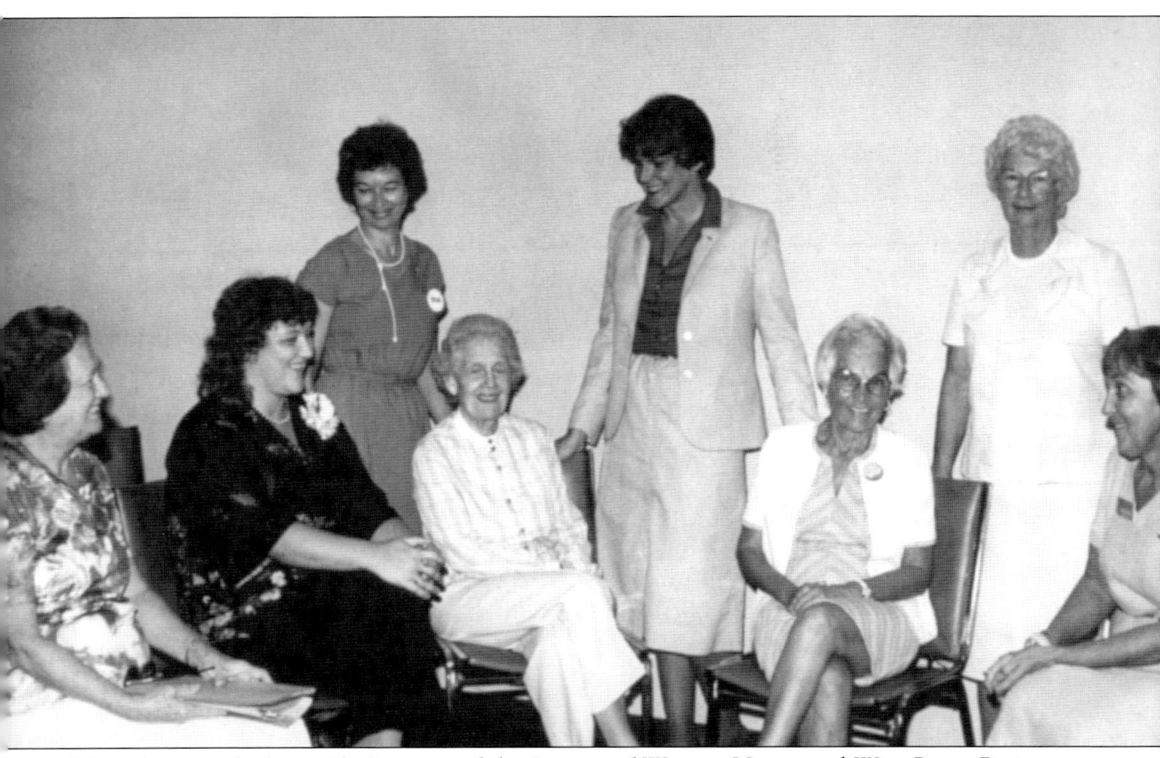

This photograph shows Ida Brunner of the League of Women Voters and West Pasco Business and Professional Woman (BPW); Janet Woods of BPW; Alma Smillie of LWV of Florida and ERA chairperson; Roxy Dillon of LWV and Common Cause; Jane Campbell and Dorothy Wylie of Common Cause; Billie Bobbit; and Clara Ann Smith, Pasco County ERA chairwoman. "We want to inspire the ERA supporters to share their support with their local legislators," said Jane Campbell. "Unfortunately, a lot of constituents are a little afraid of their legislators, and a lot of ERA supporters have never lobbied a legislator." In 1982, a group of Tampa Bay and Florida women worked for the ratification of the ERA amendment. ERA America was a national coalition of about 200 groups working for the ratification. The women traveled the state talking to business and professional groups about the amendment and why they considered it necessary. They were invited to Pasco County by the League of Women Voters, the West Pasco BPW, and the Calusa BPW and Common Cause. As time was running out for ratification of the ERA, the pressure was being felt on state legislators. The year 1982 marked the tenth anniversary of the approval by the US Congress with submission to states for ratification. It stated, "Equality of rights under the law shall not be denied of abridged by the United States of by any State on account of sex." It required 38 states to ratify for it to become the 27th amendment. As of 2021, it has been ratified by 37 states, and Florida has consistently voted not to ratify it. (West Pasco Historical Association.)

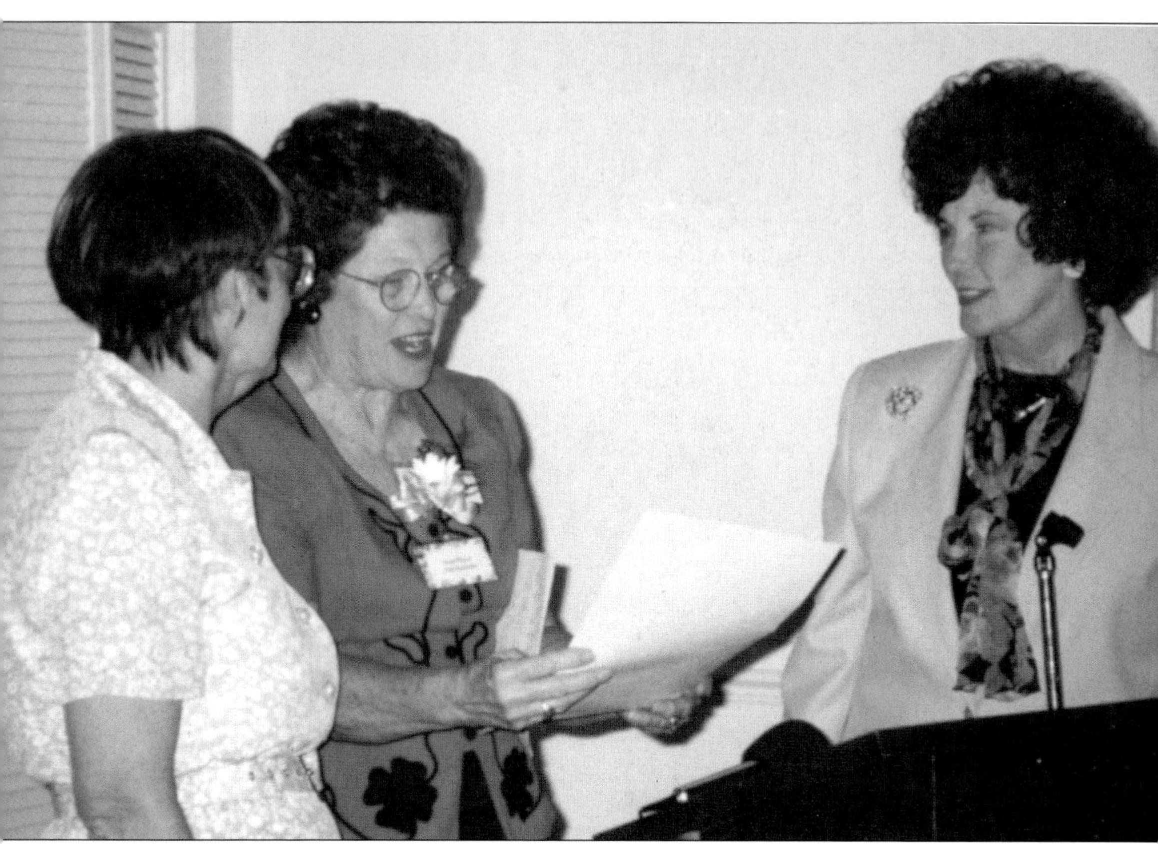

Pasco County commissioner Pat Mulieri (left) and Sylvia Miller Young (right) honored Joan Prior (center), an accomplished educator and president of the Dade City Garden Club as well as previous state president, for her work with the environment. Dr. Mulieri, elected in 2014 to the county commission and serving for 20 years, was a champion of many causes, including technological access, services for the homeless population, mobile medical units, and enhanced humane animal control services. She was known for her optimistic phrase, "We are on the cusp," often referring to thriving tourism or a robust economy. (Dade City Garden Club.)

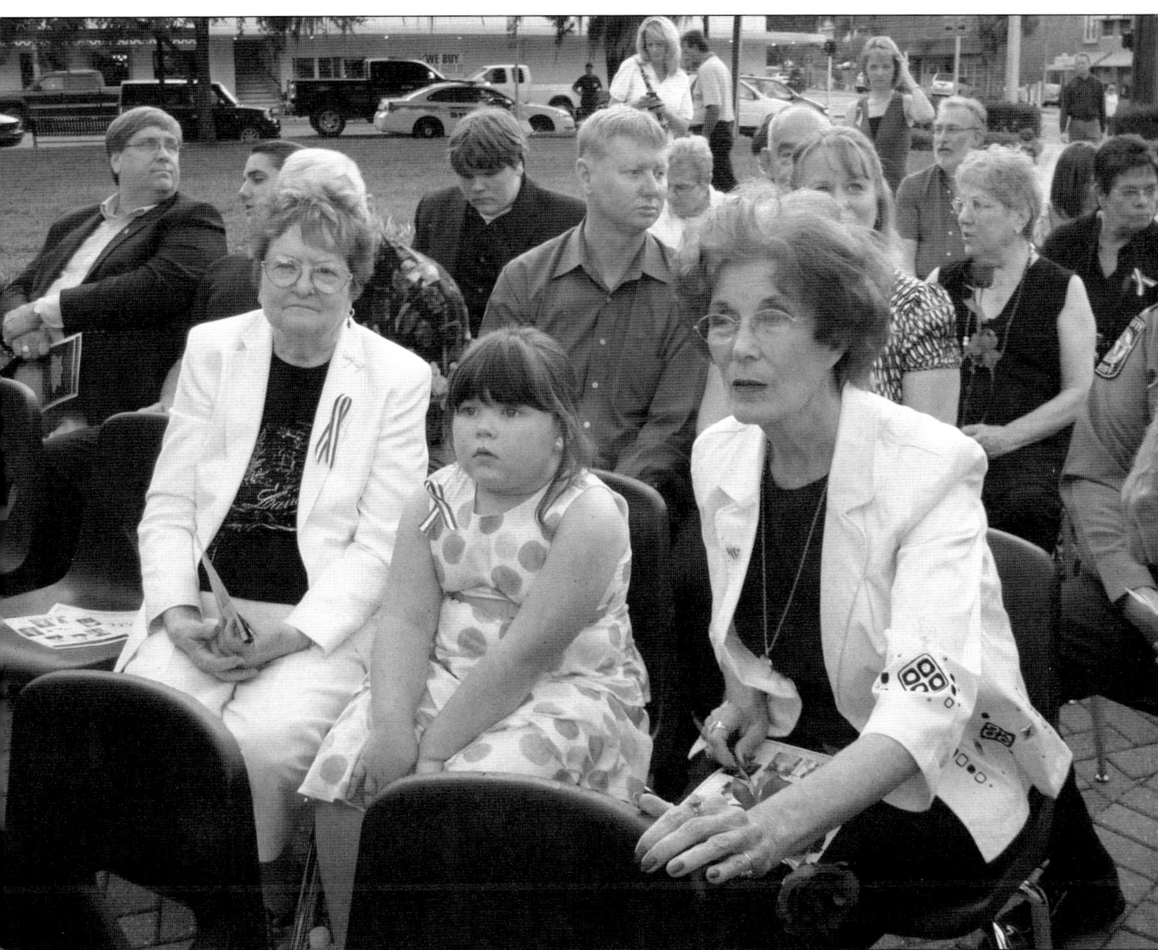

The first woman elected to the Pasco County Commission, Sylvia Miller Young, served five terms. Young said, "This has been my life, and I've spent twenty good years." Her proudest accomplishment was the over $2 million preservation and renovation of the historic 1909 Pasco County Courthouse, painstakingly overseeing the renovation, decorations, and furnishings to period-correct specifics. She was also instrumental in saving the historic train depots in two east Pasco towns. Her pride in Florida heritage was deeply rooted in her own heritage, and her style of careful consideration of all constituents paired with brutal honesty was unparalleled. She served during a period of the area's largest and fastest growth, representing Pasco on the Tampa Bay Regional Planning Council. (Zephyrhills Depot Museum.)

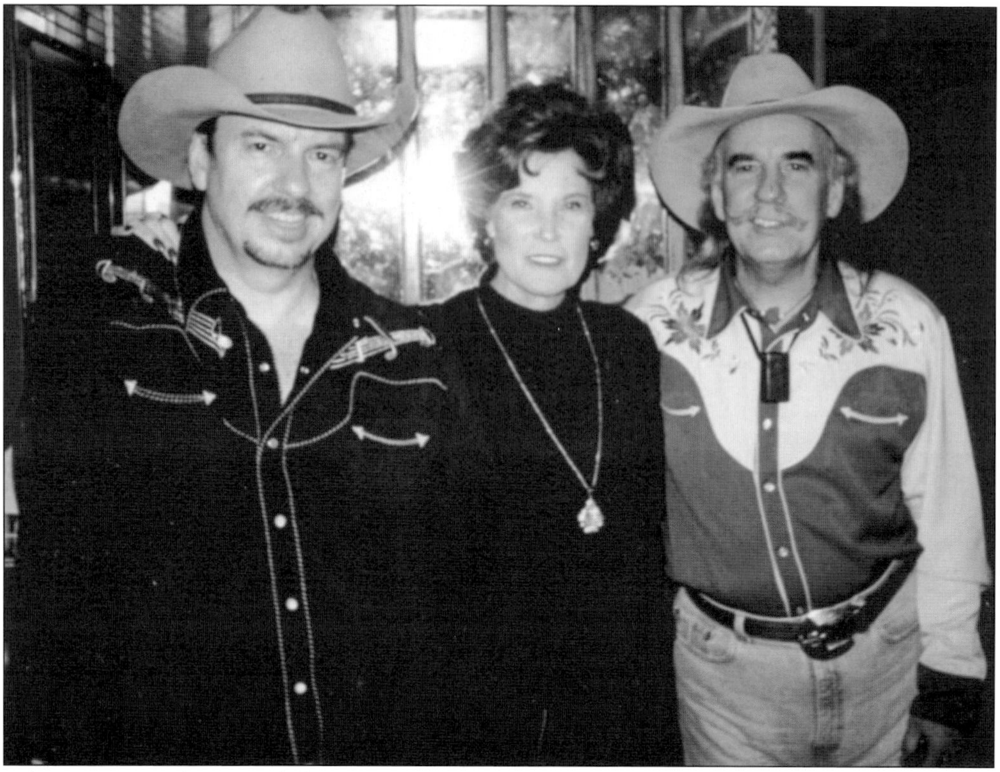

Sylvia Young is shown with her cousins the Bellamy Brothers in Blanton. A homegrown girl, she fought fearlessly for her constituents. She solicited Howard and David Bellamy to do benefit concerts to raise funds to bring more area parks and recreation development. (Jeff Miller.)

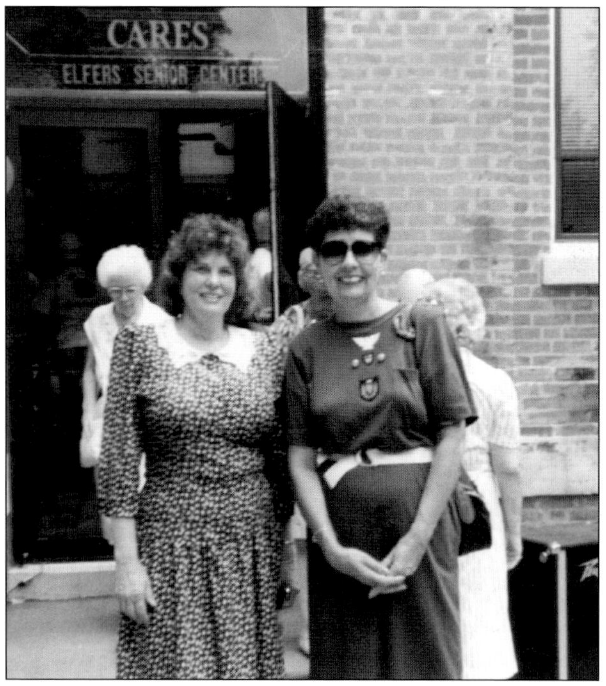

Dorothy Schluter Mitchell (left) and Ann Hildebrand are pictured at the 10th anniversary of the Elfers Senior Center. Hildebrand served seven terms on the county commission. Hildebrand was perpetually focused on social services, working on the boards of several organizations, including the Good Samaritan Health Clinic and the PACE Center for Girls. Remembered for her work in the region through groups such as Tampa Bay Water and a relatively new regional transportation agency, Mitchell served four terms on the school board and was an active community member. (Jeff Miller.)

"A phrase bounced off the walls of the Pasco County Commission Chambers this week for the first time ever: Madam Chairman," said Jeff Testerman. Sandra Werner (left) was one of the first female county commissioners. A fourth-generation member of a Tampa Bay family, she became the first chairwoman of the county commission in 1982, a position she revered in part because her great-grandfather James W. Clark and two of her great uncles, Edward Liles and David H. Clark, also served as commissioners. (Jeff Miller.)

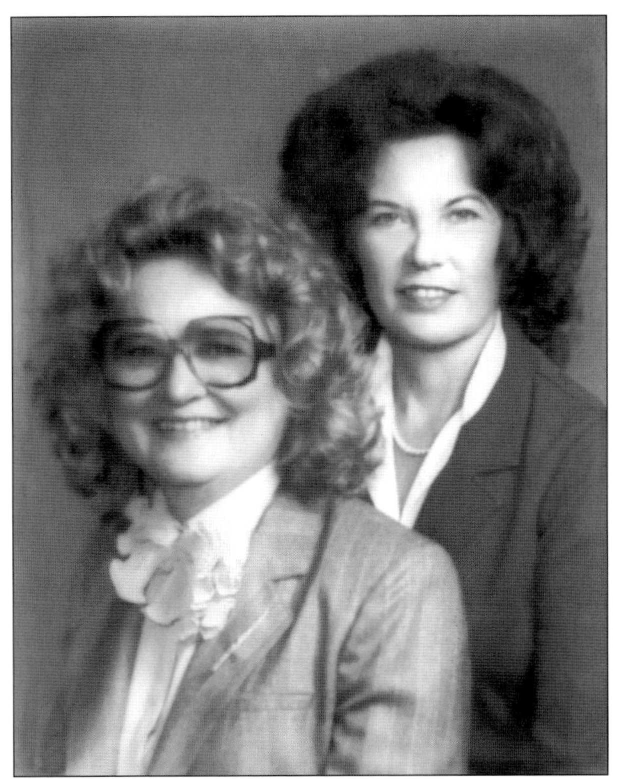

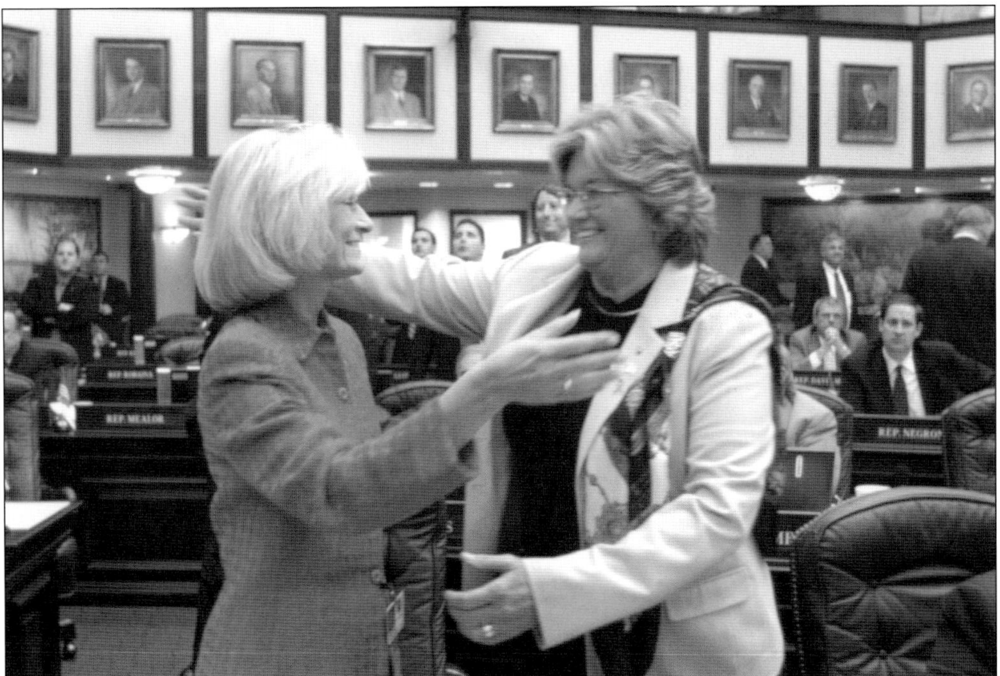

A prime bill sponsor from Tampa in the Florida legislature, Sandra L. Murman hugs Rep. Heather Rose Fiorentino when the Parental Rights Bill was approved by the House of Representatives. A bipartisan effort, the two Tampa Bay legislators worked together. (Florida House of Representatives.)

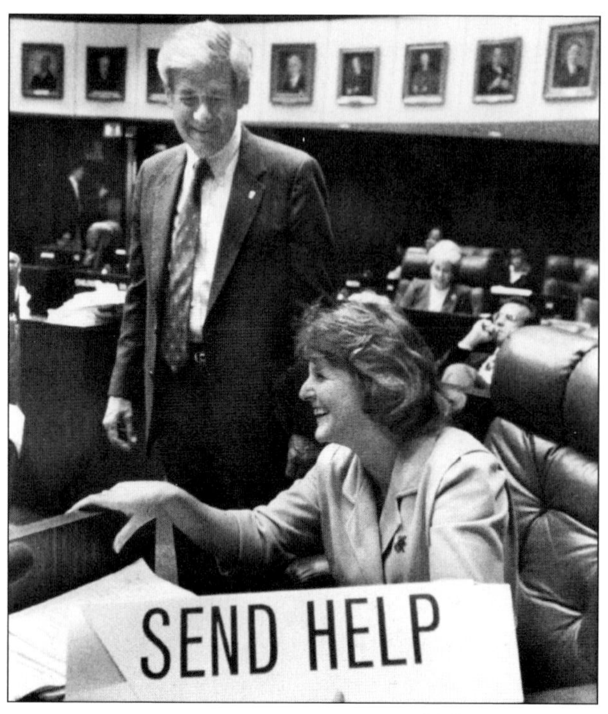

Karen Loveland Thurman of Dunnellon poses with a "Send Help" sign at her senate desk during a breakdown on the budget on a Friday night in June 1988, forcing the legislature to work until the midnight deadline with a probable extension into the following week. A middle school math teacher, Thurman got her first taste of politics when she organized her students to protest the Dunnellon City Council's plan to close the beach. She was later elected to the council, and later mayor. She went on to run for US Congress, representing several counties on the Gulf Coast. In later years, she served as state chair of her political party. (Photograph by Mark Foley, Don Dughi Collection, Florida Memory.)

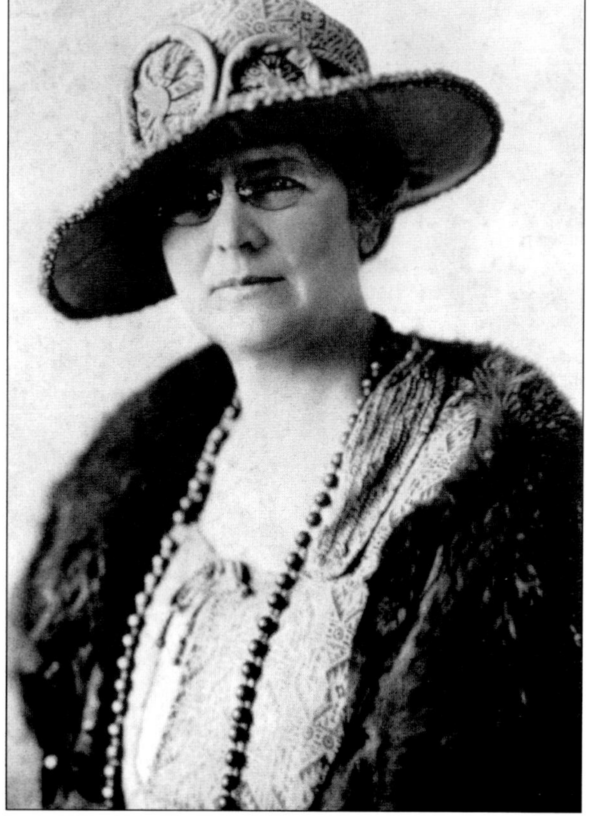

Katherine Bell Tippetts courageously ran for the state legislature in 1922 but was unsuccessful. As the second woman to run for the Florida legislature, she was a trailblazer in that regard but is better known for her work as an author, conservationist, and humanitarian. She helped create the Florida Fish and Game Commission, founded the St. Petersburg Audubon Society, and served as chair of the Florida Chamber of Commerce and president of the Florida Federation of Women's Clubs. (Florida Memory.)

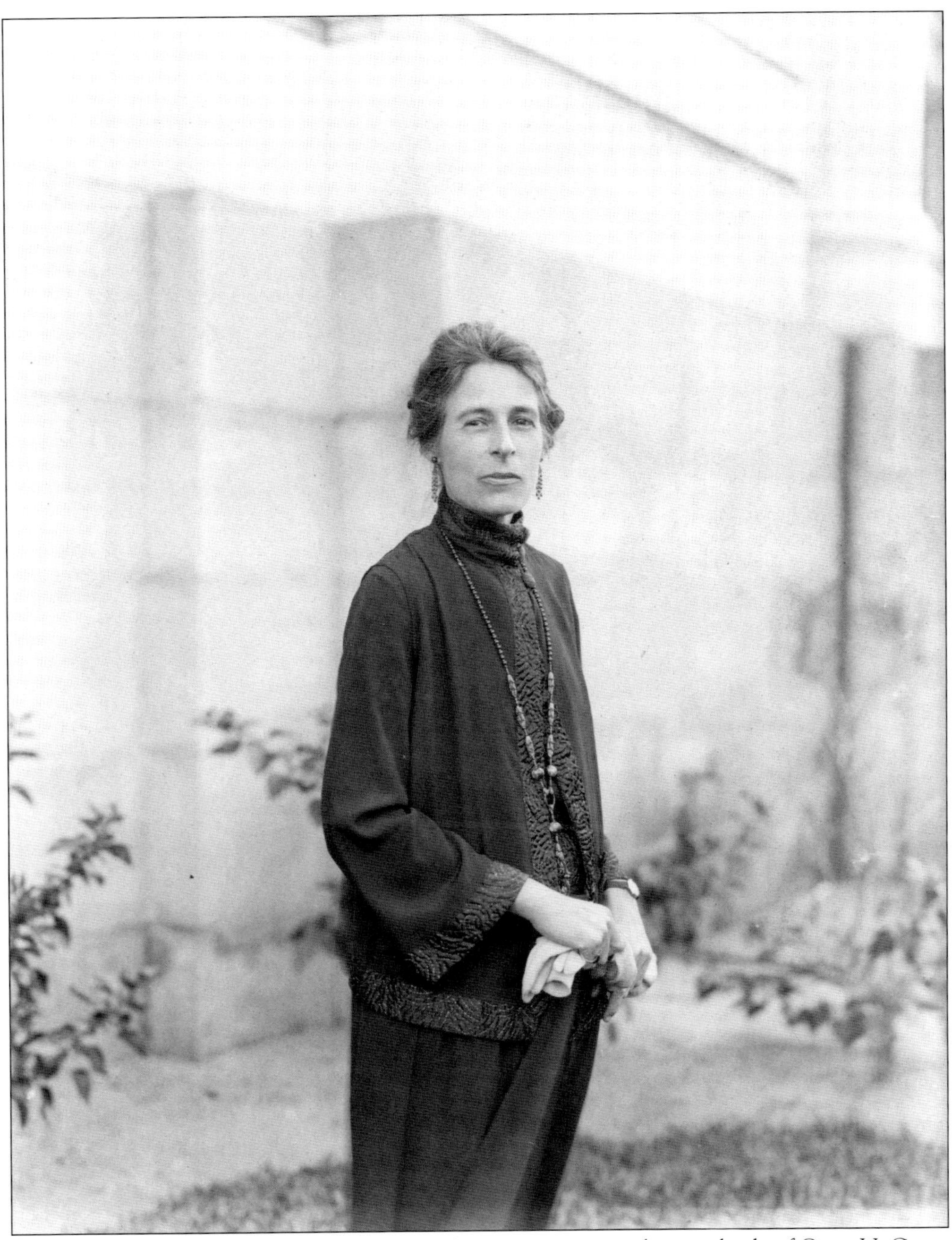

Postmaster Elizabeth Dortch Barnard arrived at Port Tampa as the new bride of Capt. U. Grant Barnard. After he died in 1906, and with two young children, she sought work. The post office told her they were not using women, but she persisted and took a business course. She worked for the post office and diligently ascended from private secretary to foreman to postmaster in 1923. She received a salary of $6,000 per year, said to be one of the largest salaries for a woman in the world at the time. Leland Hawes stated in 1984 that Barnard was Tampa's first and only woman postmaster from 1923 to 1933 and the first woman to achieve executive status in a government role. (Tampa–Hillsborough County Public Library.)

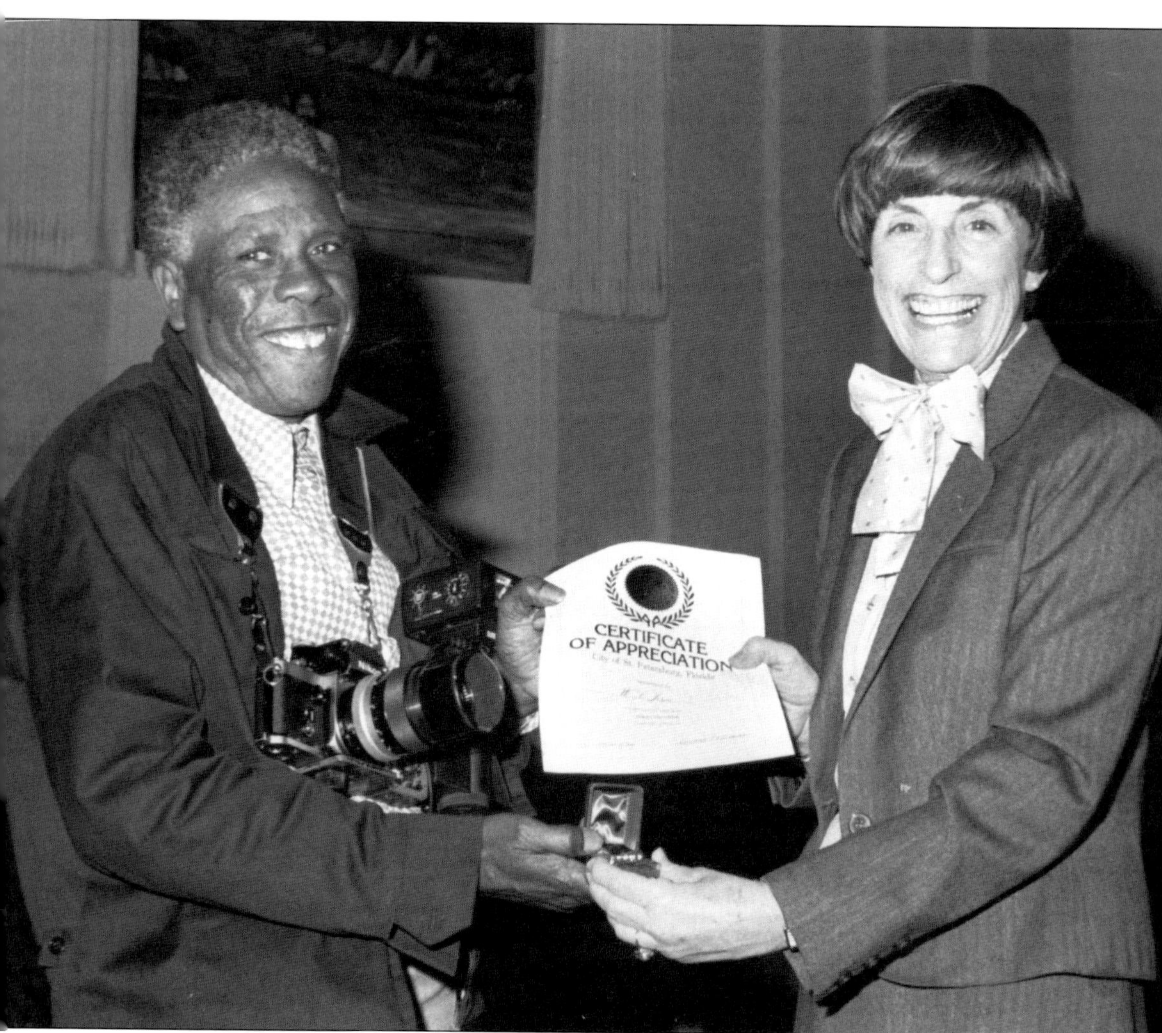

The first female mayor of St. Petersburg, from 1977 to 1985, was Corrine Freeman. Trained as a nurse in New York, she was part of Eleanor Roosevelt's Army Cadet Corps. She migrated from New York, and after years of avid membership in the League of Women Voters, she ran for and served on the Pinellas School Board for 10 years. From her mayorship, she was proud to have secured the land for Tropicana Field. In this photograph, Willie "W.L." Jones, retired photographer for the *Weekly Challenger* newspaper in St. Petersburg, receives the key to the city from Mayor Freeman. Her obituary proclaimed, "Corinne had an amazing zest for life and loved classical music, dancing and the Tampa Bay Rays. Corinne was a long-time season ticket holder of the Florida Orchestra and the Tampa Bay Rays, sitting behind home plate amongst the scouts. Corinne was an avid reader and swam laps in the morning at 6 a.m." (USF.)

Four

Acquiring the Voice

Histories chronicle that women were more overtly speaking out for community needs and formally advocating for each other by the late 19th century, largely via the club movement. Before about 1880, women's associations were primarily auxiliaries of men's groups or church-related or social societies. Women were shunned for leadership in church at the pulpit, and only a courageous few ventured from the norm as there were strict societal expectations. By 1890, the Federation of Woman's clubs was founded. Numerous groups such as Garden Club, YWCA, Grange, Home Demonstration Clubs, and others offered active discussion that opened up possibilities for expression, debate, informal education, and the facilitation of leadership skills.

Simultaneous to the suffragettes, the club movement was vital to the evolving path of trailblazers. Advocacy was gestated in this environment, and women researched needs and spoke out for social welfare, beautification/conservation, and community-identified endeavors.

For many, it was the first time that women had the floor and were not overpowered by male counterparts who, in many cases, were well-meaning. The work done by the numerous clubs in the Tampa Bay area made a difference, and many of the vital institutions continue to exist and evolve in contemporary Tampa Bay.

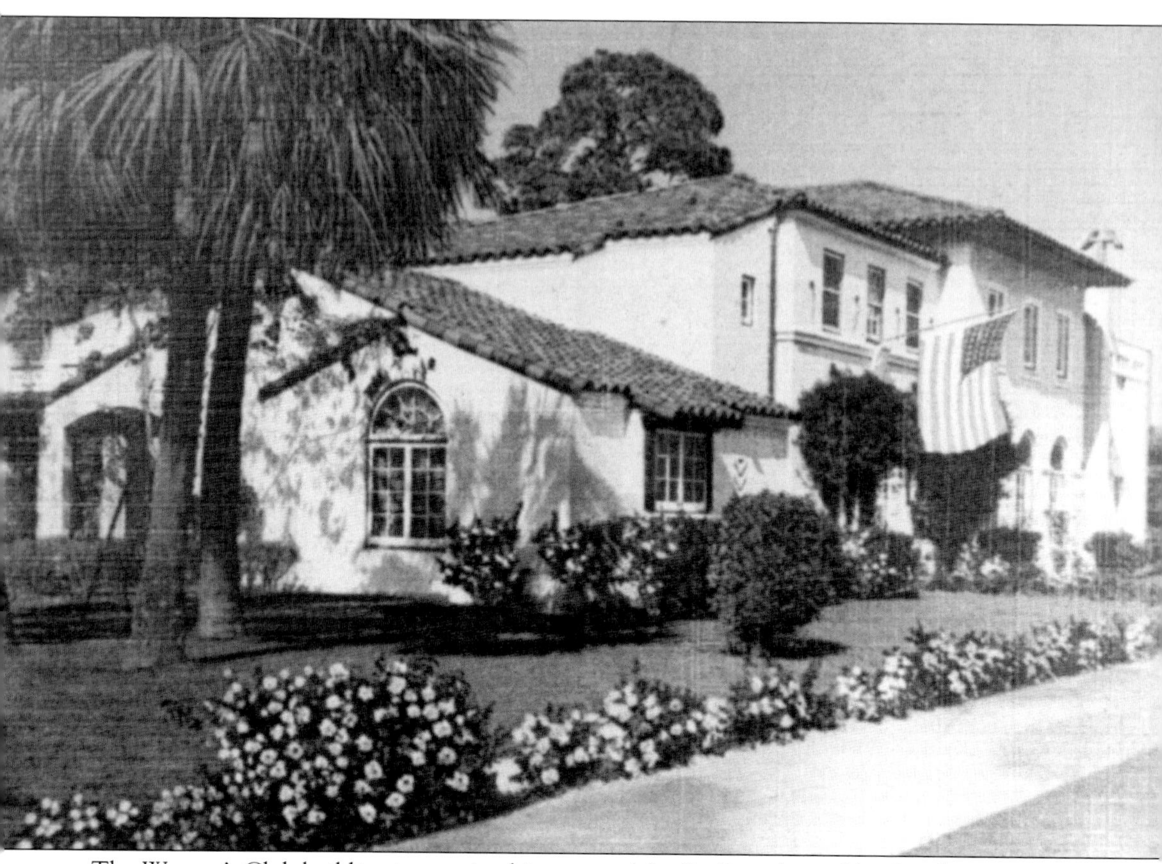

The Woman's Club building is seen in this postcard for St. Petersburg, "the Sunshine City," in 1931. Nancy Greene had been the president of the Federated Woman's Club when she moved to St. Petersburg from Illinois. She chartered the group with 14 members in 1913. The first woman's club to perform war work, with the Belgian relief effort in 1915, the club elevated women to increasing influence in their communities. The members addressed social welfare and educational issues, and the institution became an informal training school for women who sought leadership roles. It was critical to the push for suffrage. (Hampton Dunn Collection, USF.)

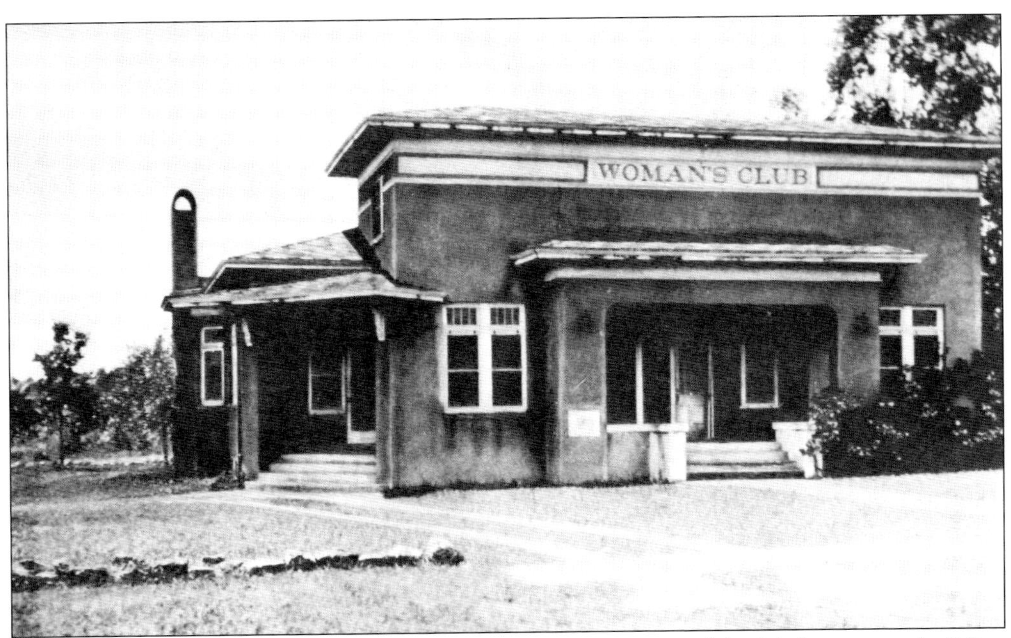

Woman's Club in Dade City raised $23,000 for the construction of the Mediterranean building that hosted community, civic, and educational events. Sallie Embry was the charter president of the club in 1910, and Dolly Hendley was president for 17 years and diligently coordinated fundraising efforts in the community. (Florida Memory.)

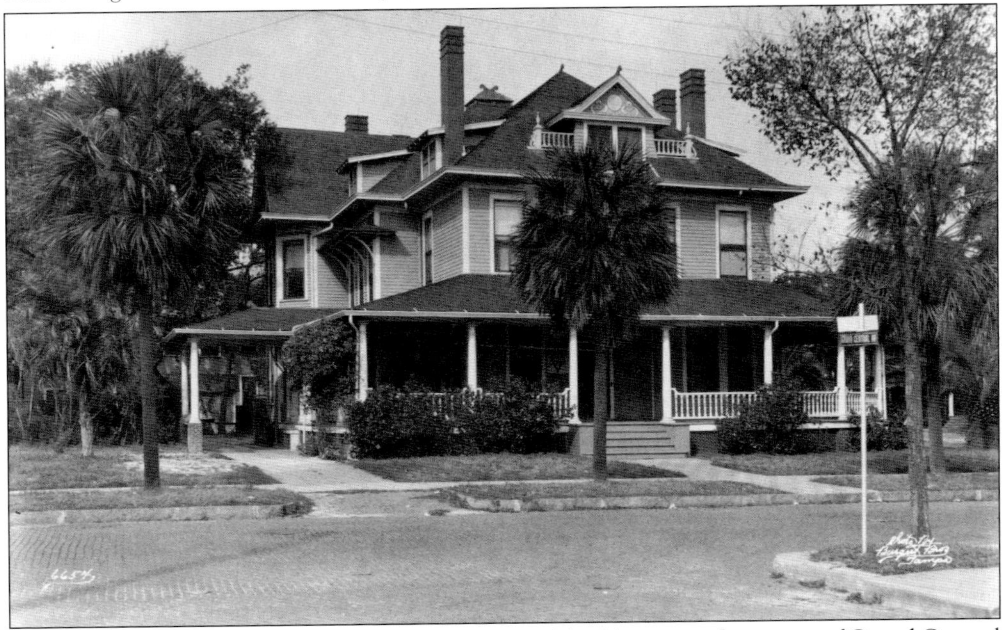

The Young Women's Christian Association (YWCA) building near the corner of Grand Central Avenue in Tampa's Hyde Park neighborhood was a burgeoning place for women. The YWCA was established locally in 1919, and in 1991, the St Petersburg and Clearwater YWCA merged to form the YWCA of Tampa Bay. "We have a long history of doing things nobody wants to do," said executive director Peggy Sanchez in 1992. "We are not afraid to push up our sleeves and get involved." (Burgert Brothers Collection, Tampa–Hillsborough County Public Library.)

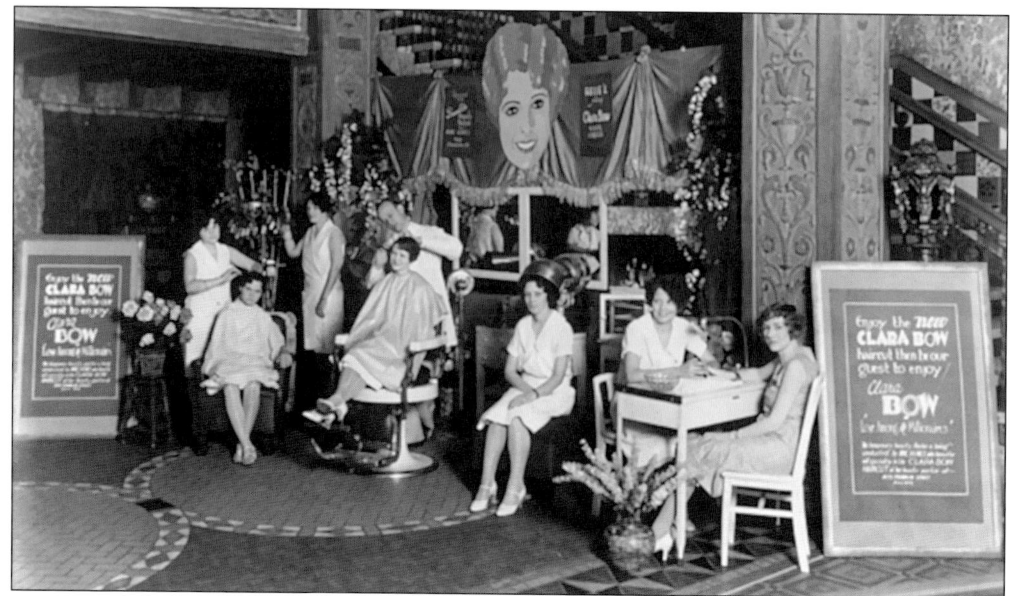

In an innovative marketing technique, the Madame Hines Beauty Parlor set up chairs and stylists in the front lobby of the Tampa Theatre in 1930 for the film *Love Among the Millionaires* so that women could get a fashionable Clara Bow haircut and style and then see the romantic comedy. Posters boasted, "Enjoy the new Clara Bow haircut then be our guest to enjoy Clara Bow in Love Among the Millionaires." Indicative of the changing nature of fashion and norms of behavior for women in the early 20th century, the movie's theme involved a young waitress who fell in love with the son of a railroad tycoon and traversed societal expectations. (Burgert Brothers Collection, Tampa–Hillsborough County Public Library.)

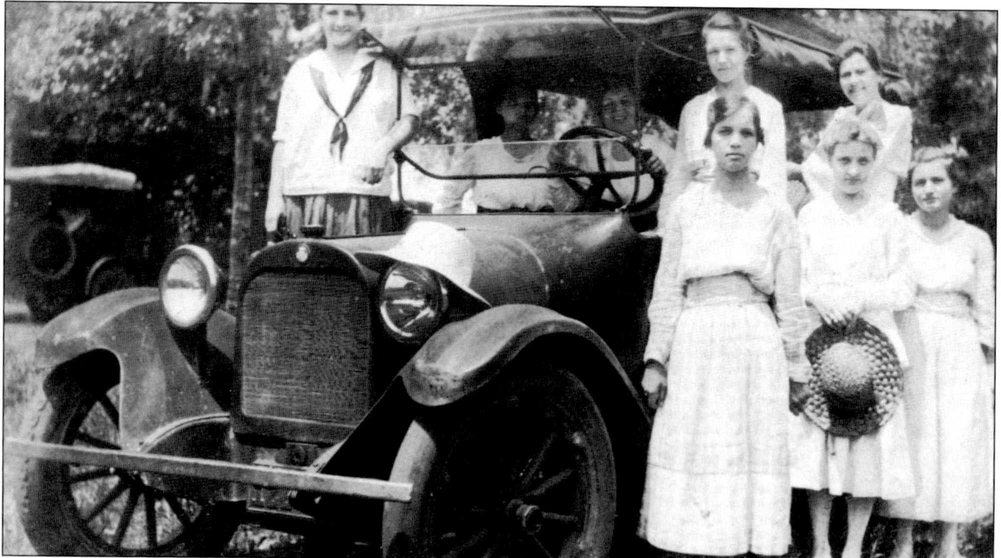

A group from Tampa prepares to attend the summer Y Camp at Rollins College in 1920. The Florida Christian Temperance Union operated the camp in Winter Park. It was led by Woman's Christian Temperance Union officers who instructed on the topics of character and preparation for women's work. Lottie Faye Mendenhall Starr is standing on the car at far left, and Annie Oren is in the group. (Florida Memory.)

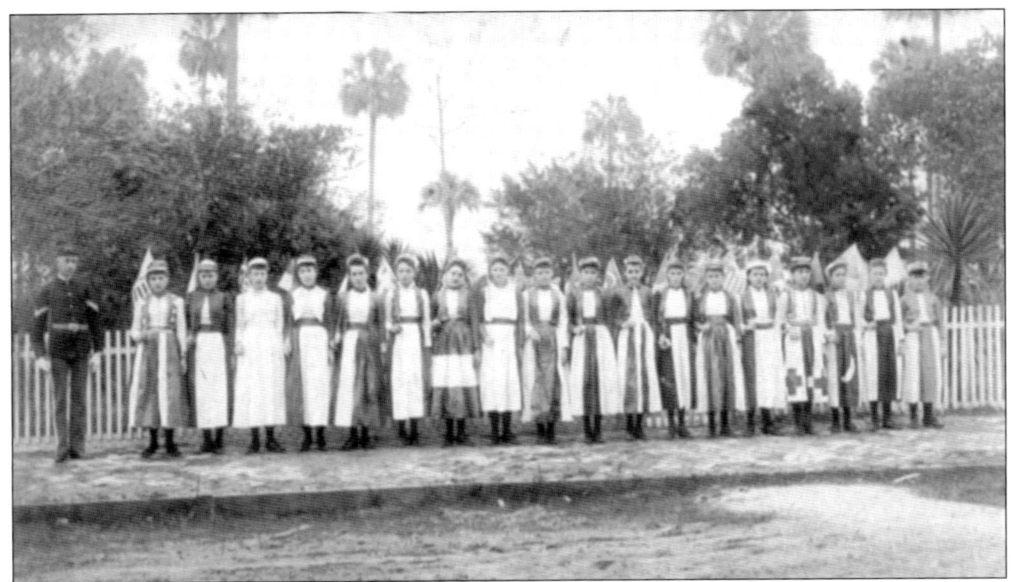

A soldier is joined by various women who hold flags of the world in 1898. The Ensminger Brothers photographers were renowned for their ability to capture not only everyday Florida life, but the troop mobilization in Tampa during the Spanish-American War. Dozens of women migrated from New York to Tampa and Cuba in 1898, and with the US declaration of war against Spain, Clara Barton, who was by then in her late 70s, arrived in Tampa to oversee the training as she offered a Red Cross short course for nurses who worked heroically. (Ensminger Brothers Collection, USF.)

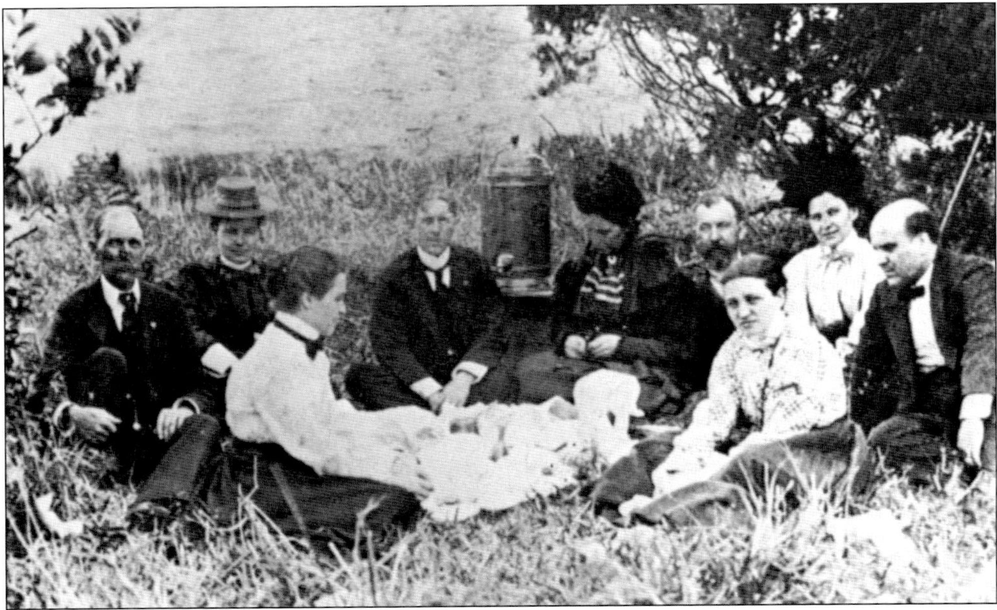

Clara Barton (center right, with head down) is shown with a group of colleagues from the Red Cross having a picnic, most likely at the Tampa Bay Hotel, built by Henry B. Plant, as they await permission to take relief supplies to Cuba. At her advanced age, Barton was ridiculed for taking on the endeavor of nurse training and coordination of health services for the Spanish-American War. Determined to lead, Barton carefully concealed her age with tedious daily make-up and demonstrated athletic vigor as she flourished in her efforts. (Florida Memory.)

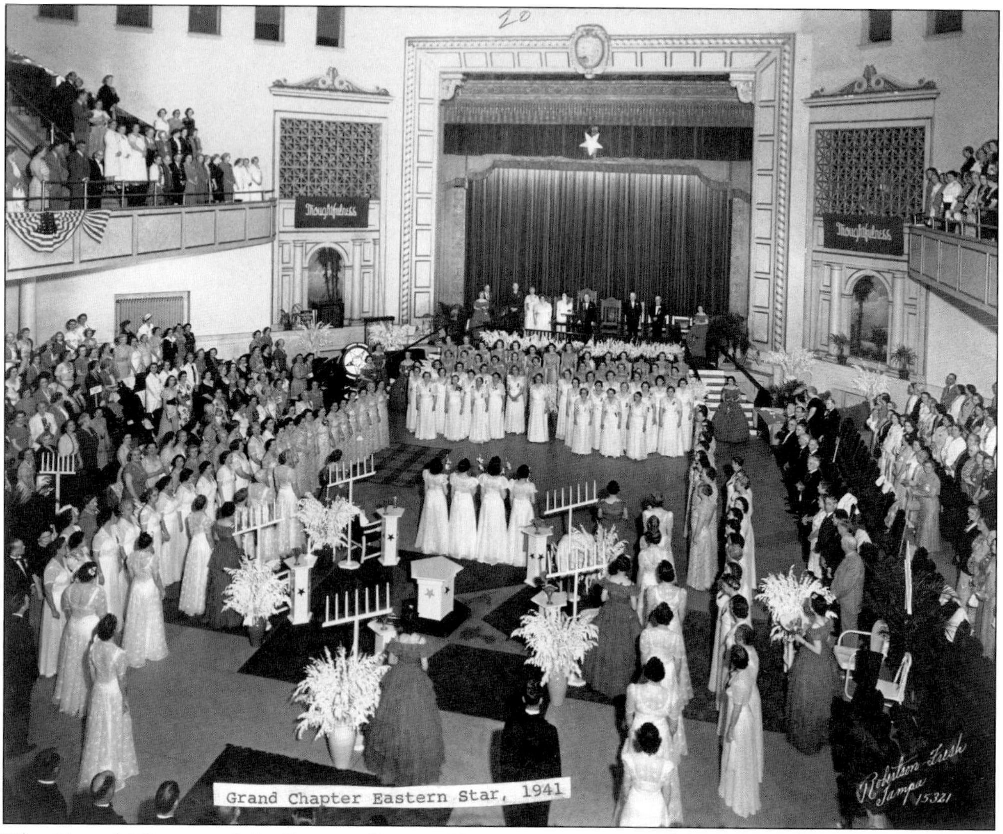

The Grand Chapter of the Eastern Star in Tampa is seen in a celebratory event in 1941. Several fraternal organizations such as Eastern Star, the woman's group associated with the Masons, and the Daughters of Rebekah (referred to as the Rebekahs), a women's group associated with the Independent Order of Odd Fellows, were significant in providing leadership opportunities for women to gain a voice and grow in societal and business endeavors. (Robertson and Fresh Collection, Florida Memory.)

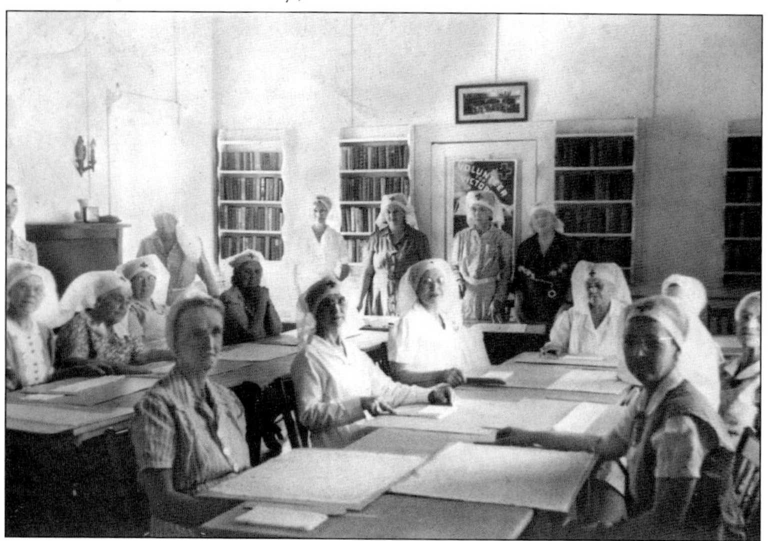

Red Cross Women's Club Volunteers during World War II were integral to assisting the war efforts. This group was photographed at Crystal River, Florida, in 1943. (Tampa Bay History Center.)

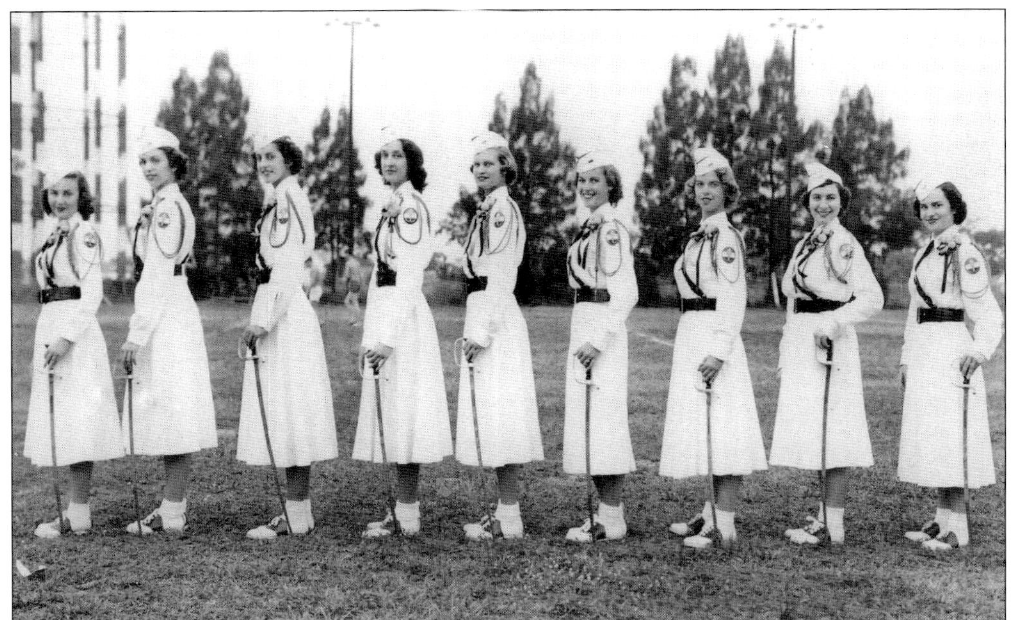

Post–World War II philosophies slowly changed regarding women in the military. This 1953 photograph of the Plant High School ROTC features nine female students in ROTC uniform, including Ann Einbinder, Aileen Wilson, Jane Perdigon, Beverly Ann Wright, Ann Cowart, Sally Villar, Anna Jo Graves, Joyce Schonbrum, and Shirley Morgan. (Tampa Bay History Center.)

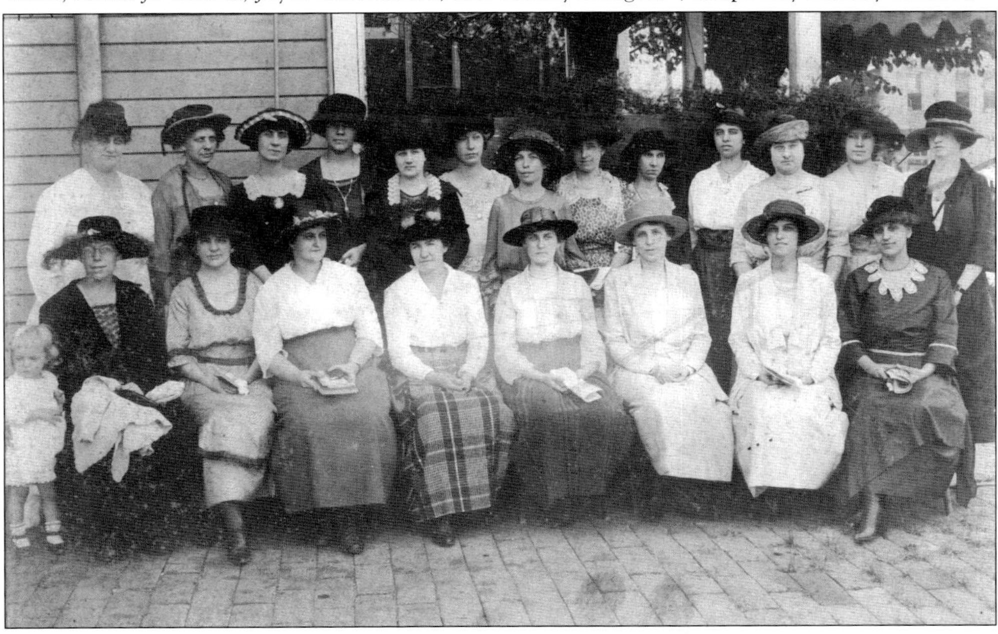

The Delta Alpha class of the First Methodist Episcopal Church, south of Tampa, poses in 1921. From left to right are (first row) Ruth Jeter, Duff Bell Jeter, Leila Stubs Jordan, Lena Wafford, Mae Drumm, Isey Drew Webb, Eva Blakeslee, Caroline Linkins, and Flora Carter Turner; (second row) Lenora Hawes Dunkle, Jessie Miller Wallace, Adine Stafford Frierson, Ann Bates Marshall, Lucy Whaley Pearson, Alma Peters Koone, Lottie Whaley, Debbie O'Neal, Maggie Gibson, Daisy Rae Smith, Myrtle Sawyer, Mrs. Hockinsmith Brown, and Willie Beatrice Hartley. (Tampa Bay History Center.)

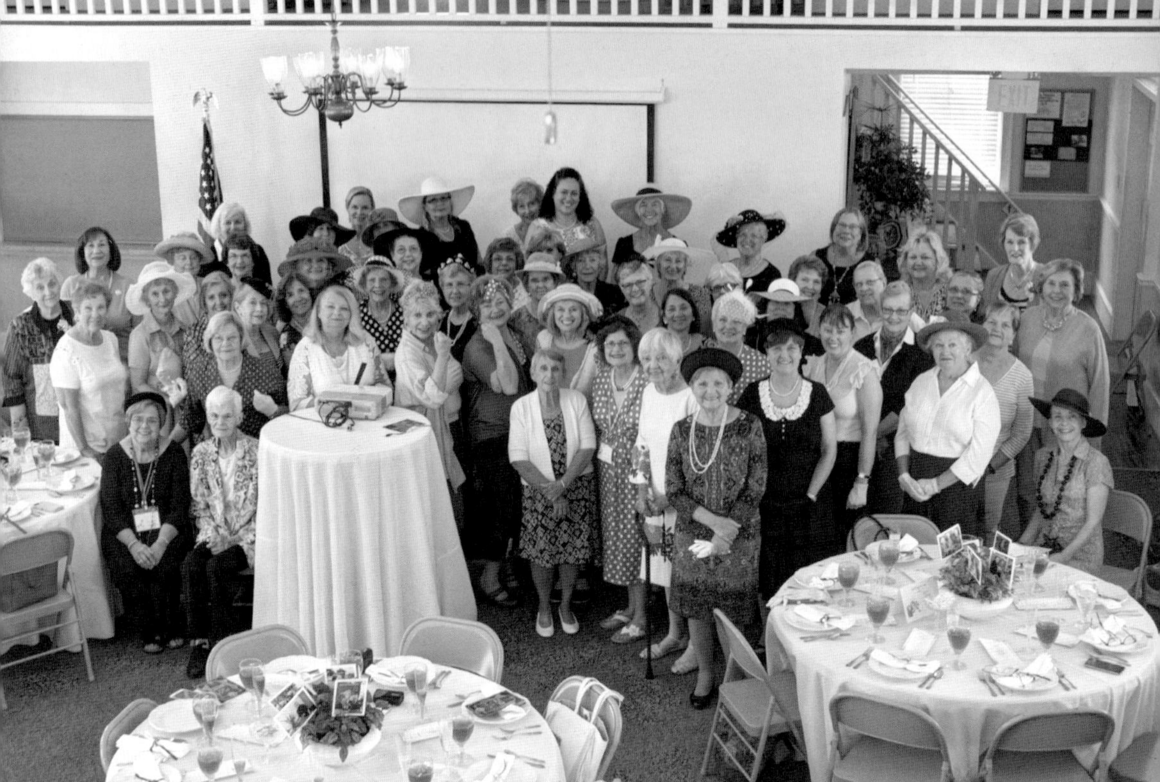

A typical Florida social club for women evolved and changed over time. Here, in 2017, the Dade City Garden Club celebrates its 70th anniversary with an array of business and professional women from all walks of life. Held in the historic Dade City Garden Club that was originally St. Rita's Mission Church, the members came together with guests and community dignitaries to celebrate the garden club as an integral component of Dade City. The first garden club was founded in Georgia. Dade City Garden Club was organized in 1947 and federated in 1948. Over time in post–World War II America, garden clubs became a voice for women in both creative expression and environmental advocacy. (Richard K. Riley.)

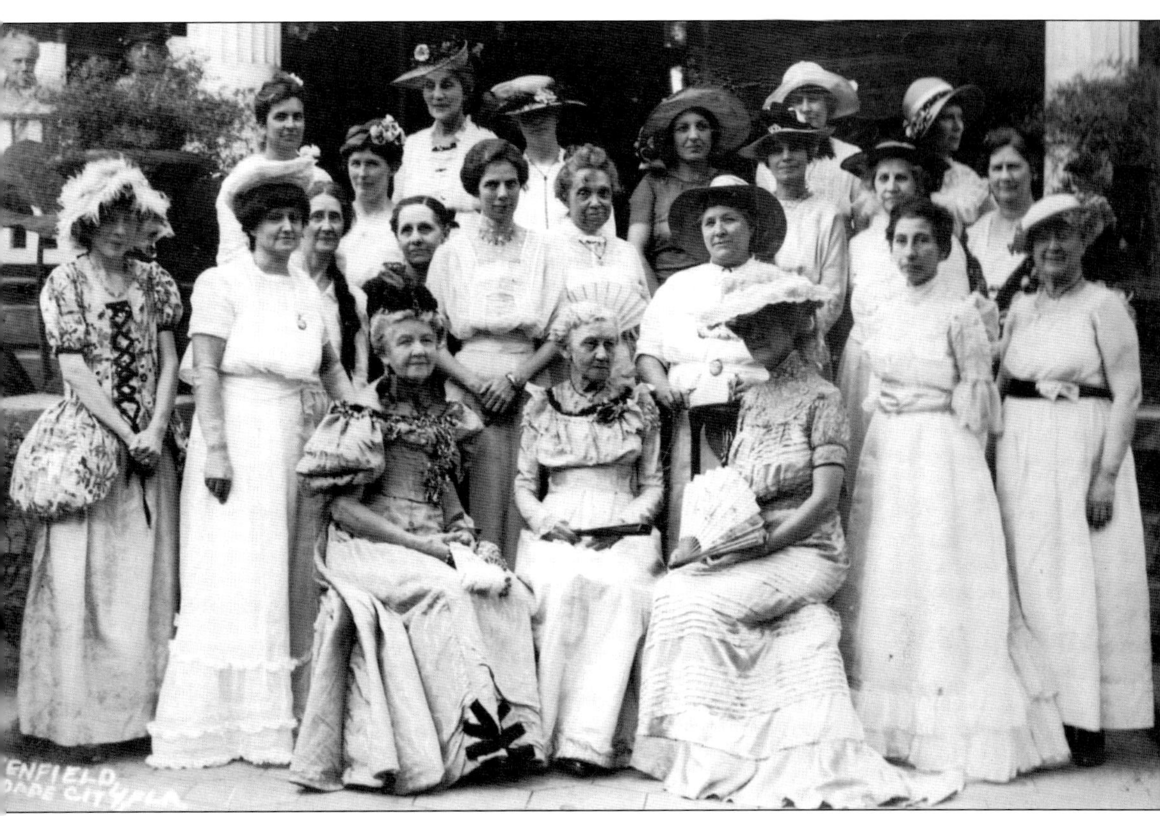

The Alpha Sorosis club was organized by Dade City women in 1909 and continued through 1968. They met regularly for intellectual pursuits. This 1928 meeting at the Edwinola Hotel marked the organization's anniversary. Each member dressed in teenage attire and answered to roll call from the latest book they had read. This photograph includes, in alphabetical order, Iva Wilder Aughenbaugh, Ella V. Bayeat, Jane Butts, Lydia Estella Paxson Butts, Sarah Carter, Mrs. Ray Cook, Alice M. Forsburg, Emily Grace Clark, Nancy Davis, Minnie Dayton, Harriett Gardner, Emma Lee Hill, Ruth Ann Parker, Ellen Richardson, Frances Sistrunk, Emma Stevenson, Frances L. Sturkie, Effie Taylor, Bertha C. Willis, Gertrude Wood, Hazel Wirt, and Mary Elizabeth Ziegler. (Susan Maesen.)

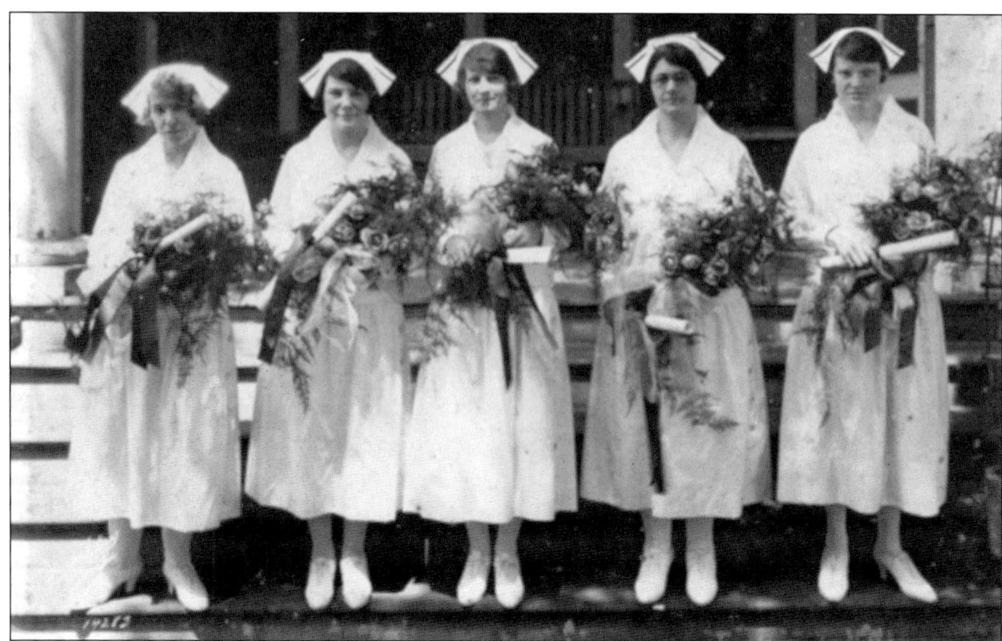

Carrying huge bouquets of roses and dressed in spotless white, graduates offer a picture symbolic of the oath to Florence Nightingale. The 1925 graduates of the Gordon Keller Memorial Training School included, from left to right, Sadie Pearl Vick, Etta Hazel Miner, Thelma Rochelle Redding, Mary Irene Wolfgang, and Zadie Ruth Bravo. The nursing school was established in 1910, named for downtown haberdasher Gordon Keller, and operated until 1972. About 1883, Keller came to Tampa and acquired an interest in the clothing business of Charles L. Jones, which became Keller Clothing Co. on the corner of Franklin and Lafayette Streets. Keller was community-minded with great empathy for others, so when he died in 1909, there was unanimous support that his memorial legacy would be Gordon Keller Memorial Hospital. Later, when a larger hospital was erected on Davis Islands (now Tampa General), an inscription was etched reading, "Memorial to Gordon Keller." In 1953, his two daughters, Susie Harris and Sara Hobbs, obtained the cornerstone of the old Gordon Keller Hospital and gifted it to the Gordon Keller Nurses' Alumnae Association, who placed it at the hospital nurses' home on Davis Islands. (Both, Burgert Brothers Collection, USF.)

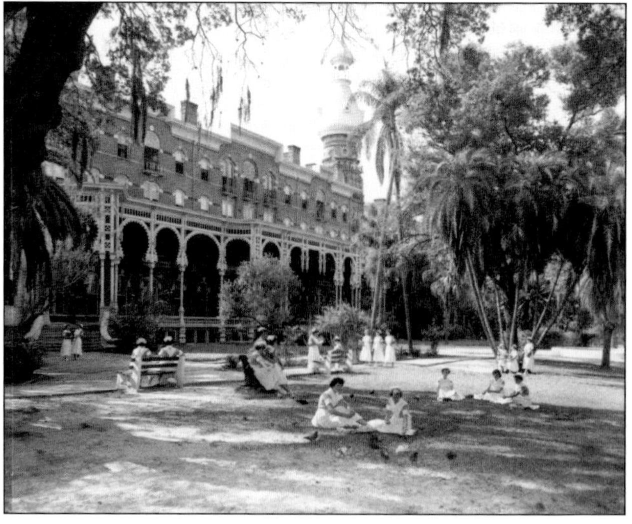

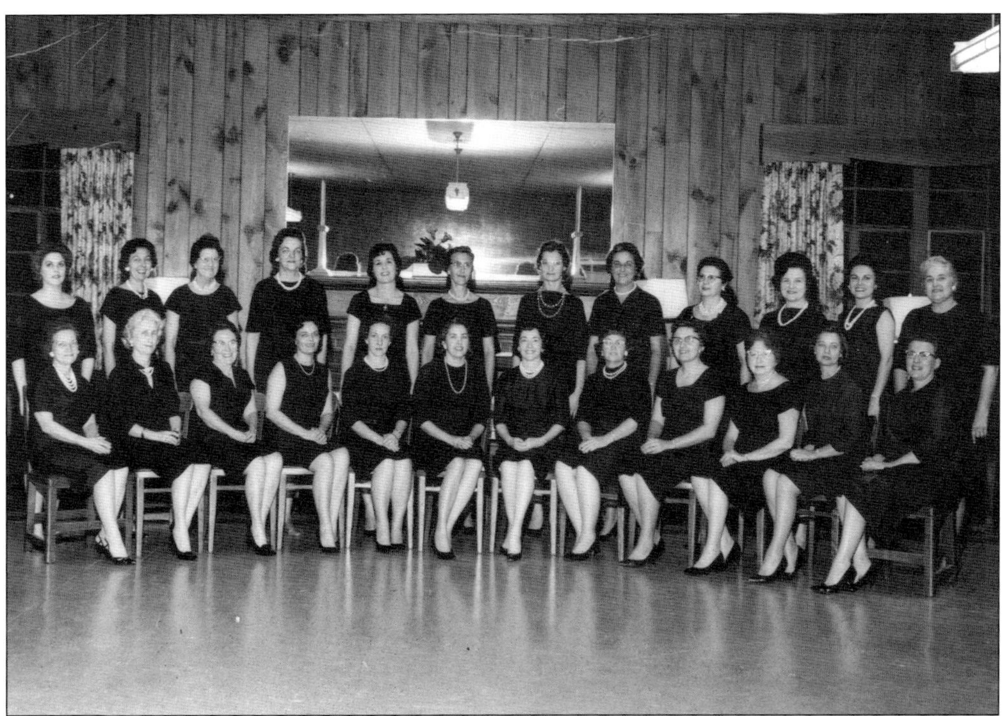

The Tampa Professional and Businesswomen's Chorus and soloists are pictured on March 2, 1965, at the North Boulevard Recreational Center next to the state fairgrounds. Chartered in 1919, the group hosted workshops and lecturers, contemplated professional attire, and provided camaraderie. Frances Stearns was the new president in 1922 and served under the inaugural president, Nellie H. Macfarlane, while Irene Rovira, telegraph editor for the *Times*, was elected a director. The club met at the Tampa Gas Company at the corner of Madison and Tampa Streets. (Tampa Bay History Center.)

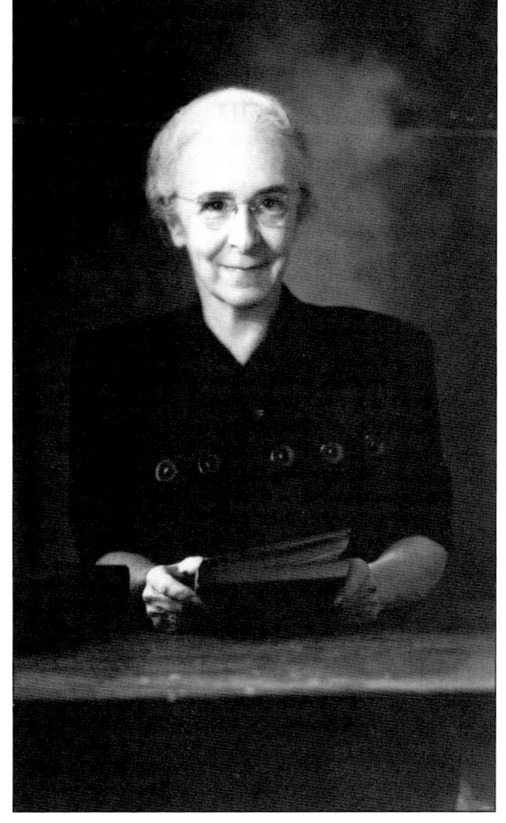

"Known to thousands of library users in Tampa, particularly school children in whom she took a particular interest, she always saw that none of their questions went unanswered," read Helen Virginia Steele's 1947 obituary. Steele took charge of the Tampa Public Library System for over 30 years. She organized the Florida Library Association and was active in professional organizations, including as an officer in the Southeastern Library Association. (Tampa–Hillsborough County Public Library.)

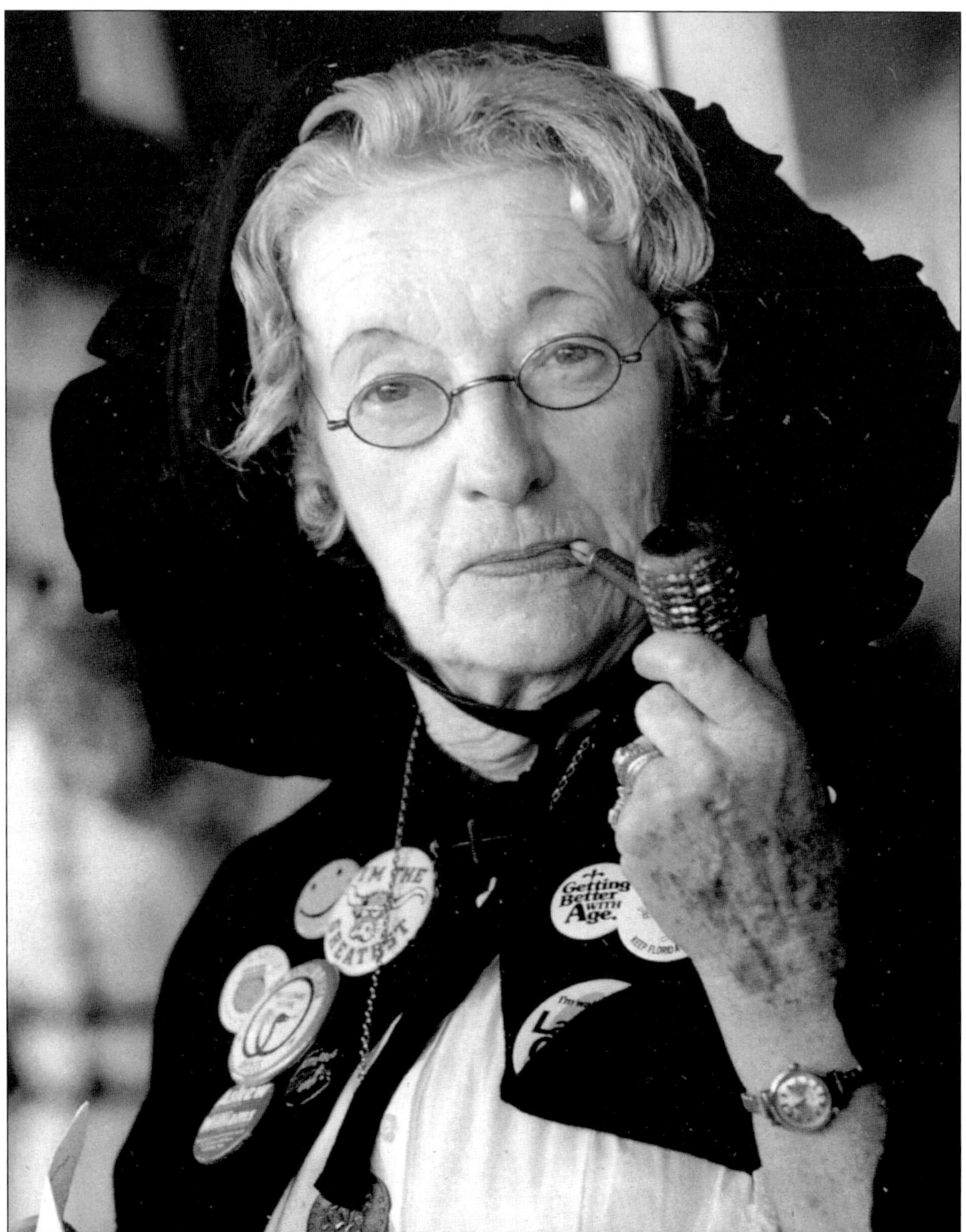

"Alice Hall has made a living doing what people say cannot be done," wrote Paul Hogan of the *Tribune* in 1990. Active in the chamber, Garden Club, and Veteran's Associations, a goal was to bring a hospital, which she facilitated in the 1980s. Later, she equipped the facility with cardiovascular equipment from funds she raised. Shown in the 1976 Founder's Day Parade in period costume, she retired as a writer at age 86 for the *Tribune*, where she worked from 1953 until 1990, chronicling local news. "Without her, gone would be the hospital, the city's first nursing home, first bank, its first emergency rescue equipment, its blood drive, its floral displays, Krusen Field, the Pioneer Florida Museum and even the continuation of Founder's Day. What she does, she does with her whole heart," said councilwoman Gloria Brown. (Zephyrhills Historical Society.)

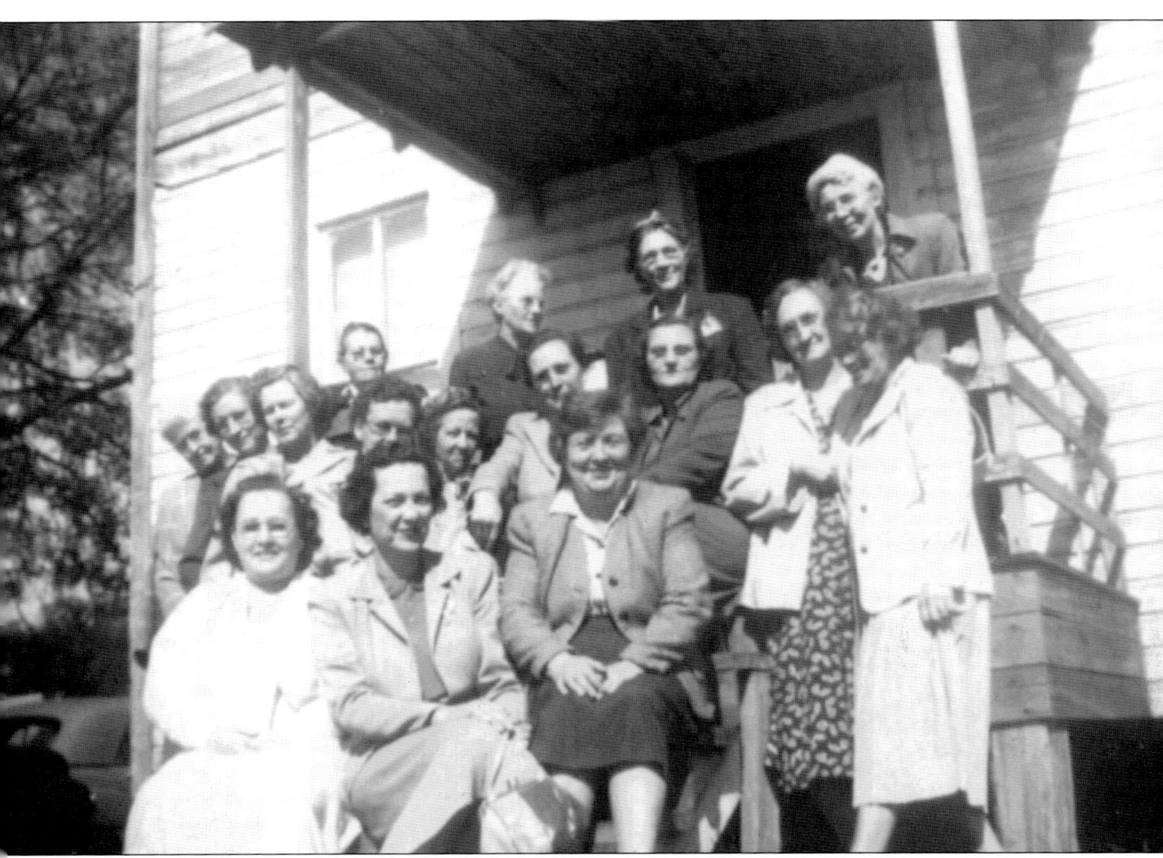

Part of the Progressive Era, home demonstration clubs were a component of the US Department of Agriculture's Cooperative Extension Program with the goal of improving women's lives by imparting research and information on the latest technology with skill-building. In the bay area town of Trilby, the club poses in front of the Trilby Masonic Lodge in 1951. Members pictured are Bessie Cannon, Bernadette Chesbro, Myrtle Davis, Flossie Edwards, Verna Free, Gertrude Greshem, Ethel Mingus, Jesse Moore, Allie Prevatt, Lenessa Richardson, Mary Stearns, Leota Whittington, Elizabeth Wilkes, and Georgianna Woodburn. Not shown are Velma Burney, Katie Carlisle, Thelma Farr, Essa Davidson Gould, Exa Hicks, Minnie Hopkins, Missie Morgan, Ruth O'Berry, and Hattie Tyer. (Pasco County Fair Association.)

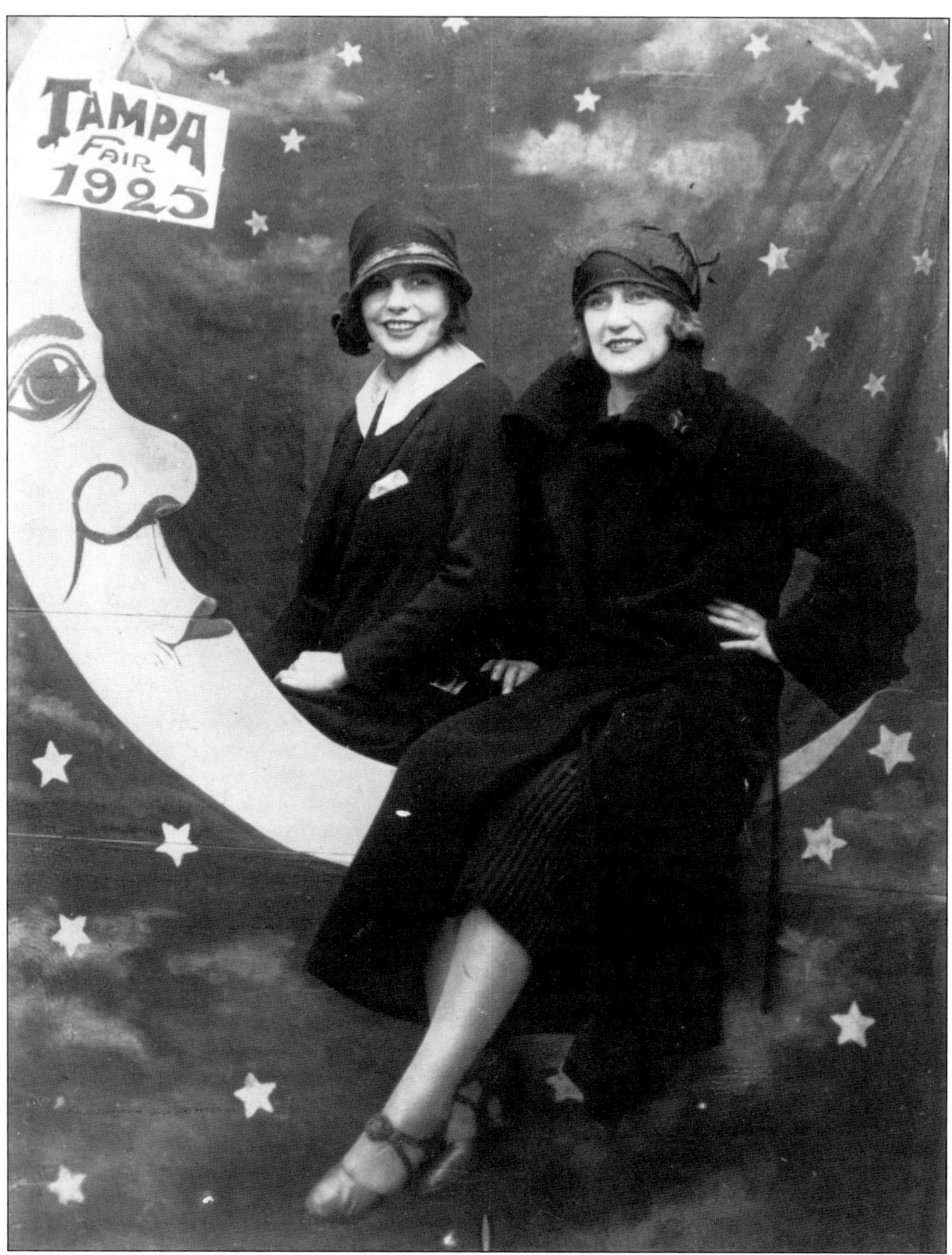

This image from the Tampa Fair in 1925 shows women posing on a moon prop. The *Tribune* on February 20, 1925, reported that the Tampa Fair broke all attendance records, and the fair this year was unanimously voted best ever. For home demonstration clubs, the local fairs and the state fair were opportunities for instructional gatherings and displays of the latest innovations and projects. (Tampa Bay History Center.)

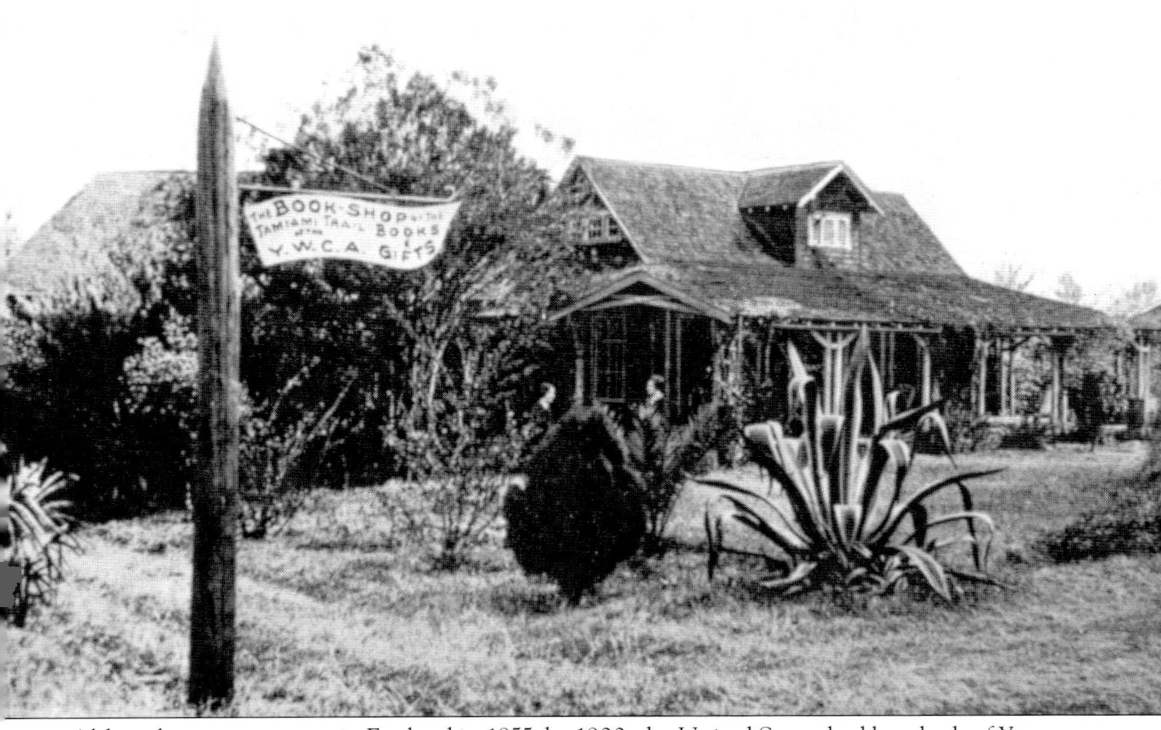

Although its origins were in England in 1855, by 1900, the United States had hundreds of Young Women's Christian Associations. This postcard proclaimed, "The Hill City-A Jewel in the County of Hills," and shows the YWCA building. In 1931, Lenora Beck Ellis of the *Times* reported, "By the fifth birthday of this beneficent enterprise, the Bookshop of the Tamiami Trail is found in spacious quarters on the historic highway . . . built originally for a motion picture place, the large store space in front, is now lined with volumes of books." The bookstore and YWCA facility provided a meeting place for various local women's groups. (Florida Memory.)

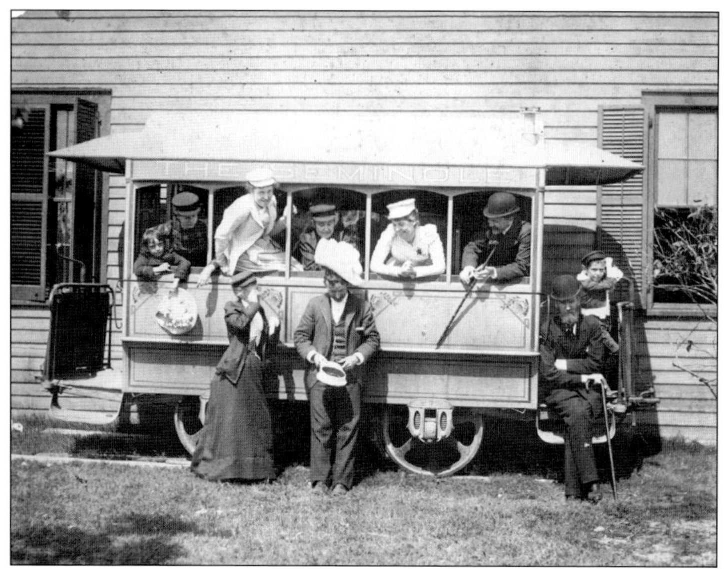

An open trolley car named the *Seminole*, seen here in 1892, provides an opportunity to frolic for young people in Tampa. Leaning out of the windows are, from left to right, Gladys Crocker, unidentified, Kate Walker, Jennie Fassett, Margaret Bender, and unidentified. Standing are Crete Couch and ? Ledwirt. On the platform are Truman Fassett and unidentified. (Florida Memory).

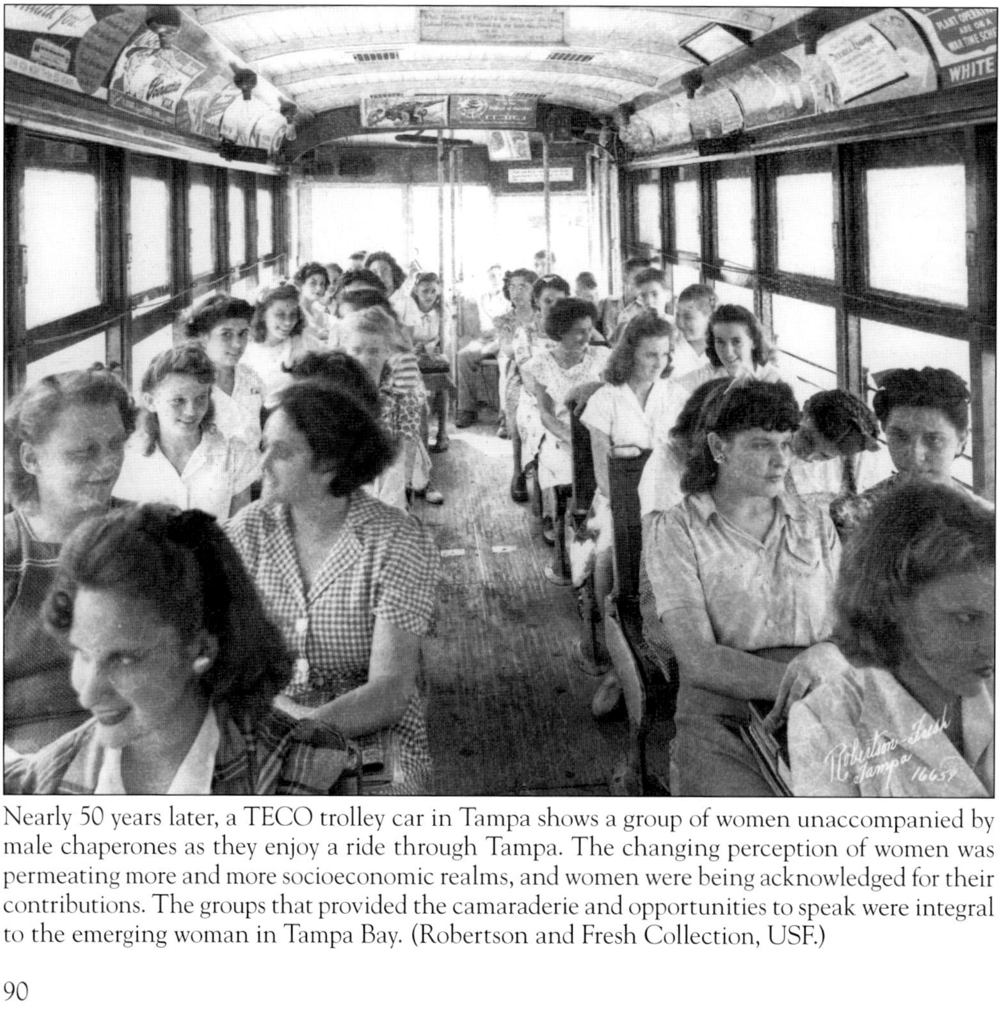

Nearly 50 years later, a TECO trolley car in Tampa shows a group of women unaccompanied by male chaperones as they enjoy a ride through Tampa. The changing perception of women was permeating more and more socioeconomic realms, and women were being acknowledged for their contributions. The groups that provided the camaraderie and opportunities to speak were integral to the emerging woman in Tampa Bay. (Robertson and Fresh Collection, USF.)

Five

Courage under Fire

Courageous women have stepped up throughout history in Tampa Bay. Frequently, they remained nameless, and their humble stories were untold. Their selfless sacrifice, however, sustained families through employment inside and outside the home and improved living conditions, as they literally saved lives and simply made a difference. This chapter offers a glimpse at a few Tampa Bay women who charted paths of service, stepped out in work environments, and sometimes even risked their well-being and comfort to grow the community.

In the workforce of contemporary America, about 76 percent of working-age women are in the workforce, but this percentage has evolved from only 18 percent in 1900. The Center for Creative Leadership recognized that Fortune 500 companies with higher representation of women in leadership outperformed companies with low representation. Although the roles of women have evolved with, for example, a nearly equal amount of women training in professional fields as men, women lag in salary and benefits. Women remain the central workers in the service fields. Unfortunately, working conditions and safety have not always been prioritized, and a few of the examples reveal the tireless fortitude of workers who sought improvement.

Women in this chapter range from modern-day Joan of Arcs to Mother Teresas, and their humility is admirable, as they were motivated to recognize need and serve others.

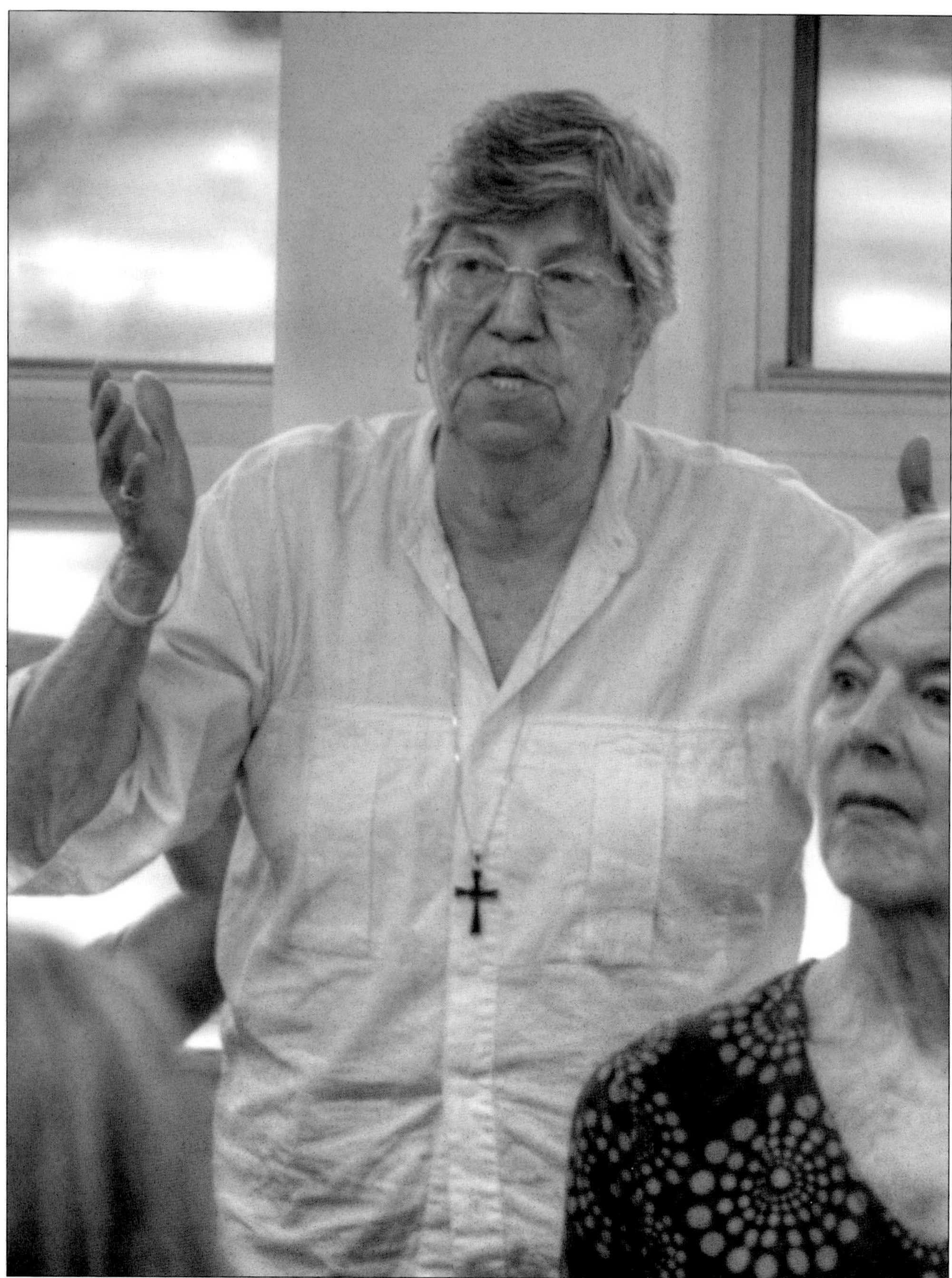

"This is what God planned for me, and I will be here until the day I die," Margarita Romo proclaimed in 2010 when she was honored as Hispanic Woman of the Year by the Tampa Hispanic Heritage. Romo is best known for advocating and lobbying for improvements to Tommy Town, a poor farmworker community on the north end of Dade City, and organizing Agricultural Women Involved in New Goals (AWING), a self-help program designed to help women create better lives for themselves through education. Romo stands beside Anne Johnson, a nurse and educator who contributed greatly to education as director of vocational education. (Richard K. Riley.)

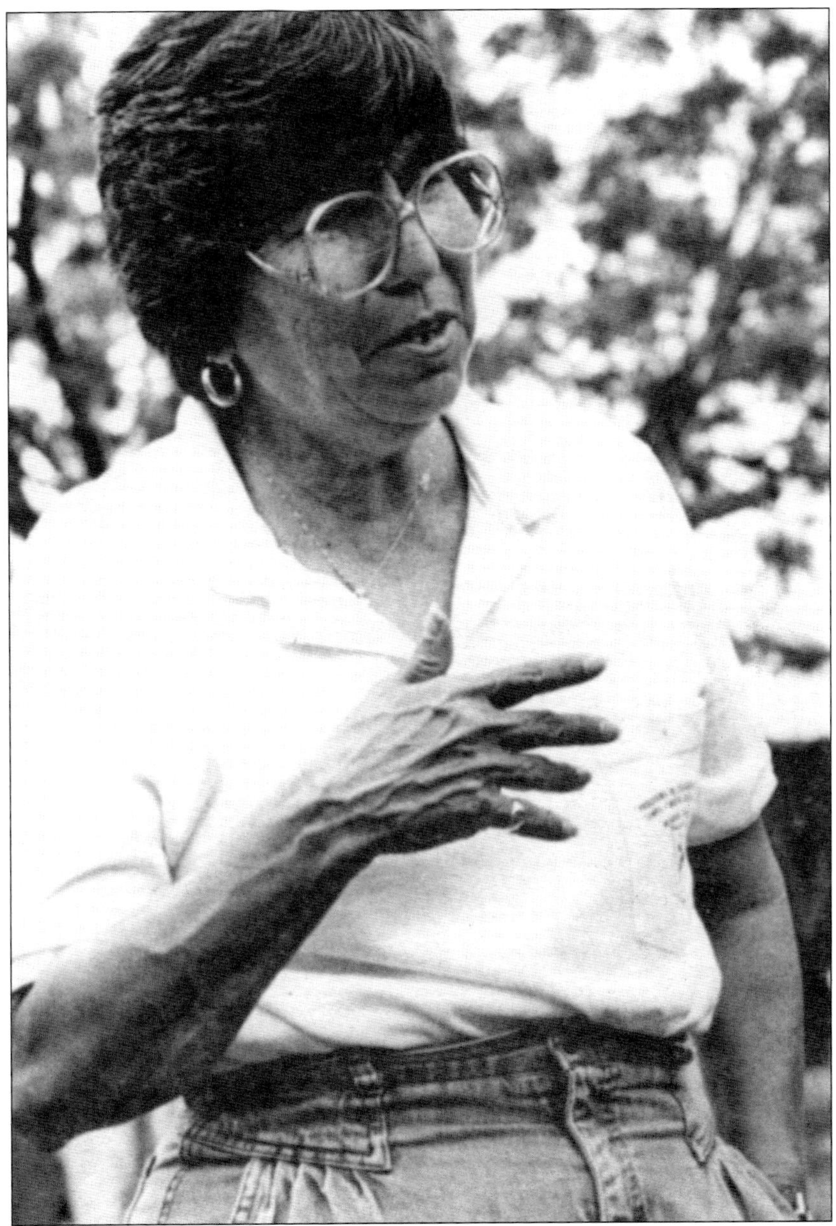

Margarita Romo was named to the Florida Civil Rights Hall of Fame in 2012 by the Florida Commission on Human Relations. Candace Samolinski wrote, "Embrace her, quarrel with her, but don't try to ignore her . . . this petite mother of six children has been spreading her message of equality for farmworkers. She has gone head-to-head with commissioners and other political leaders including Governor Jeb Bush." Romo said, "I started in 1971, not because I'm some Joan of Arc. I'm just a regular person." Romo was raised in a Texas convent from the age of three after her mother died. Explaining that she grew up believing women could only teach, she became a translator for ministers in the migrant camps, which evolved into a ministry. Later, after attending Pasco Hernando State College, she partnered to provide food and clothing banks. Her role of advocacy expanded her reach as she assisted workers in learning the process of filing immigration papers when migrant camps were raided by border patrols in the 1980s. (Farmworkers Self-Help Inc.)

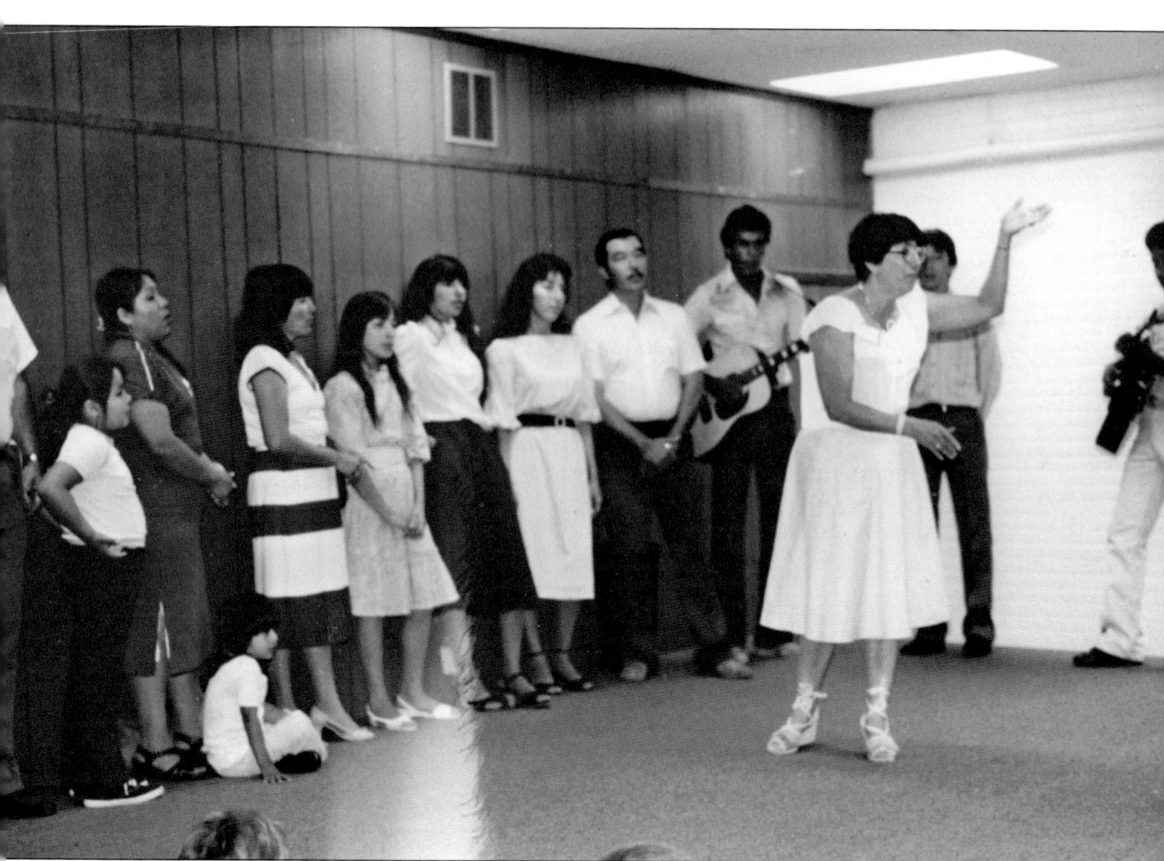

As founder of Farmworkers Self-Help Inc., Margarita Romo committed over 50 years for migrant families in the Tampa Bay area with free medical clinics, after-school programs for teens, food support, and an educational learning center. Former governor Rick Scott said, "She has acted on her conviction and truly made a difference in countless lives in our state and around the country." Romo is shown here with her English class. (Photograph by Davida Johns, courtesy of Farmworkers Self-Help Inc.)

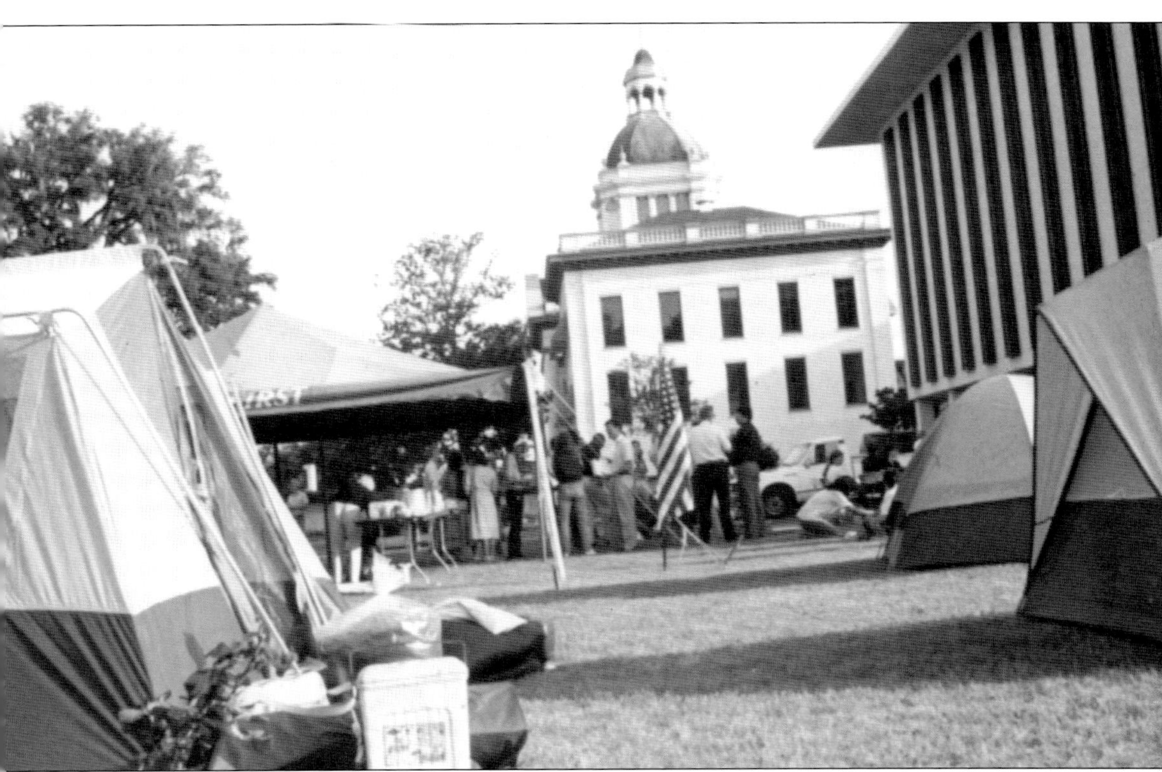

Marching with civil rights advocate and co-founder of the National Farmworkers Association, César Chávez, in her early years, Romo is an unequaled spokesperson for the underprivileged and a community treasure and unequaled role model in the Tampa Bay area. Today, Farmworkers Self-Help is a lifeline that provides English classes, translation services, and a soup kitchen. To Romo, education is paramount, and she is proud that children who have passed through the organizations have become doctors and lawyers. In addition, Self-Help, as well as the Coalition of Immokalee Workers and others, have fought to help workers with insurance, living conditions, and work relations. This photograph is of workers in Tallahassee advocating for needed funding and legislation. (Farmworkers Self-Help, Dade City, Florida.)

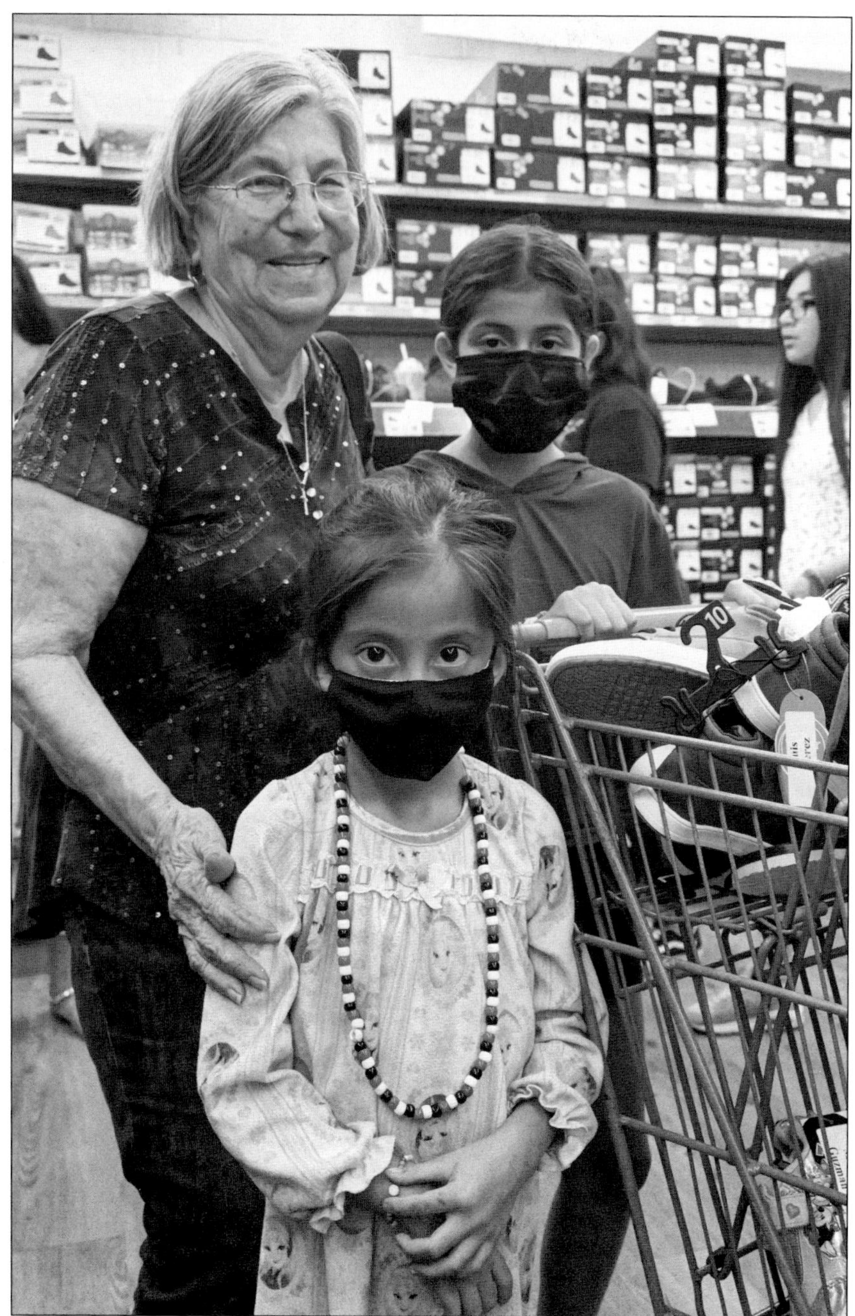

Ordained in 2003, Romo considers this commitment her highest achievement, and divinely inspired. In 1996, she related that her mission was to help young Hispanics and farmworkers by fighting the poverty, disease, and violence many of them face every day. Tax collector and longtime senator Mike Fasano said, "I have come to realize the zeal she has for people she serves shows how truly committed she is to helping them." This image shows Romo with Hilan Luna (front) and Arlene Luna at Farmworkers Self-Help and Resurrection House and Park at an event that was sponsored by the Nativity Lutheran Church of Weeki Wachee, which has donated school supplies and new shoes for the past 10 years. (Richard K. Riley.)

Betty Mae Tiger Jumper, who also had the Seminole name Potackee, was the first female chief of the Seminole Tribe of Florida in 1967. Appointed to the National Congress on Indian Opportunity, she was a prominent lobbyist for Native Americans. As the first health director, she was beloved for her incredible tribal storytelling. (Florida Memory.)

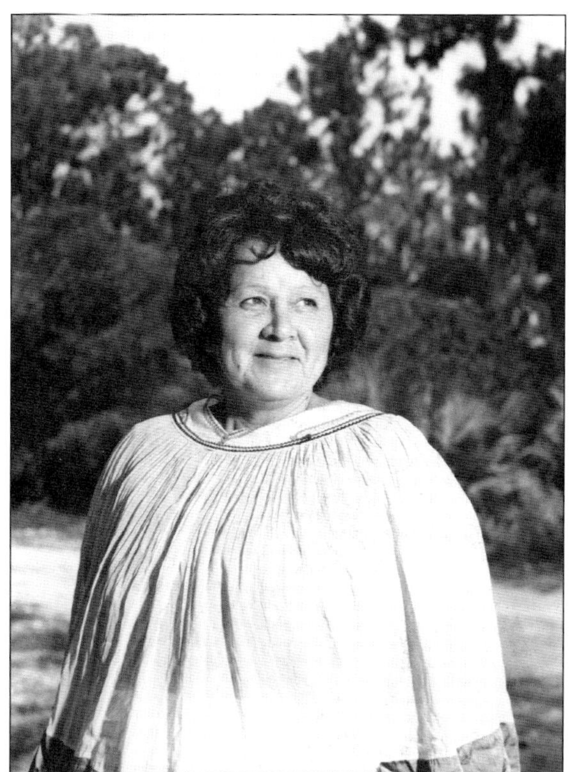

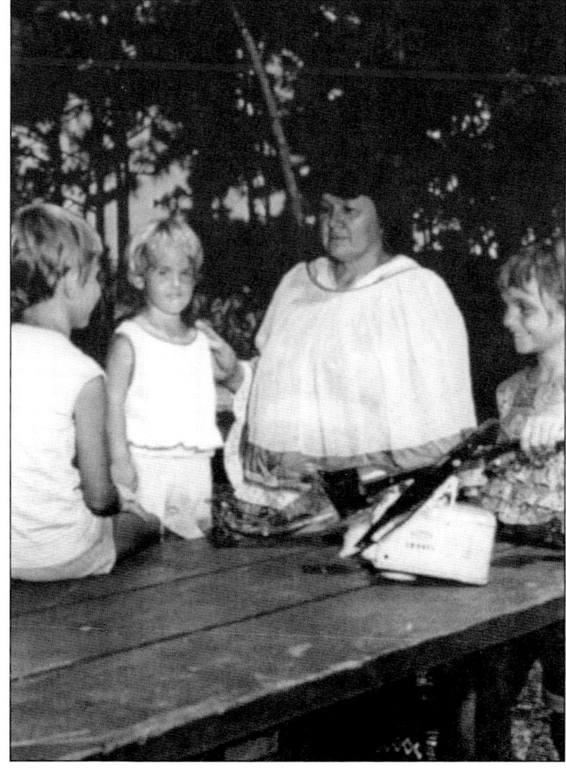

Awarded an honorary doctorate from Florida State University, Betty Mae Tiger Jumper was appointed by Pres. Richard Nixon to the National Congress on Indian Opportunity. Jumper edited the *Seminole Tribune* and authored two books: *And with the Wagon—Came God's Word* as well as *Legends of the Seminoles*. (Florida Memory.)

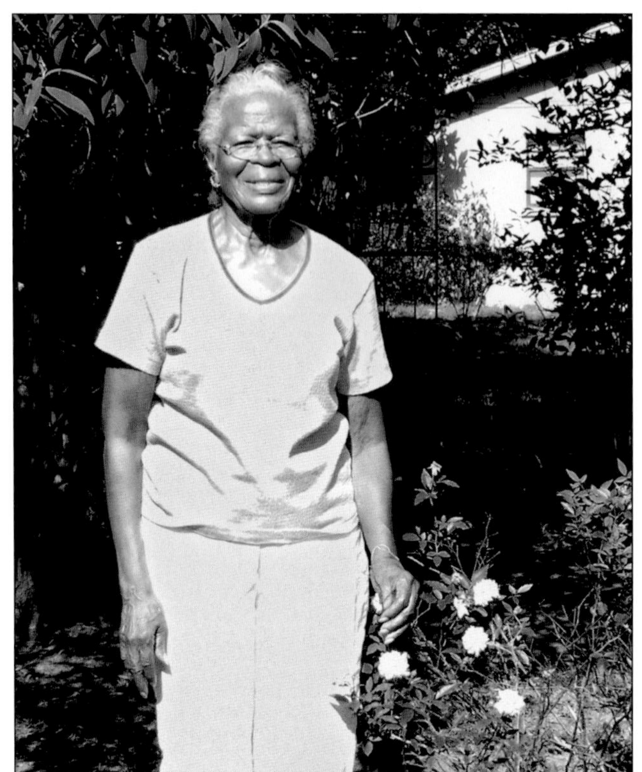

Irene Dobson was one of Tampa Bay's outstanding community activists during the last 40 years of the 20th century and the first decade of the 21st century. Her purpose in life has been to make her community a better place. Racial and economic barriers never soured her pursuit to encourage youth, politicians, ministers, and law enforcement personnel to do the right things. Born in Georgia during the height of Jim Crow, she moved to Florida in 1946 with her husband, Robert, who worked for the Hercules Powder Company, the largest employer in Zephyrhills. "She is a leader who gets things done such as paved streets and streetlights for Moody Subdivision and MLK Street recognition," said Imani Asukile. (Dobson family.)

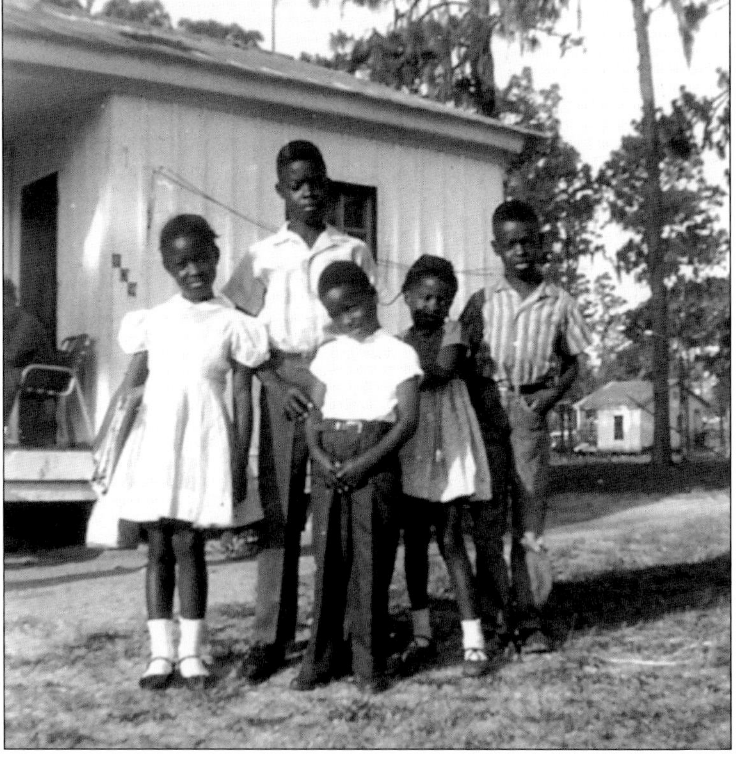

A Hercules Powder Company home in the days of segregation is seen here, with, from left to right, May McKenzie Pickett (mother of professional football player Ryan Pickett), E.J. McKenzie in back, Van McKenzie, Celia Dobson, and Alvin McKenzie. (Dobson family.)

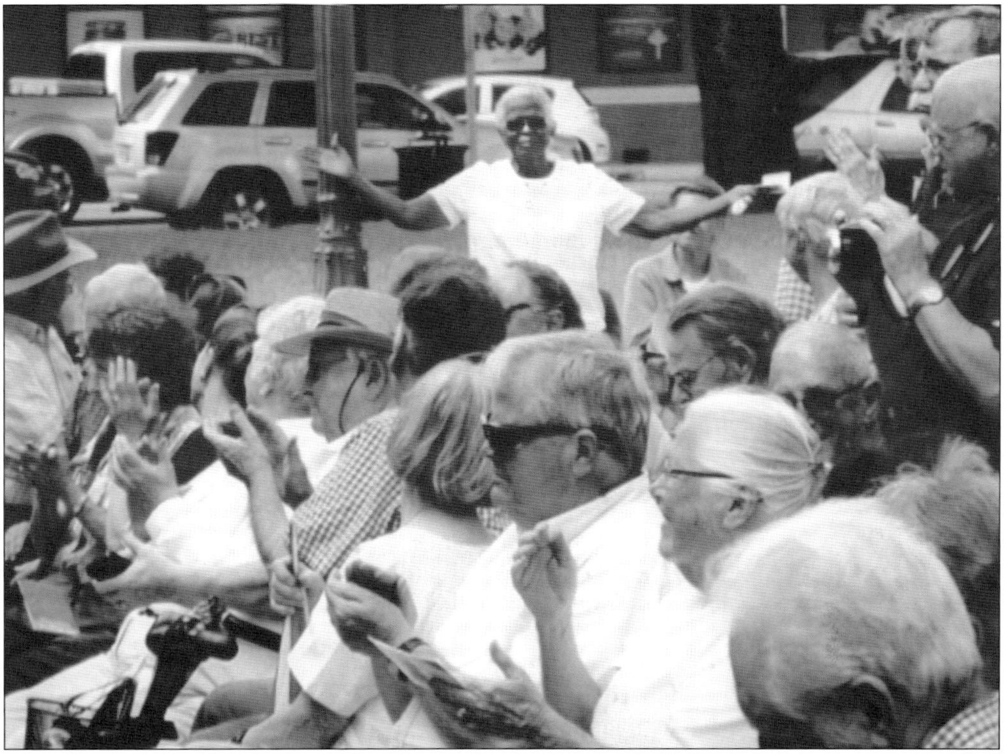

Irene Dobson is shown in front of the Dade City Courthouse as a crowd acknowledges and welcomes her. A founding teacher of the Head Start Early Childhood Program, her outspoken and well-researched persona made her a regular member of the school advisory council, PTA, and community groups in Tampa Bay, as she voiced concerns and identified needs to problem-solve. (Richard K. Riley.)

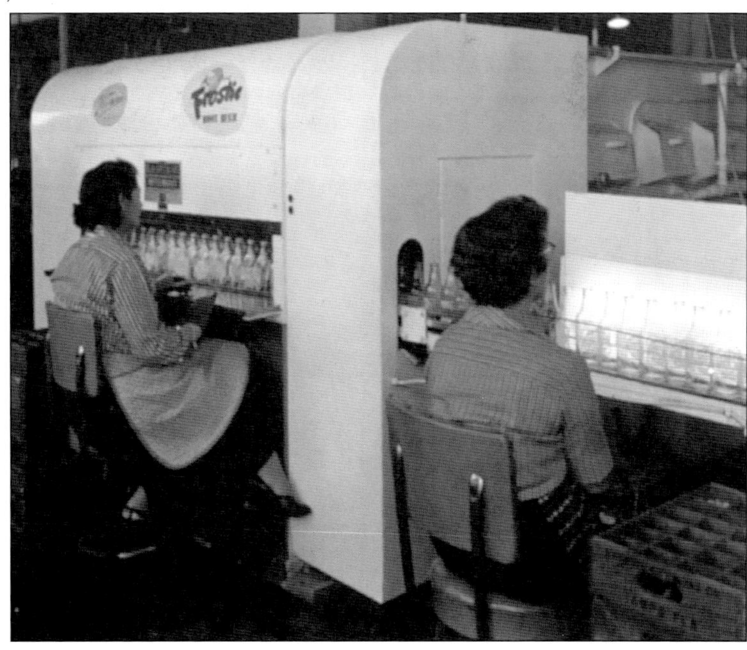

Women workers attentively inspect the glass bottles that were filled with root beer at a bottle washing machine station at the Frostie Bottling Company in Tampa. At the time of this photograph in 1958, one in three women participated in the labor force. (Burgert Brothers Collection, Tampa–Hillsborough County Public Library.)

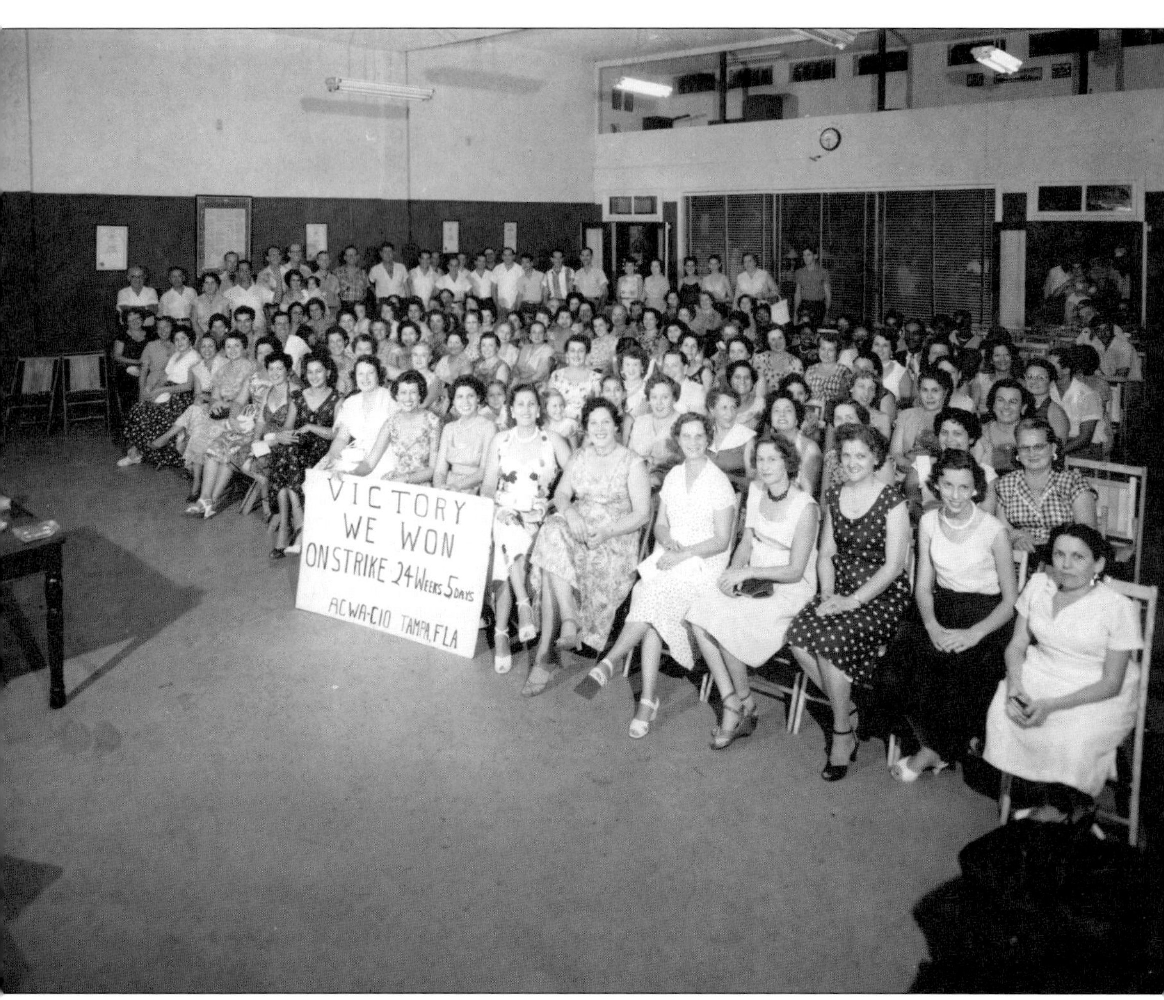

The women of the Amalgamated Clothing Workers of America, a member organization of the Congress of Industrial Organizations (CIO), staged a brave labor strike that was marked by violence, threats, and even an explosion in 1955 after Sunstate Slacks Inc. on North Howard Avenue in Tampa cut the hourly rate of female workers. It began on January 5, when 170 women walked out with the backing and full support of all CIO unions in the country, including auto, brewery, furniture, paper, steel, stone, and oil workers, and the Florida State and West Coast Industrial Union Councils, which stood by the female workers. They published notices in the local newspapers urging all Tampa residents to respect the picket lines and offer active support, stating it would contribute to making Tampa a better place to work and live for all citizens. The debacle originated when Sunstate Slacks won a National Labor Relations election and, with 17 negotiation attempts, presented a 10 percent cut in wages to the women. After six turbulent months, the workers gained a near 15 percent increase in wage and fringe benefits. In a time in which only approximately 33 percent of the labor force was women, this episode represented courageous action. (Burgert Brothers Collection, Tampa–Hillsborough County Public Library.)

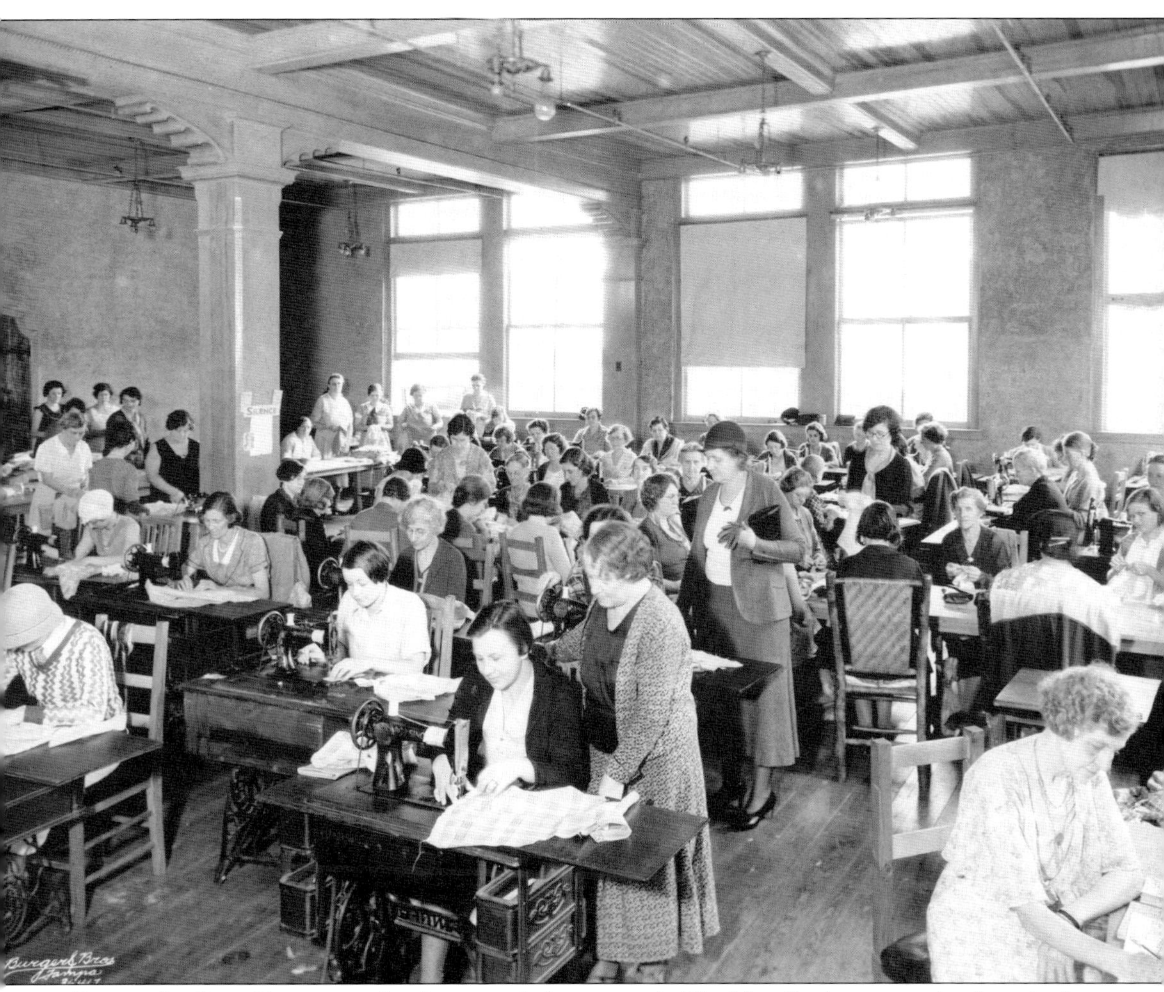

During the Great Depression, families struggled enormously. The New Deal recovery plan launched by Pres. Franklin Roosevelt put many women to work, including women in Tampa in the Civil Works Administration. This photograph shows some of the more than 300 women employed in four sewing rooms maintained by the Hillsborough County Emergency Relief Council, who typically labored 30 hours a week in two shifts to sew clothing for unemployed families. The sewing room was in the *Times* building. Established in 1932 as part of the Junior League, they made 2,000 garments each week. Marjorie Fish was the director of the Relief Council of the Social Service Department and was responsible for the distribution of the clothing. This image was printed in the *Tampa Daily Times* on January 25, 1934. (Burgert Brothers Collection, Tampa–Hillsborough County Public Library.)

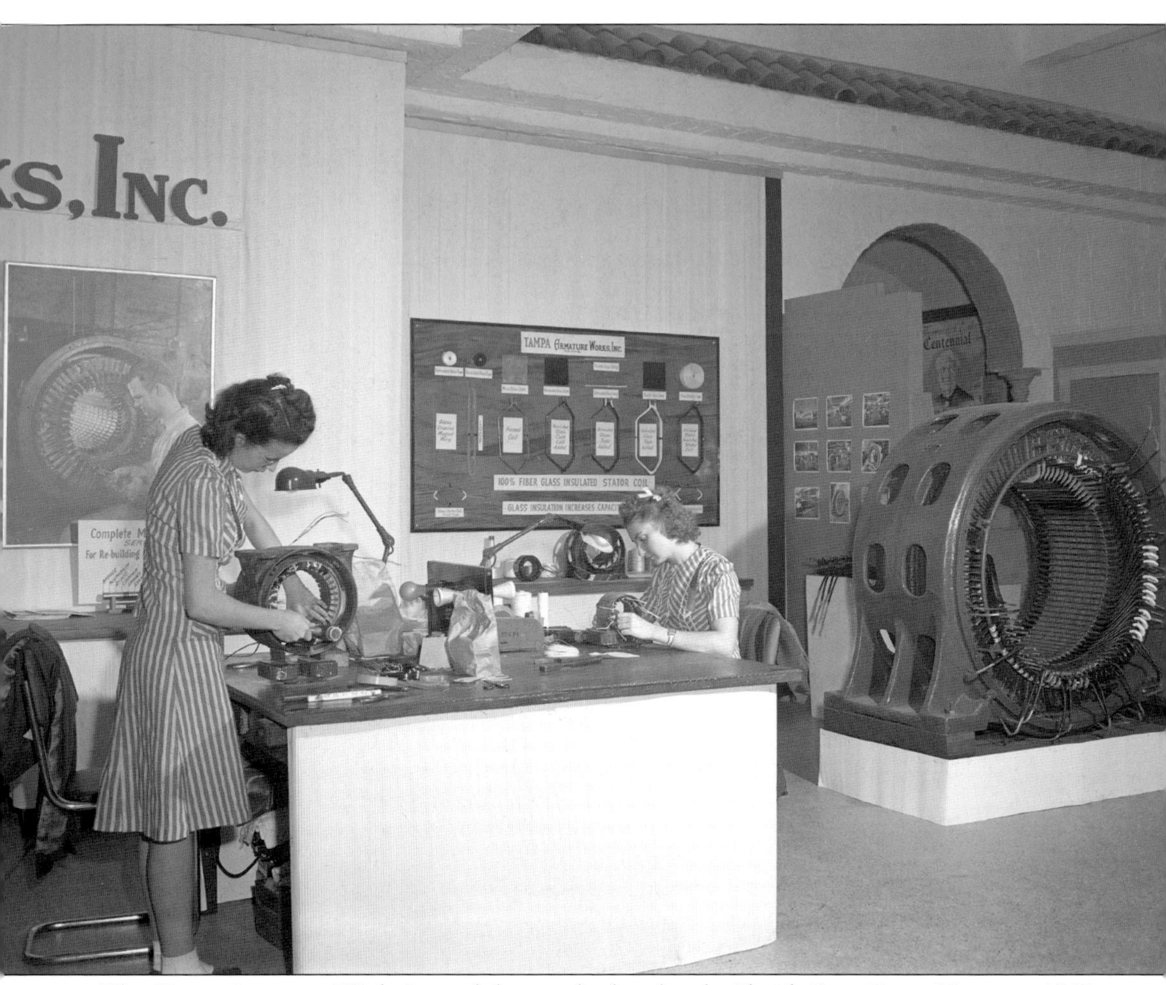

This Tampa Armature Works Inc. exhibit was displayed at the Florida State Fair in Tampa in 1947. Opened in April 1921 at 203 Tampa Street, the firm was a partnership between James Arthur Turner, William H. Garlets, and Claude Mein, who were experienced in construction and repair of switchboards, motors, and generators. Employing area female workers during World War II, they recruited Alla Mae Hurlston and Maxine Musselman to host the exhibit. (Florida Memory.)

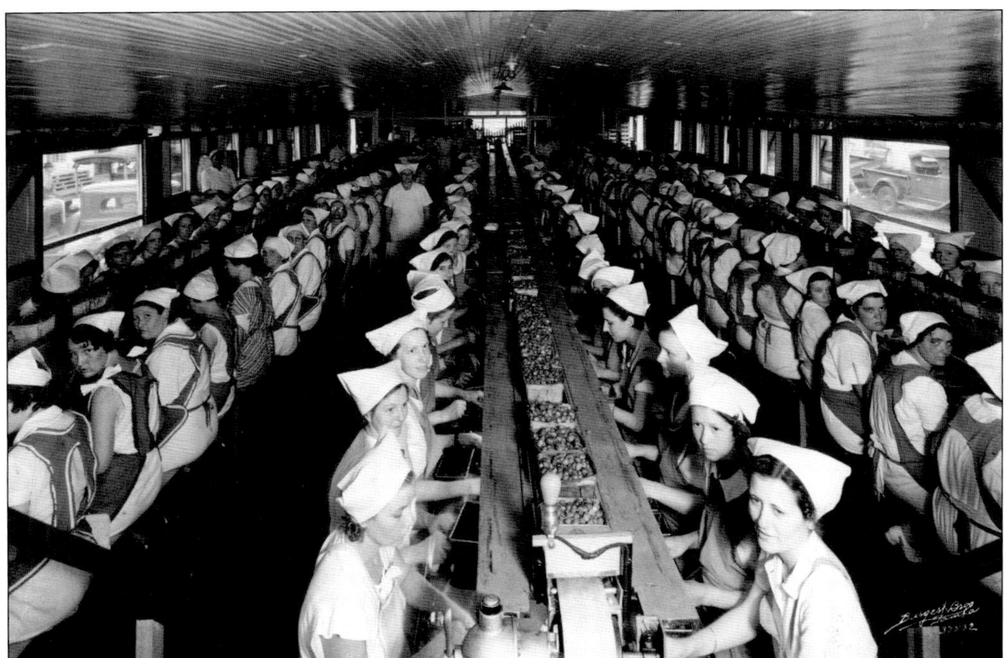

The C.H. Kruse strawberry plant in Plant City offered fruit processing as work for women in the mid-20th century. Women frequently chose seasonal work in the 1940s and 1950s because only about 30 percent of the labor force was female. At this juncture in history, women were frequently not employed in professional work except teaching and nursing. Childcare for women working outside the home was not readily available. This photograph reflects the camaraderie of the women working together. In that era, Plant City was developing strawberry planting and harvesting as Florida was evolving into the largest strawberry-producing state. C.H. Kruse, who owned the operation, was also experimenting with strawberry packing and transportation while he worked on other commodities in the northern states. (Burgert Brothers Collection, Tampa–Hillsborough County Public Library.)

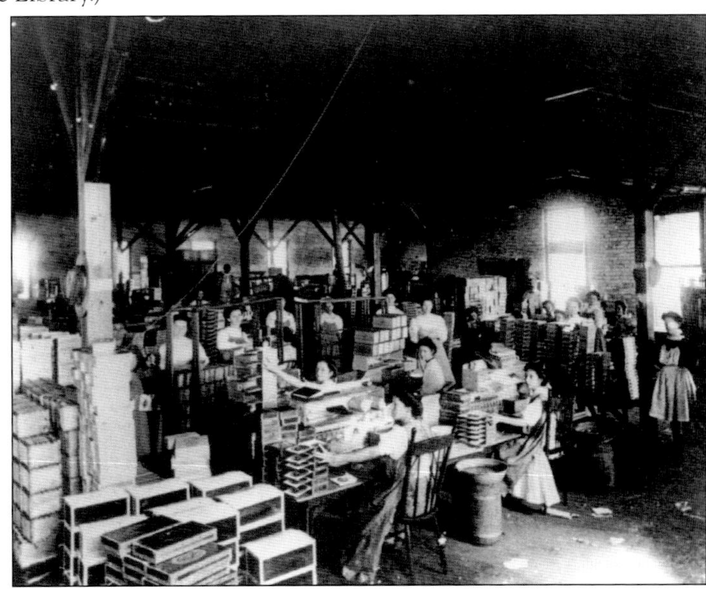

Young women are at work gluing elaborate brand labels onto boxes that contained cigars from the nearby Cuesta Rey factory at the J.W. Young Cigar Box Company in 1917. The factory was on Frances Avenue and Ponce de Leon Street (now North Albany and Beach Streets) in West Tampa. All the employees were women. (Tampa Bay History Center.)

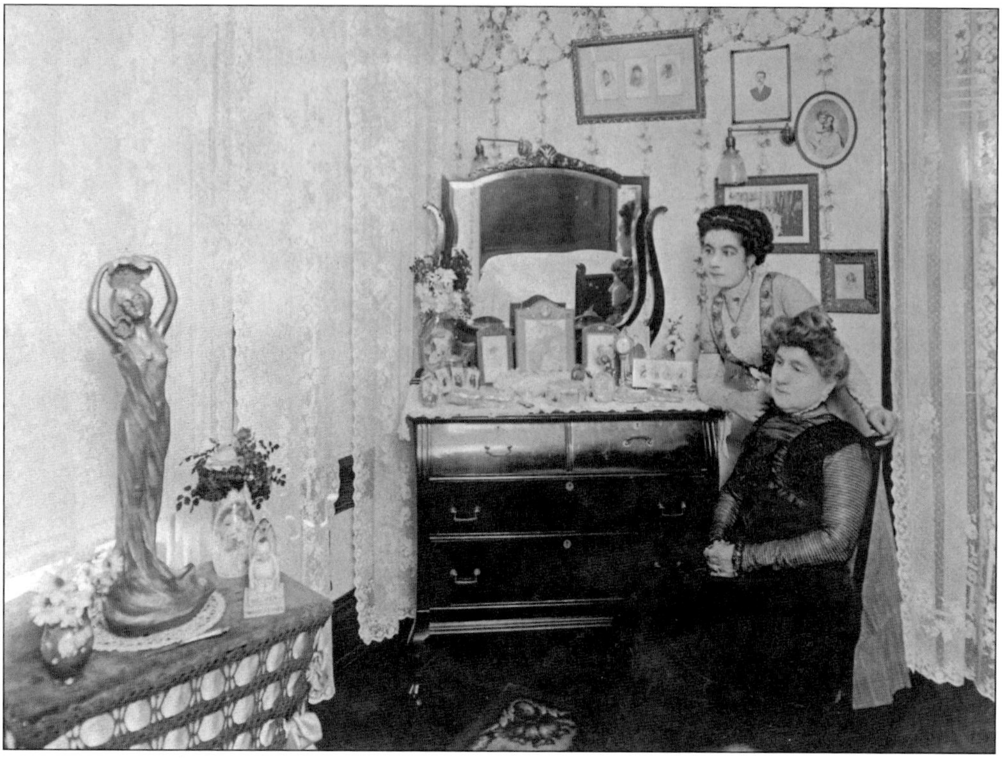

Fannie Haya and a visitor are pictured in her home at 605 Magnolia Avenue in Hyde Park in 1895. A female entrepreneur, Haya was president of the Sanchez & Haya Cigar Company, one of the first cigar factories established in Ybor City. She came to the Tampa area in 1885 from New York with her husband, Ignatius Haya. She was also the founder and president of the Sanchez and Haya real estate firm. After her husband died in 1906, she carried on business affairs, including large holdings of Tampa real estate. She passed away in 1930. (Florida Memory.)

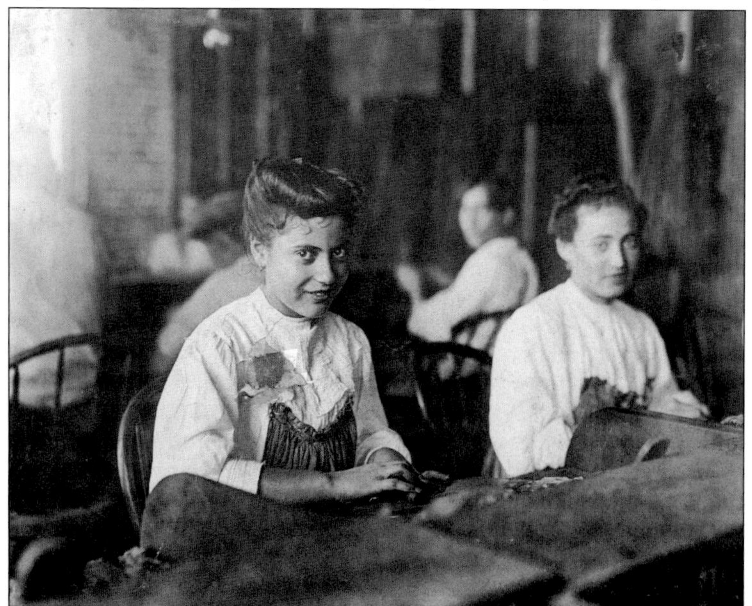

The tobacco industry employed women and children in the Tampa Bay area. This 1909 photograph captured a teenager working in the tobacco industry, which was heavily dependent largely upon girls and women. (Photograph by Lewis Wickes Hine, Library of Congress.)

In the midst of World War II, three US Naval Women's Reserve machinists work diligently on a Navy plane in Tampa in 1944. In 1942, Franklin Roosevelt signed legislation with the goal of freeing up male servicemen for sea duty. By the end of recruiting in 1945, about 86,000 had enlisted, and 8,000 were officers. (Library of Congress.)

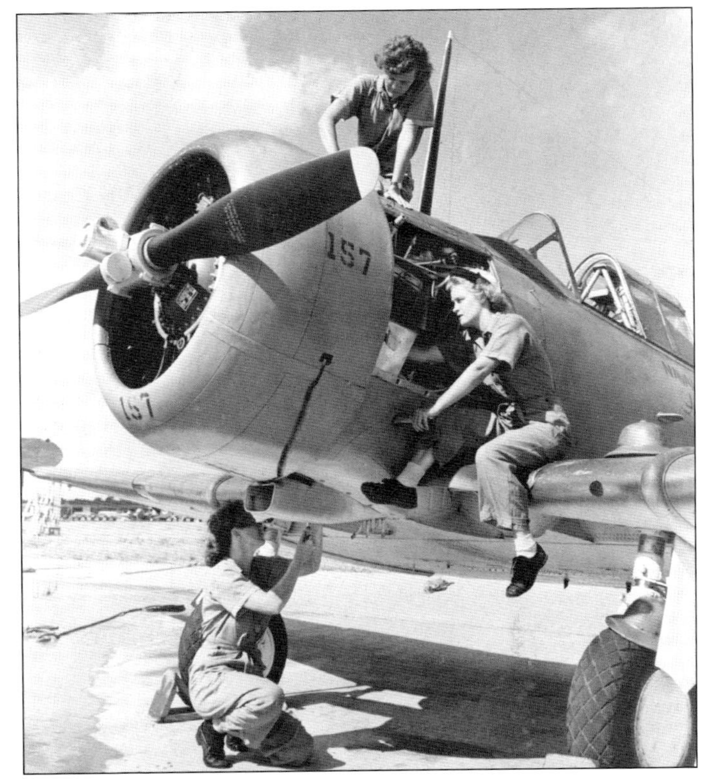

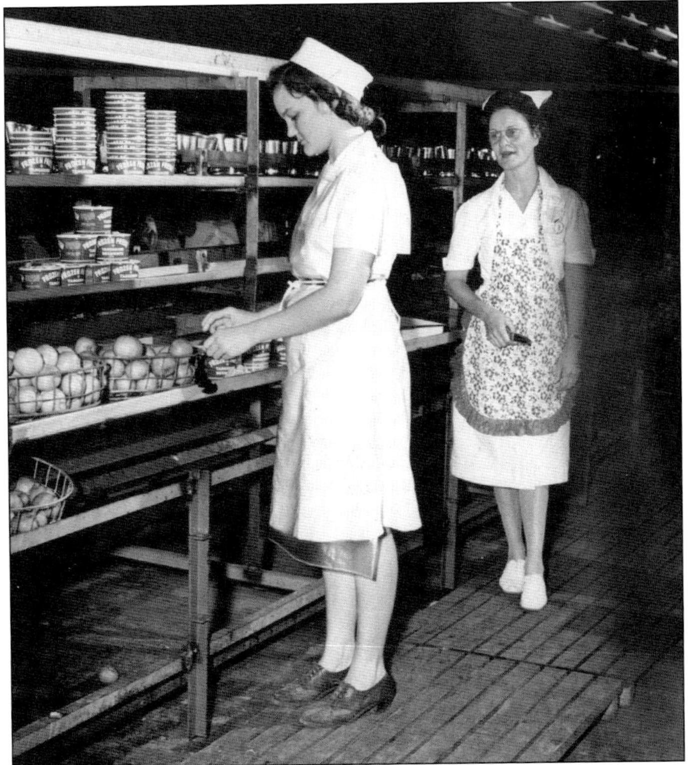

Two women prepare tangerines at Pasco Packing, a citrus processing plant. At the beginning of World War II, many packing employees left to join the armed forces, and changes were made, including hiring many female employees. During the war, the US military purchased 50 percent of the plant's products, and Pasco Packing won the War Food Administration's "A" Award for massive production of citrus juice. (Tampa Bay History Center.)

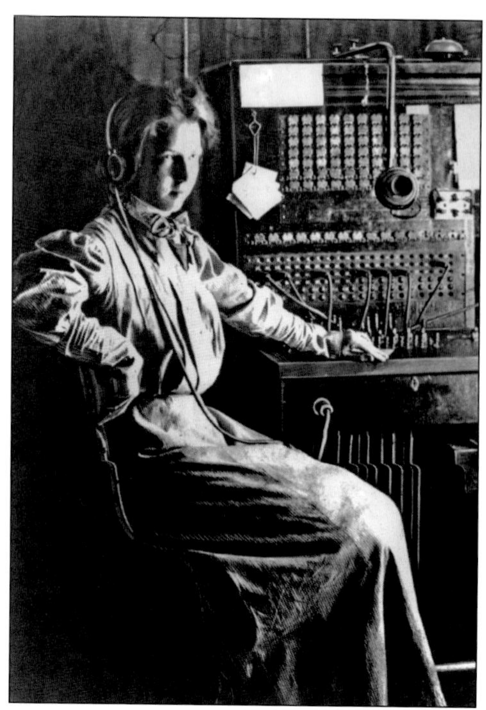

Elsie Hart wore a high-necked long dress and a benign smile as she was photographed as the first telephone operator for the Peninsular Telephone Company. A *Tribune* article of October 17, 1902, states, "The Peninsular Telephone Company with over one thousand subscribers, has its service in good working order now and the lines are kept warm day and night. Everything is new now, and consequently . . . in a short time, say two weeks, it will be working like a charm." (Burgert Brothers Collection, Tampa–Hillsborough County Public Library.)

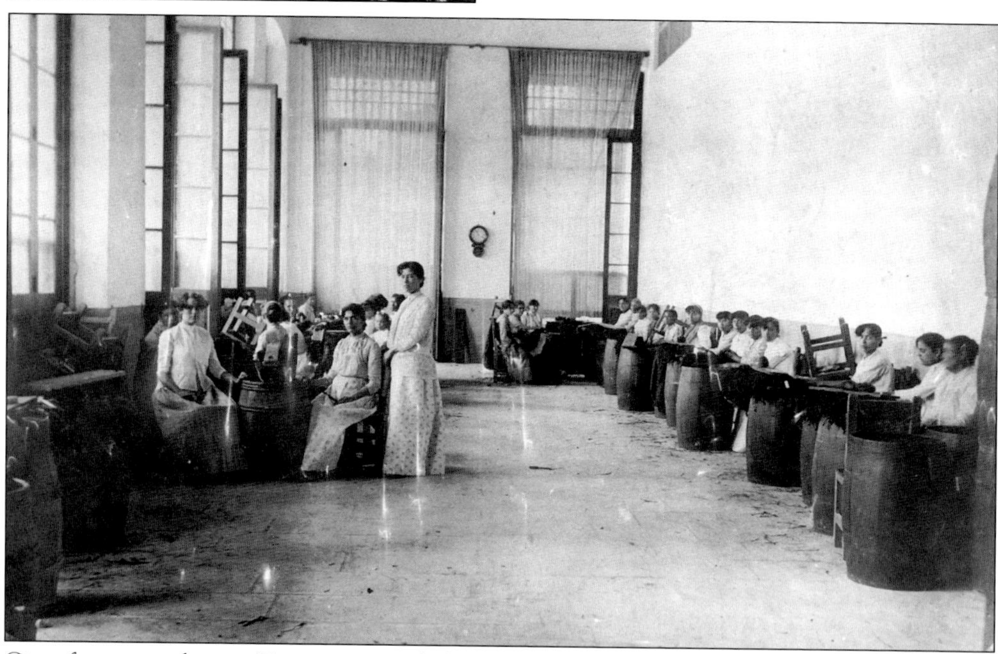

Cigar factory workers in Tampa, primarily female with one young child, are shown stripping the tobacco, which entails removing the stem that divides the two sides of the tobacco leaf. This picture was taken in a cigar factory building. Wet tobacco leaves can be seen piled atop most of the barrels. In 1939, Dr. A. Stuart Campbell documented in *The Cigar Industry in Tampa* that 51 percent of tobacco workers in Tampa were women, comprising all of the stripping tasks and most of the banding and cellophane duties. The average weekly wage was $13.86, and the hourly rate was 39¢. (Tampa Bay History Center.)

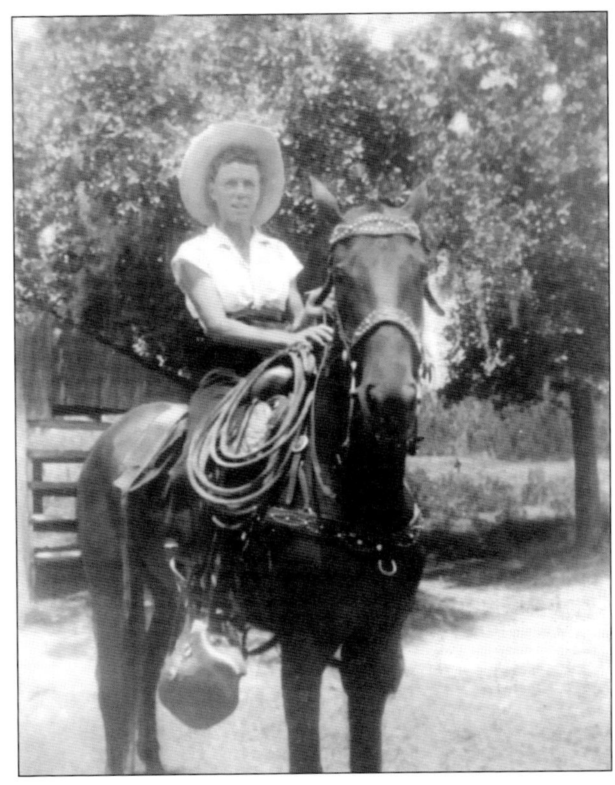

On the trail, Thelma Hale is pictured on her horse Penny. She was the cook for the roundups in the Wesley Chapel area, where agrarian life was the norm on the open range. The wife of the foreman who served K-Bar ranch for 37 years and the mother of the next foreman, she was a rugged country girl with an incredible work ethic. When the cowhands were working cattle in the area that is now Bruce B. Downs Highway, Thelma provided the sustenance and delivered the chow and was said to be one heck of a good cook. (Clarence Hale.)

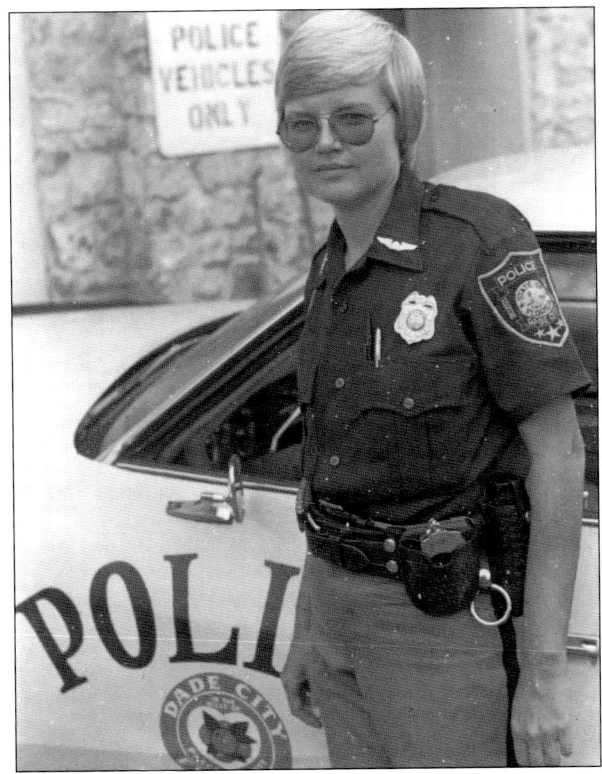

Margaret Angell is a trailblazer. After reading Nancy Drew and Hardy Boys books as a child, her mission to become a private investigator provides a modern-day inspiration for girls seeking non-traditional careers. Active in local law enforcement and the sheriff's office, Angell obtained her private investigator license and spent years tracing missing persons, doing surveillance in domestic matters, and all nature of rigorous and risky work. Anyone wanting a formal tea in Tampa Bay can visit her lovely and refined establishment, Angel Tea Room & Heavenly Treasures. She is also president of the Merchant's Association. (Courtesy of Dade City.)

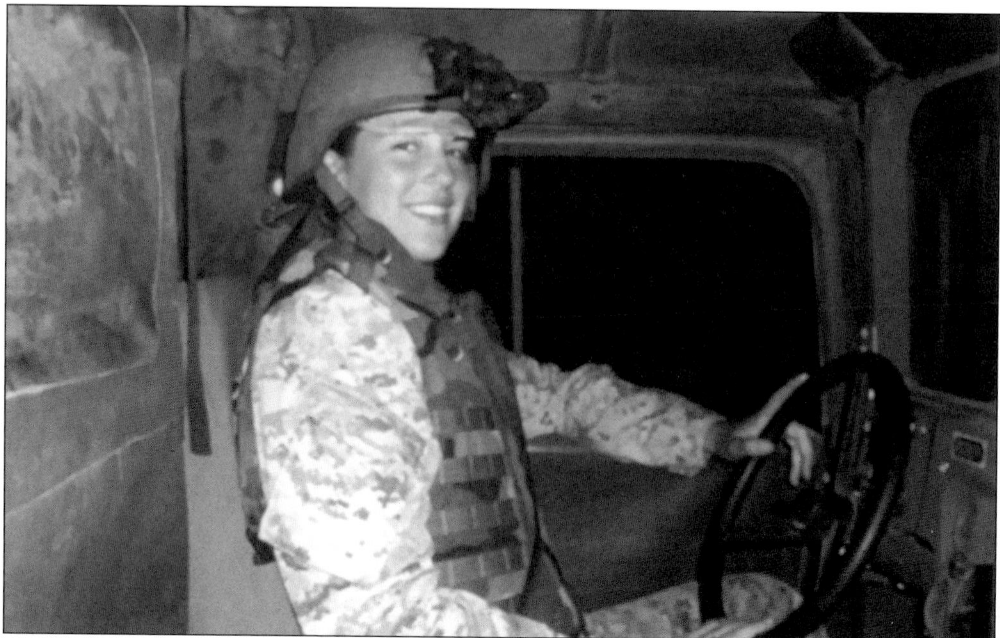

"I didn't get to finish my victory. You don't want to come back without your unit," said Marine Mary Katherine Mason-Sauter. She spent two months in Kuwait and then drove military trucks into Iraq. On March 25, 2003, the 507th Maintenance Company was ambushed as Mason's unit headed toward Nasiriyah to resupply troops during a sandstorm. "I was running around trying to refuel everyone and get them out of there," she said. When orders came to leave, she stepped off the truck while under fire. She spent grueling hours being transported out for recovery from her injuries. The Marine Corps Women's Reserve was established in February 1943, and as Congress passed the Women's Armed Services Integration Act in 1948, women became a permanent part of the Marine Corps. A proud veteran, Mason became an entrepreneur in Dade City with her business Lanky Lassie's Shortbread, next door to Angel Tea Room & Heavenly Treasures. (Both, courtesy of Mary Katherine Mason-Sauter.)

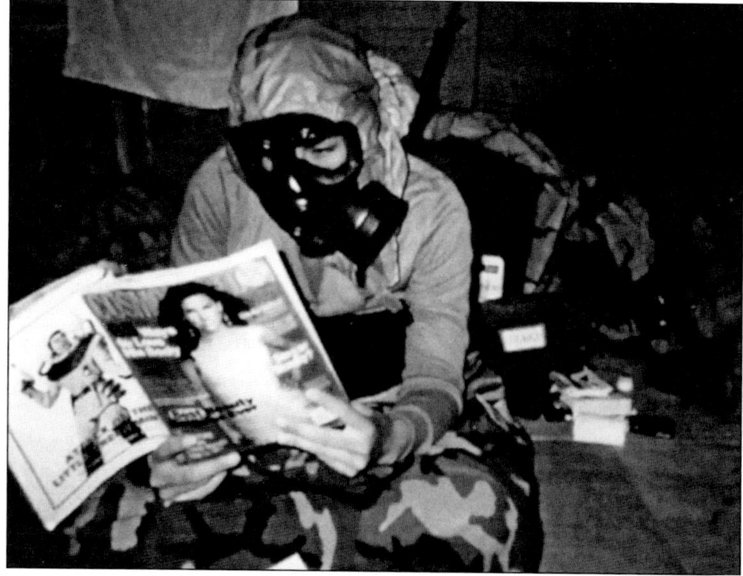

Six

Gracing the World with Style and Art

"I do not understand how anyone can live without some small place of enchantment to turn to," wrote famous author Marjorie Kinnan Rawlings, who resided near Tampa Bay in Cross Creek and penned descriptive cantos of the Florida experience in minute detail in her books.

Art, music, and drama unravel the complex and diverse history of the Tampa Bay area, and trailblazers came from all kinds of amphitheaters to the land of enchantment—the very place that Ponce de Leon thought might contain the Fountain of Youth. From the colorful history of the indigenous peoples to the exquisite beauty of the Seminoles and the opulent Hispanic history of Ybor, the imagination runs wild with color, flavor, and sound. Added to this were the strong-spirited Cracker Cowboys, the majestic, rugged country of frontier Florida, and the romantic beaches. One's mind's eye is overwhelmed with the yearnings of art and culture.

A sampling of the remarkable women in the art world from Tampa Bay are glimpsed in this section. Many of the women profiled in this book in regard to leadership in other fields possessed incredible artistic skills as well. Often, their talents are highlighted with other achievements, such as Pat Weaver, Agnes Lamb, Betty Barker Watkins, and many others. Expressions of music and art forms provide the common denominators for opening up one's perspectives. As opera star Jeanette Thompson described the impact of the arts on courage, "I was not really from this world for quite a while, because I knew no fear. I would try anything and go anywhere—all over the world, but you have to be fearless to do that, you know."

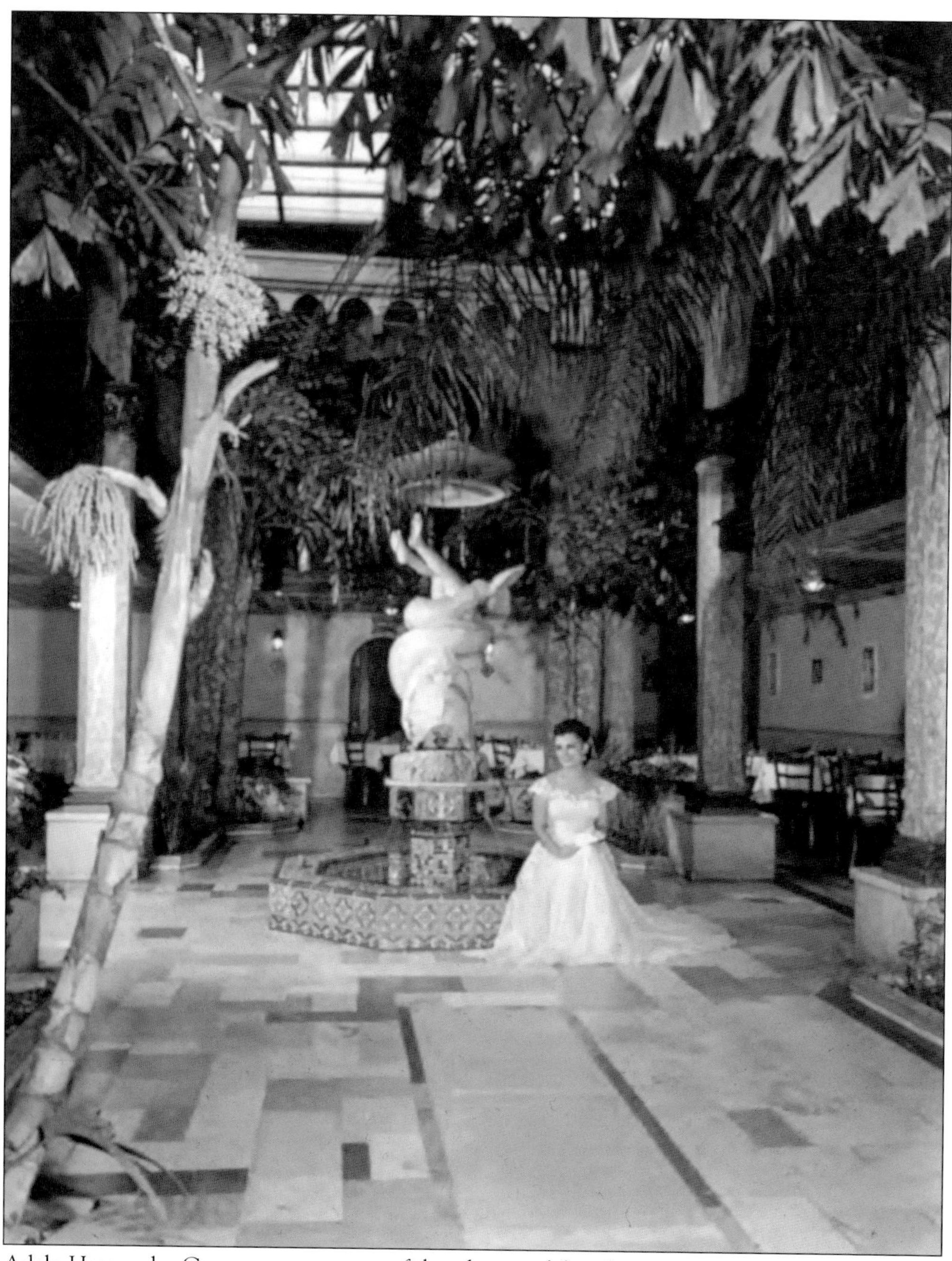

Adela Hernandez Gonzmart was a graceful and revered female entrepreneur in Ybor City. She and her husband, Cesar, developed and opened Columbia Restaurant. Gonzmart was a concert pianist, trained at the Julliard School of Music. For the 115th anniversary of the treasured Latin restaurant, which is the oldest running restaurant in Tampa, a selection of Gonzmart's original recipes were shared with interested patrons. The traditions of the woman sometimes called "the Queen of Ybor City" live on in the fifth generation of the restaurant ownership and management, and her music and dance remain as the cherished flamenco dancers perform regularly. This image was captured during a piano concert in 1945. (Gonzmart Family Collection, USF.)

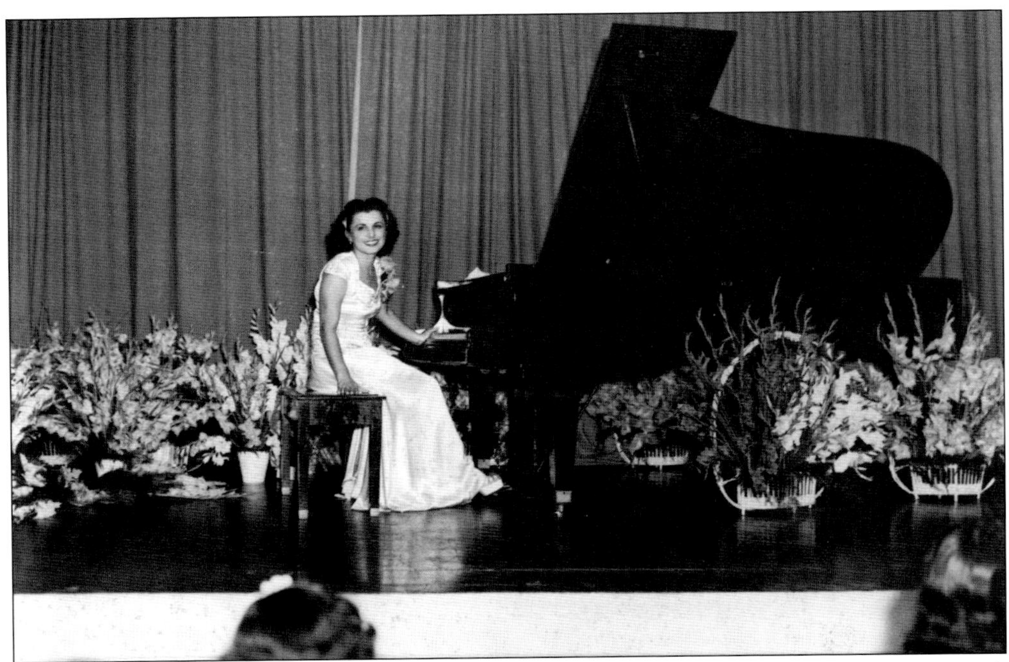

As Ybor City changed over the years, Adela Gonzmart kept the iconic restaurant operational. A fierce supporter of the arts, she worked to preserve historic buildings in Ybor and helped form the Tampa Symphony Orchestra. She was president of the Ybor Chamber of Commerce for three consecutive terms and co-founded the Latino Scholarship Fund at USF. A child prodigy, she went on to train as a concert pianist at Julliard and tour the United States and Cuba. She organized the Ballet Folkloric of Ybor City, the Tampa Ballet Sociedad Teatral de Tampa, and the Ybor City Museum. The national magazine *Vista* celebrated her as one of 13 Hispanic women in the United States recognized for accomplishments and community service. These photographs are from 1945. (Both, Florida Memory.)

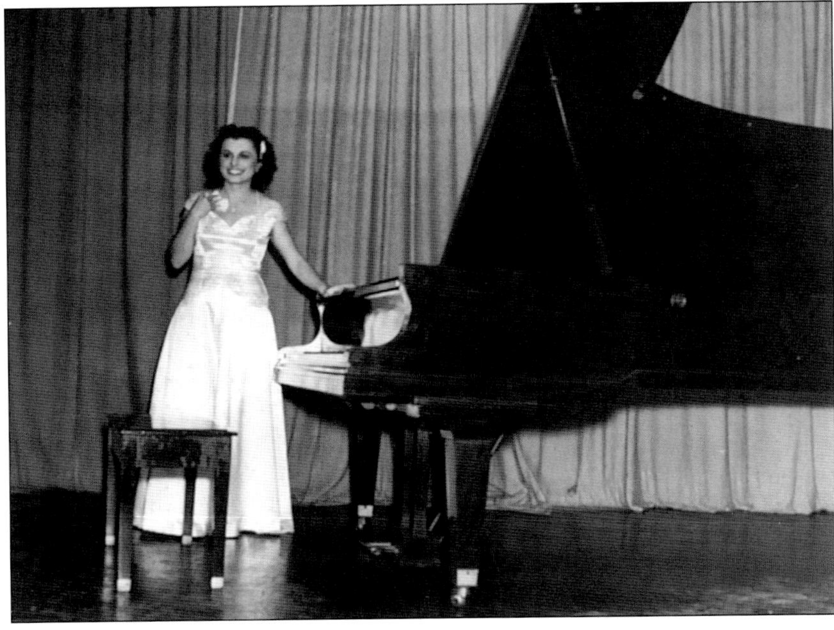

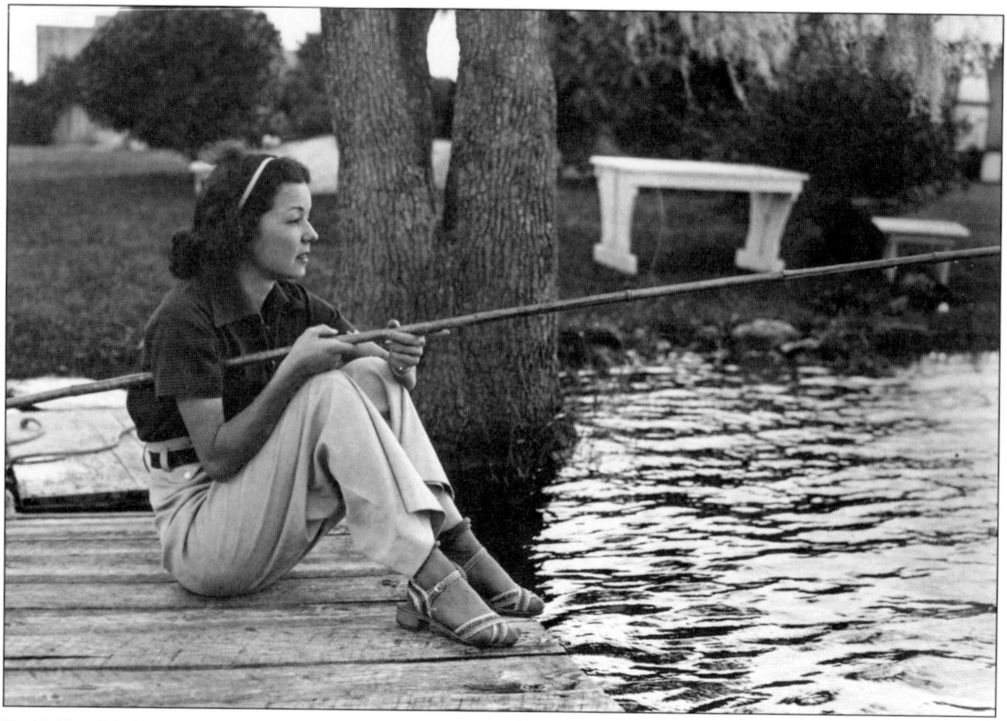

Frances Langford was a popular singer, radio performer, and actress. Born in Lakeland, Florida, the classically trained singer was discovered by Rudy Vallee while performing on a Tampa radio station. She worked on the radio with Vallee and Dick Powell. She was known as Bob Hope's vocalist on USO shows, entertaining in World War II, Korea, and Vietnam. She worked in theater and on stage, including at the Rialto Theatre in Tampa. She is seen here in a publicity photo from 1940. (Florida Memory.)

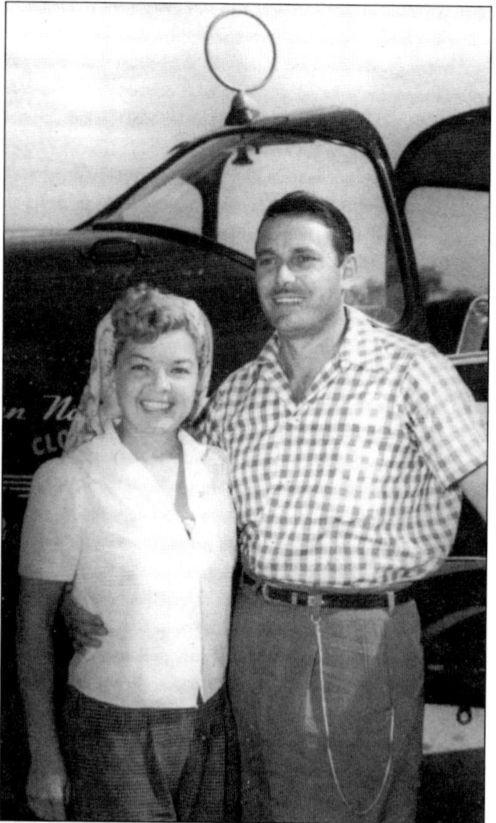

Frances Langford poses with her husband, matinee idol John Hall, in Lakeland. Her most prominent role was as an entertainer for GIs both at home and abroad, as her steadfast patriotism and empathy were greatly admired. She earned the iconic nickname "the Sweetheart of the Fighting Fronts." (Florida Memory.)

Zora Neale Hurston was an author and anthropologist and considered one of the foremost female authors of the 20th century. Born in Alabama, she relocated with her family to Florida and was not only a writer but a huge advocate of the arts. She collaborated with Langston Hughes on a play and wrote from the perspective of African Americans and women. The Zora Neale Hurston stamp was the 19th in the Literary Arts series. The design on the 37¢ stamp depicts a Florida background from the setting of her most renowned novel, *Their Eyes Were Watching God.* (Tampa Bay History Center.)

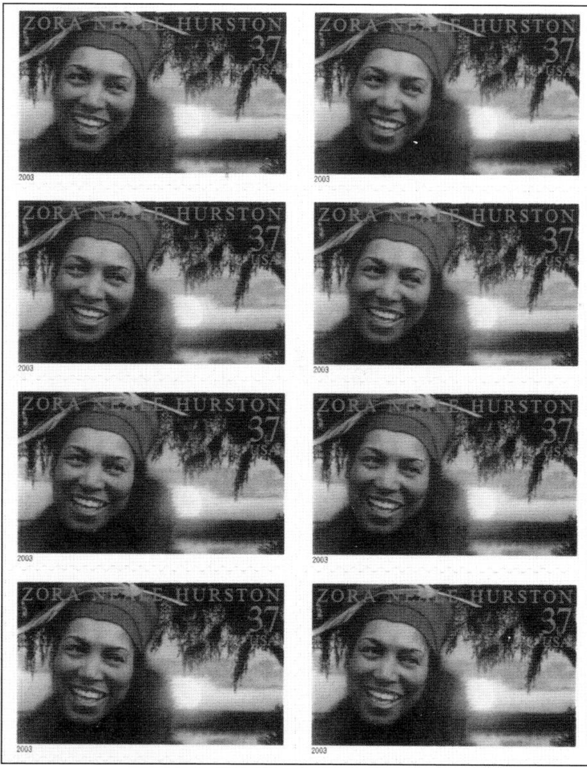

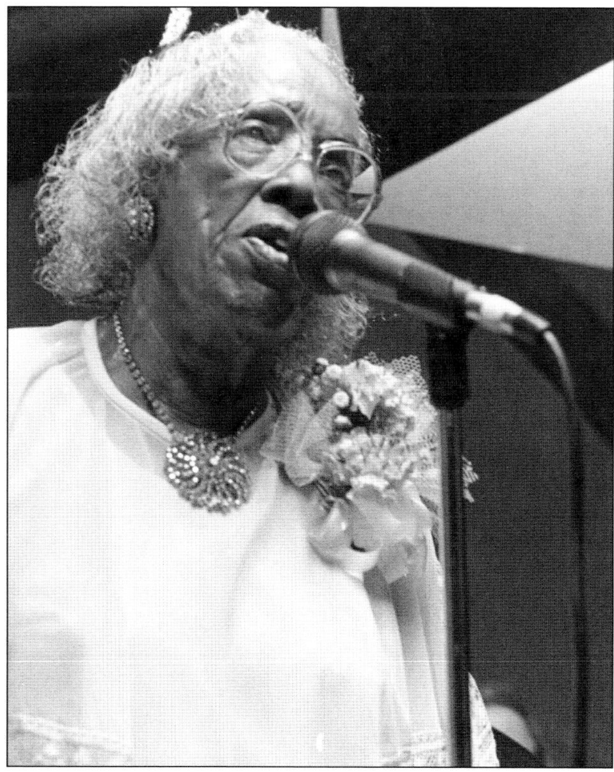

Mary Smith McClain was known as "Walking Mary" and later "Diamond Teeth Mary." McClain was a blues and gospel singer who sang with her sister Bessie Smith as well as Billie Holiday, Sarah Vaughan, Ray Charles, and Duke Ellington. She hailed from Bradenton, Florida, and performed in USO tours as well as singing in the White House for Pres. Ronald Reagan. She was photographed in 1982 performing at the Stuffed Pepper. (Ormond Loomis, Florida Memory.)

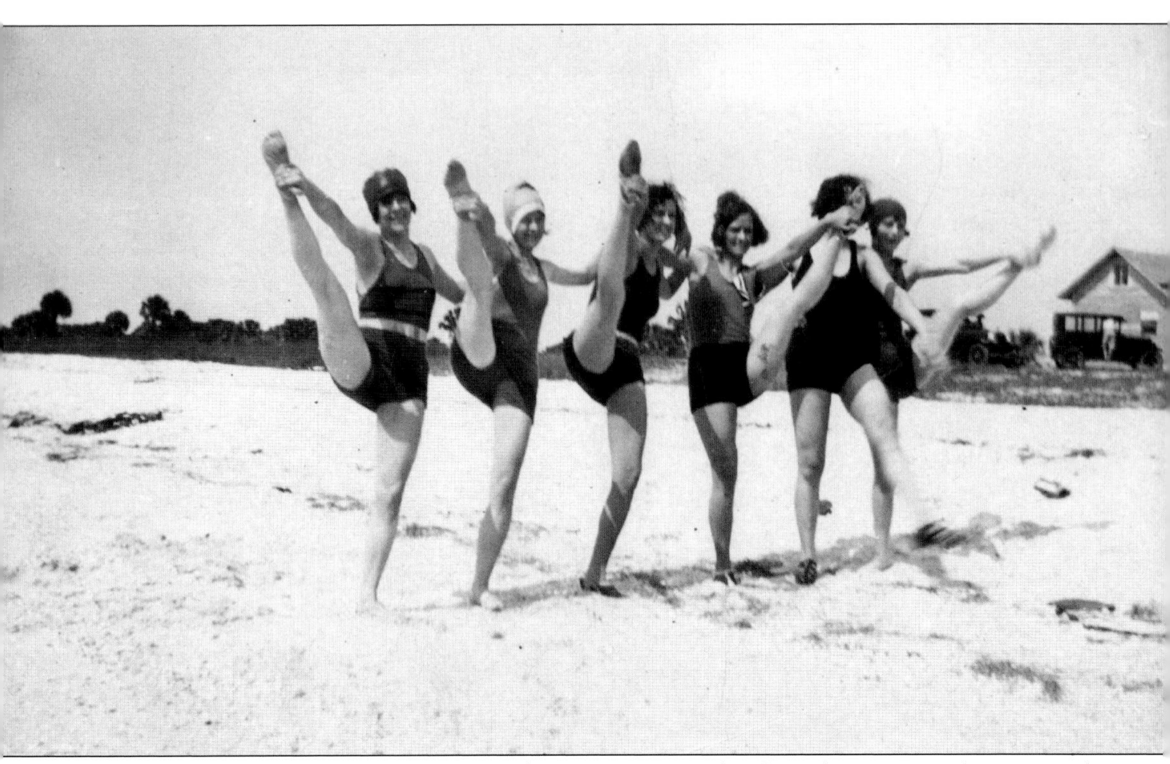

Women in Vaudeville and on stage in the 1920s were multitalented as singers, dancers, and comedians. They were some of the highest-paid women in the country and enjoyed a level of independence not available to most women. However, they had little political power. The Rialto Theatre Company was organized and financed by a group of Tampa businessmen who built the stage theater at Henderson Avenue and Franklin Street in Tampa in 1924. This photograph shows a group of women from the theater troupe posing on a beach in Tampa Bay. (Tampa Bay History Center.)

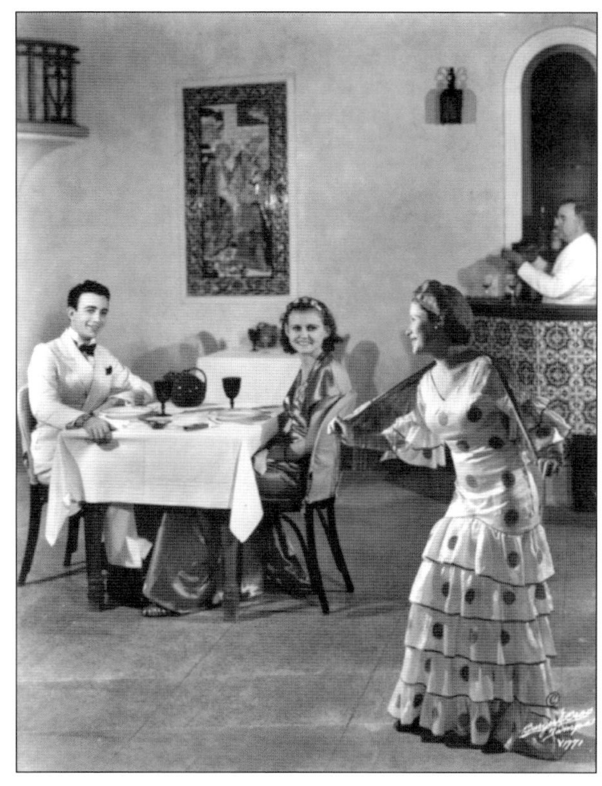

Rose Esperante performs at the Columbia Restaurant in Ybor City during the LaVerbena del Tabaco Festival in 1936. The three-day annual festival began in 1935. The *Times* wrote, "What Tampa owes the cigar industry and what the cigar industry owes to Tampa is based upon mutual responsibility which each has for the welfare of the other." The trademark Tampa-Made-Cigars, with its accompanying regalia of international culture including the entertainment industry, solidified the identity of Ybor City and Tampa. Rose was one of six daughters born to well-known Spanish entertainers Ernesto and Carmen Ramirez. Ernesto was a famed musician and arranger of Latin music. The family originated the Carmen Ramirez Theatrical Company and toured various countries presenting flamenco and theatrical Spanish dramas. (Burgert Brothers Collection, USF.)

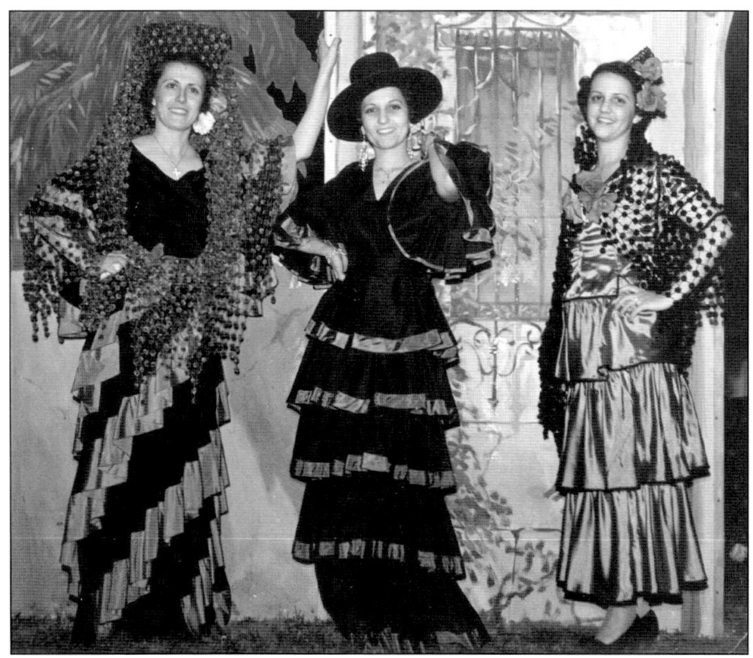

Flamenco, which encompasses song, dance and guitar, was brought by settlers from southern Spain who incorporated tambourines, bells, and wooden castanets into their unique style of performance. In this photograph, three flamenco dancers appear in Tampa. (Tampa Bay History Center.)

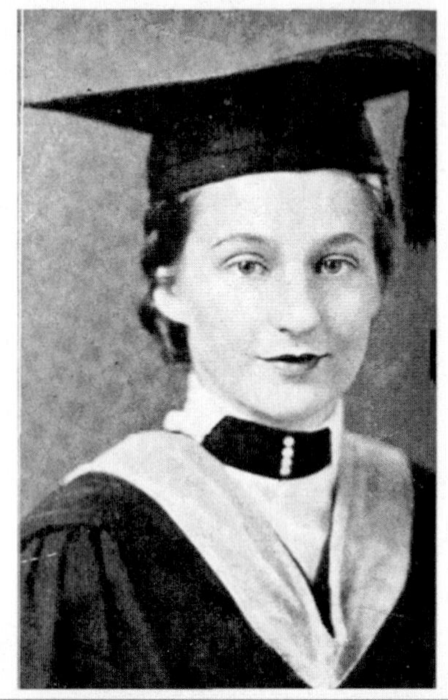

A remarkable designer, Margaret Rogers Ghiotto was honored as a Great Brooksvillian and served as grand marshal at a Founder's Day parade. A sharp businesswoman who marketed the idea of year-round Christmas in a tropical climate estimated that 450,000 would visit her village annually. The innovative concept grew from her involvement in Rogers Department Store, a community fixture founded by her father in 1912. While creating store displays, she perfected her Christmas-house concept. She graduated from Florida State College for Women (now FSU) and studied at the New York School of Interior Design. Her diverse interests included world traveling and the restoration of historic houses. Often also called "the Dogwood lady," she gave away up to 8,000 seedlings to interested community members. She was a popular physics teacher at Hernando High School before the entrepreneur spirit took over. In a 1994 *Times* interview, she shared, "I remember reading that Helen Keller once said, Christmas is the time when we dare to love.' That's saying a lot, I think. There's almost a feeling that you let yourself go and show someone you care about them." At left is her 1938 graduation photograph, and below is a sign for her business. (Left, author's collection; below, *Hernando Sun*.)

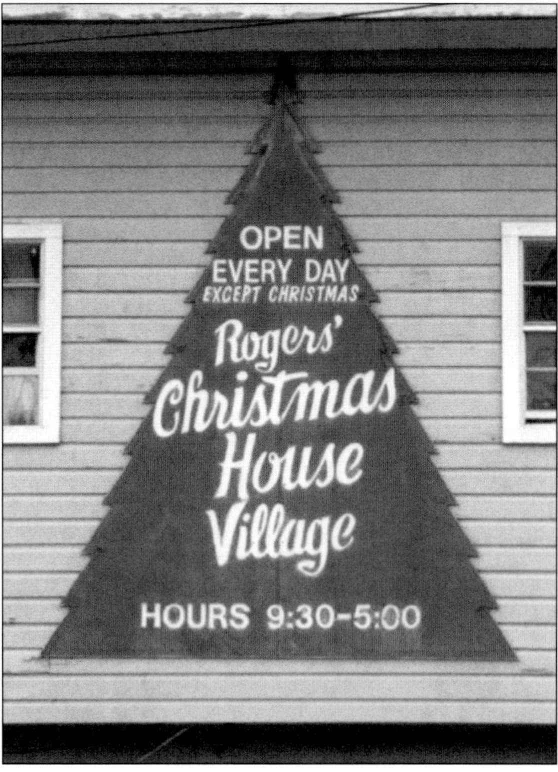

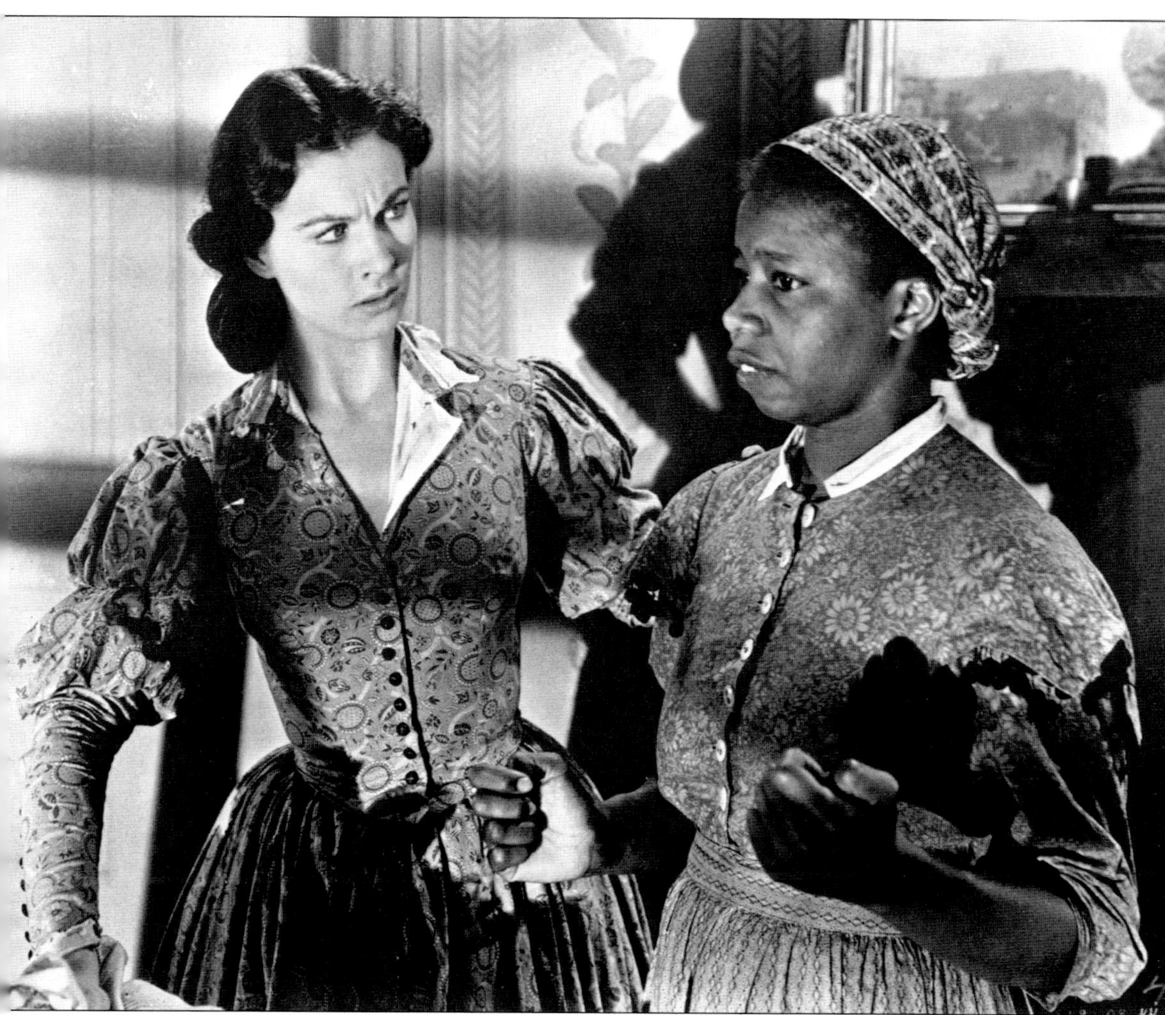

Thelma "Butterfly" McQueen was born in Tampa and attended St. Peter Claver School for a short time. Her most well-known motion picture was *Gone With the Wind* with actress Vivien Leigh in 1939. The role of Prissy was one that McQueen felt conflicted about in later years. She won an Academy Award in 1940 for the performance and said in her speech, "I sincerely hope that I shall always be a credit to my race and to the motion picture industry." She was appearing on Broadway when David O. Selznick spotted her and asked her to audition for the 1939 classic. She starred in a variety of movies and stage plays and later earned a degree from City College in New York. (Florida Memory.)

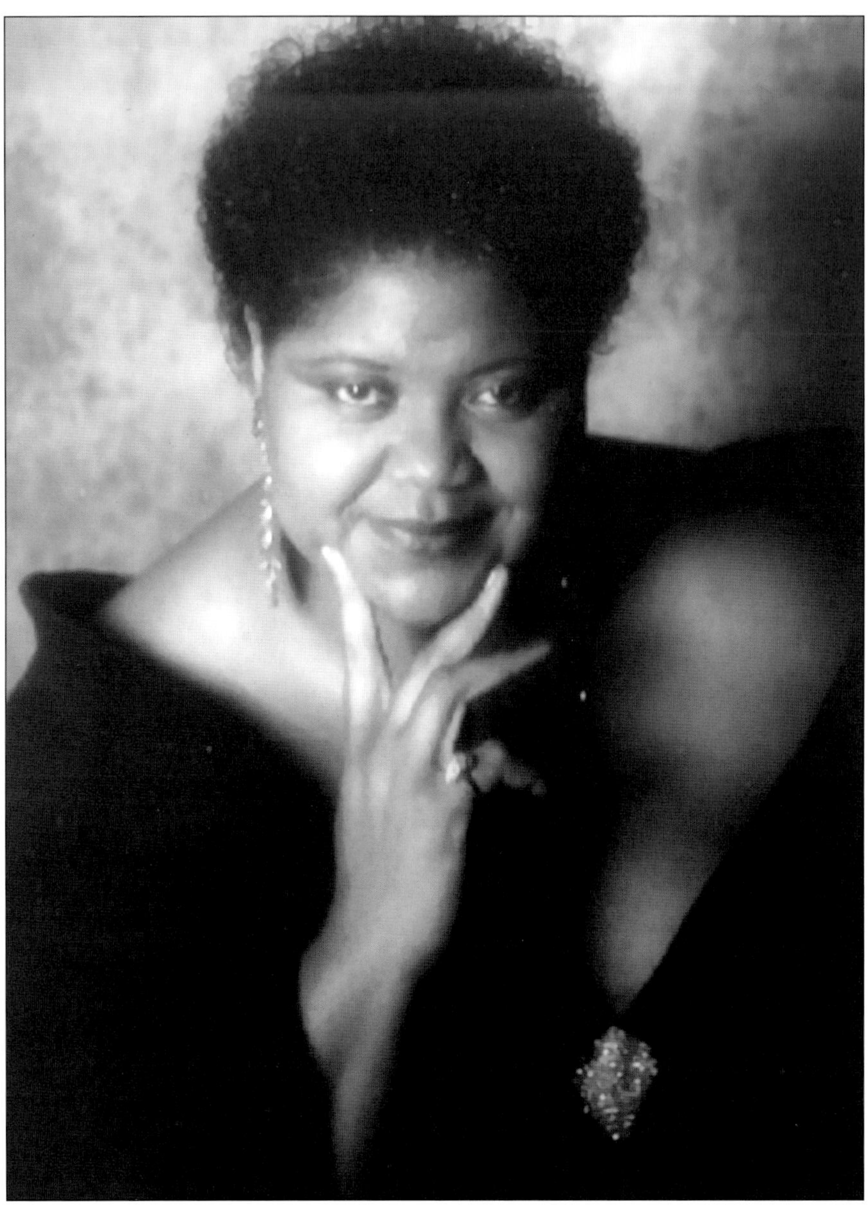

Jeanette Thompson, an international opera star of high acclaim, made her singing debut at Carnegie Hall singing Verdi's *Messa da Requiem*. Noted composers David Winkler, Craig Bohmler, Steven Sametz, Ricky Ian Gordon, and Thomas Cipullo have written works expressly for her extraordinary voice. Winning competitions around the world, she holds a gold medal from the famed Queen Elisabeth Competition in Brussels. Her career has taken her all over the globe with recitals, orchestra concerts, and operatic performances in Belgium, Germany, France, Luxembourg, Turkey, Spain, Italy, Austria, Japan, Slovenia, Croatia, Canada, Tunisia, Greece, Cypress, Cameroun, Zaire, Kenya, Latvia, Czech Republic, and Puerto Rico and throughout the United States. Thompson has taught music throughout the world from Vassar to Izmir State Conservatory in Turkey and many places in between. In recent years, she is sought after as a lecturer and instructor. She is a product of East Pasco, where she graduated from Pasco High School and then earned degrees from FSU and Rice University. (Jeanette Thompson.)

Seven

MAKING A DIFFERENCE IN THEIR COMMUNITIES

"Never doubt that a small group of thoughtful, committed citizens can change the world; indeed, it's the only thing that ever has," said renowned anthropologist Margaret Mead. A record of community involvement has become an expectation for entrance to reputable universities and is sought after by most organizations. The process of giving one's time, talents, and resources does bring an intrinsic reward that builds character and understanding.

The sampling of women in this section represents a few models who shifted paradigms by their behaviors. All were steadfast in their commitment to the community and not afraid to step out to take ethical steps for betterment and improvements, from beautification to equity to health care. To have been around any of them, one has been enriched, as they served as examples of service in Tampa Bay.

Anchoring this group of representatives is Hazel Land of Brooksville who utilized her professional training in the Peace Corps and later in founding a chapter of the NAACP. Martha McDonald Porter's passion for healthcare services in rural Florida inspired her children and grandchildren to fund a hospital and medical training. Others worked on environmental issues and toiled to beautify the communities of Tampa Bay.

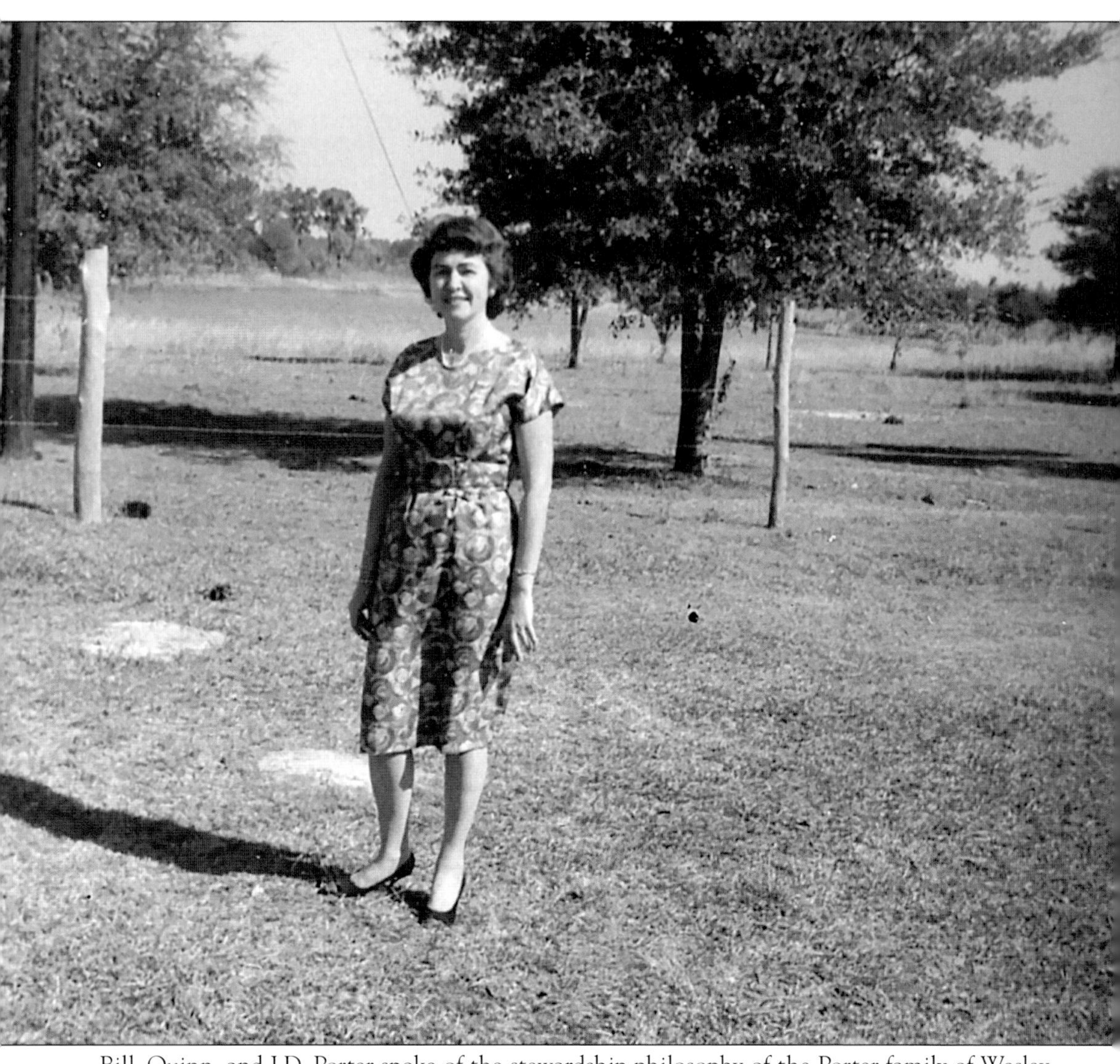

Bill, Quinn, and J.D. Porter spoke of the stewardship philosophy of the Porter family of Wesley Chapel. As it became obvious that the community was moving from totally agrarian to suburban, beginning as early as 1963 with the building of Interstate 75, Bill said his family was thinking about how they could assist. They particularly wanted to honor Martha McDonald Porter, a registered nurse who was passionate about the need for state-of-the-art health care. She was the wife of James Hatcher "Wiregrass" Porter, and her family donated land for both the Pasco Hernando State College campus in Wesley Chapel and the Florida Hospital Wesley Chapel. The college opened a nursing program, and the state-of-the-art hospital serves healthcare needs, which include education on prevention, and both are legacies to Martha's nursing career and her commitment to serving others. (Quinn Porter.)

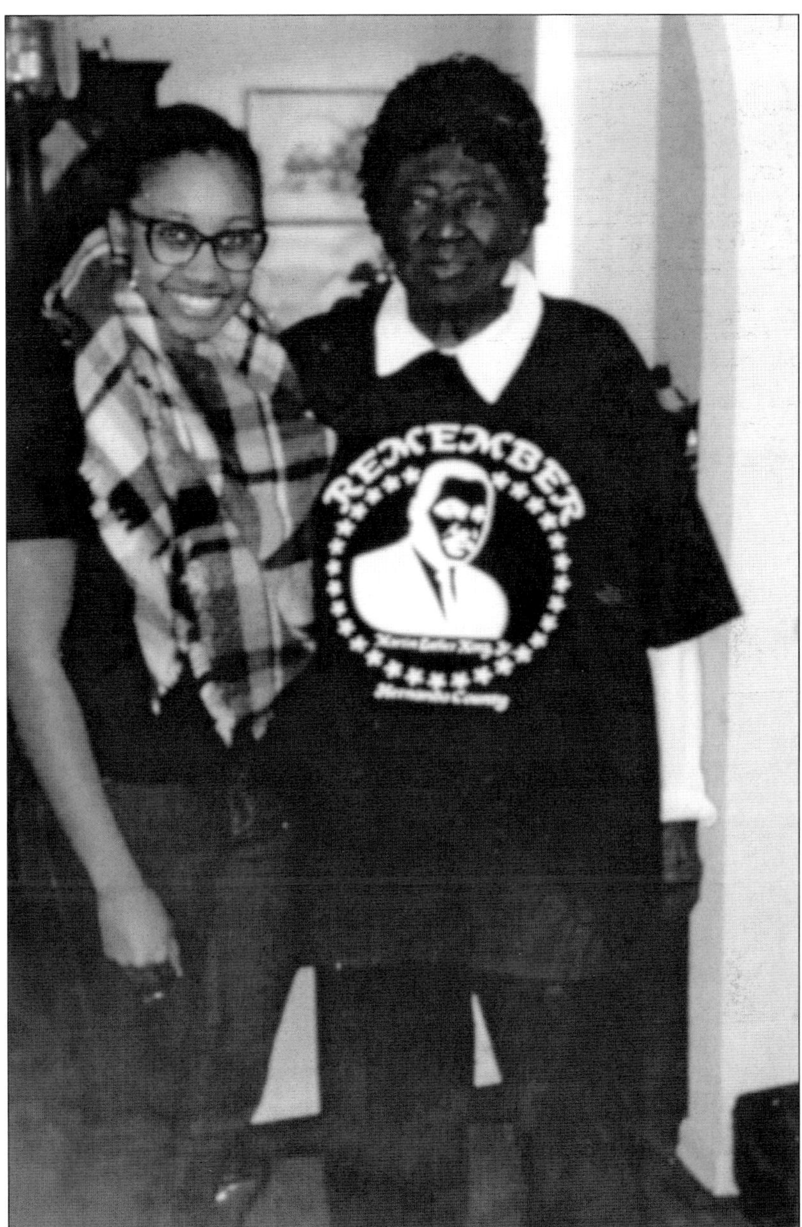

Imani Asukile explained that Hazel Land, a native of Brooksville, was valedictorian of Morton High School in 1949. "She enrolled at the world-renowned Tuskegee Institute University in Alabama. After a short stint teaching, she answered President John F. Kennedy's call and served in the Peace Corps in the Philippines and Nigeria. In 1966, she returned home to Brooksville and founded the Hernando County Branch of the National Association for the Advancement of Colored People. Because of the good work she was doing, she was promoted to the position of State Field Secretary for the State of Tennessee, the position that civil rights martyr, Medgar Evans held in Mississippi. In 1973, she became the first African American female to graduate from the University of Florida College of Law. Hazel worked many years as a staff attorney for Withlacoochee Area Legal Services. Hazel has been instrumental in researching and studying African American life and history in Hernando County." (University of Florida.)

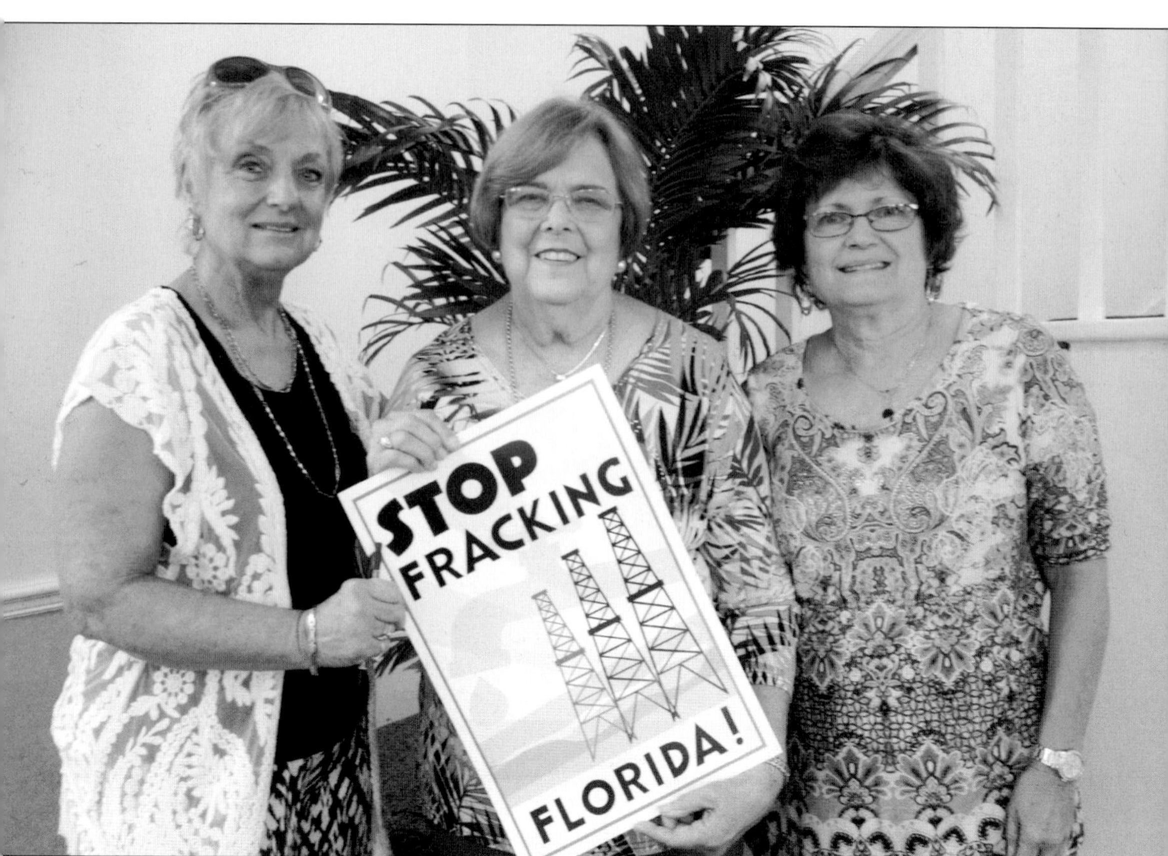

The Florida Federation of Garden Clubs, with 13,000 members, was a vigorous advocate of important environmental issues. It adopted the position of promoting the ban of hydraulic fracturing, or "fracking," in Florida as a risk to the health of citizens. Three former Garden Club presidents—Diane Scott, Pat Carver, and Gail Stout—were out with signs and educational information on the dangers of fracking in the Tampa Bay community and were eager to speak out on its impact on the environment. (Sally Redden.)

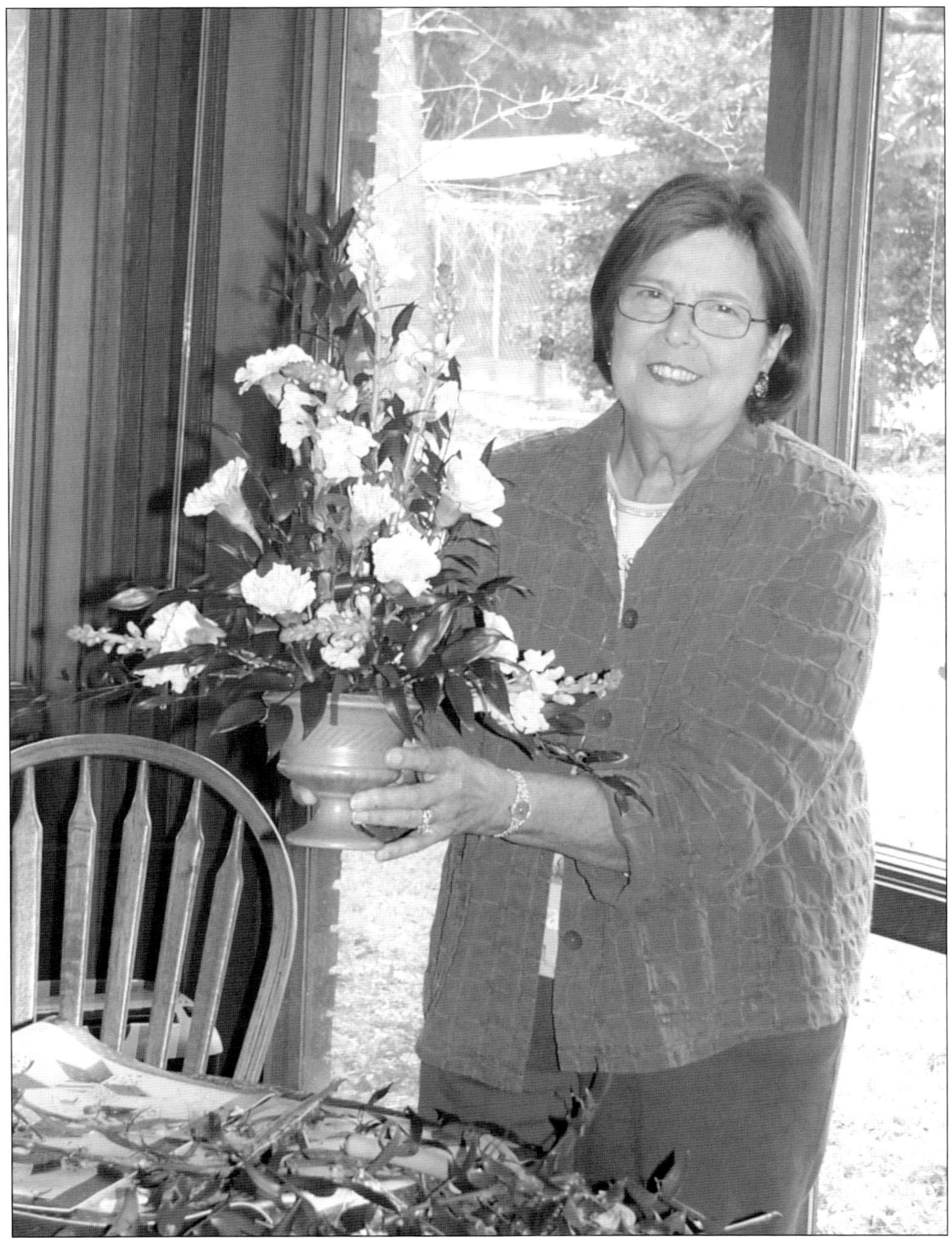

Patricia Ann Smith Carver has been a member of the Garden Club for 50 years. She is shown in 2007 conducting a workshop on floral design. Carver is a staunch environmentalist who served as the state water and wetlands chair for Florida at a time when the whole of Tampa Bay was becoming cognizant of the amount of water being pumped out of various rural areas of Tampa Bay. She initiated the memorial tree program and beautification of numerous public spaces. "Pat Carver is the heart and soul of the Garden Club. She singlehandedly inspired so many people to join the club and in the blink of an eye they realize how dear the organization is to them . . . it truly becomes one of their favorite organizations," said Jill Wiemer. (Sally Redden.)

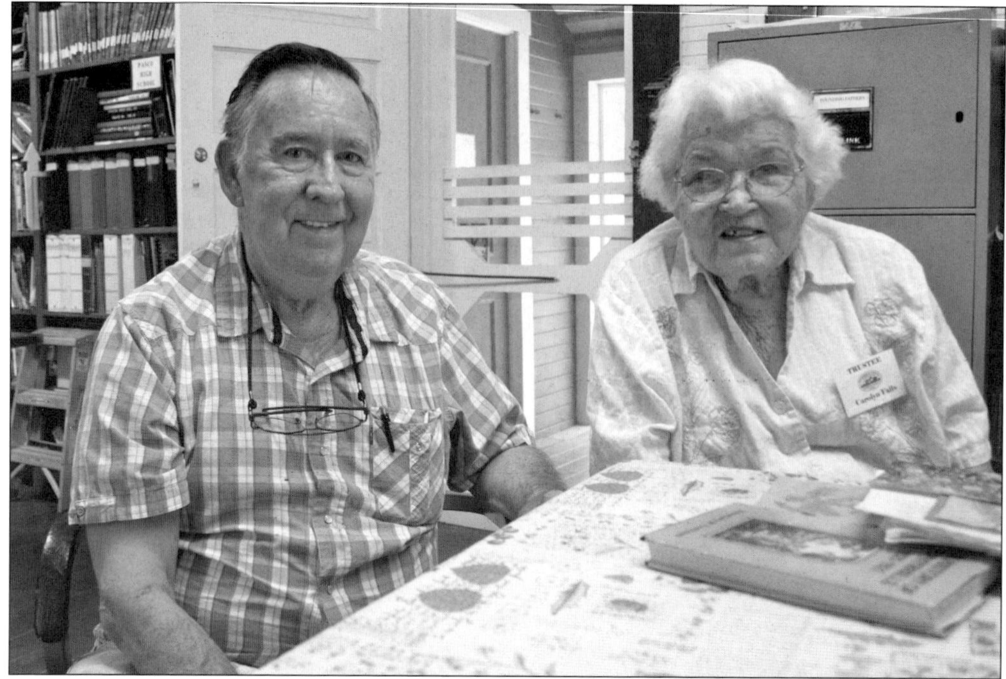

Carolyn Falls created the historical archives that were housed in the Pioneer Florida Museum & Village. In this photograph, she is shown working with fellow historian Eddie Herrmann. A real-life "Rosie the Riveter," Falls was born in Blanton and, after studying at Brewster Vocational in Tampa, worked during World War II for Vance Iron & Steel in Chattanooga, Tennessee. She served as clerk of the circuit court. In retirement, she worked tirelessly as a volunteer at the museum, where she was trustee and coordinator of the archives. (Jeff Miller.)

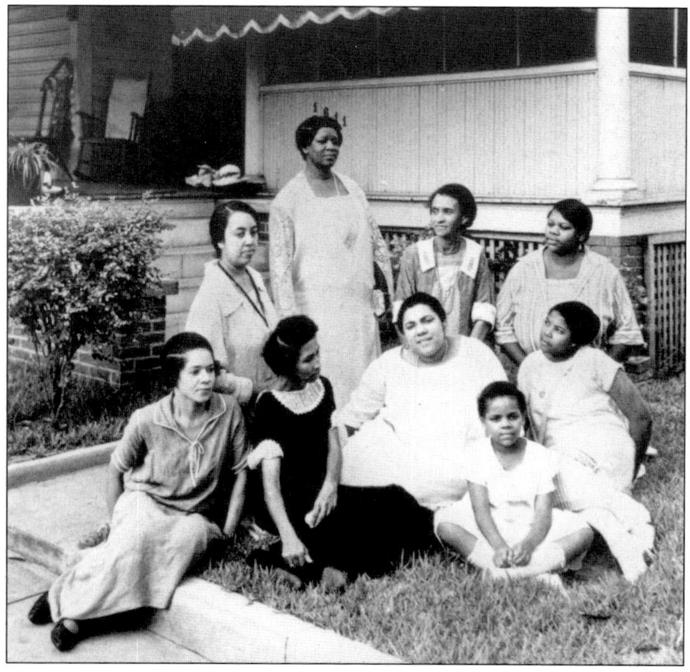

Blanche Armwood organized the Tampa Urban League, which worked on behalf of Blacks in Florida. This image of members of the Tampa Urban League, at 1615 Lamar Avenue, includes Armwood (second row, far left). "Educator, author, public servant, attorney and organizer, Blanche Armwood left her stamp on the future," said Marlene Boggs in 1993. A flier from Memphis referred to her as "the most powerful woman orator in the south, when she spoke on Reconstruction in 1922." (Tampa Bay History Center.)

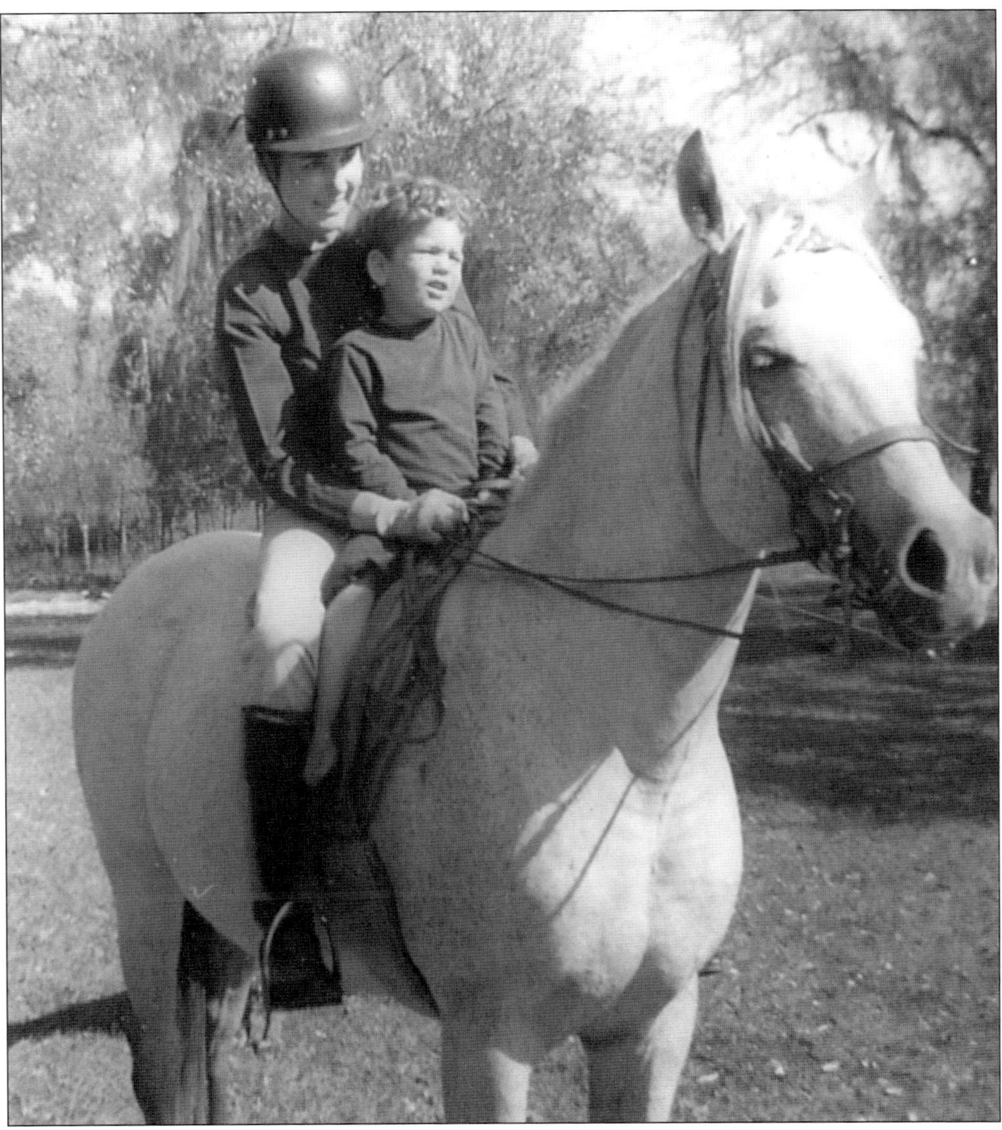

Mabel Healis Bexley was an extraordinary community helper with a 30-year career in social service in Tampa Bay. Perhaps most known for the 19 years she served as executive director of The Spring of Tampa Bay, she previously coordinated education and job training for women prisoners in Hillsborough County in the 1970s at the Women's Resource Center, which introduced her to domestic violence and its trauma. Bexley was a powerhouse fundraiser, public speaker, and change agent. In addition, she enjoyed a variety of interests, including equestrian sports of all types; this photograph shows her in 1966 riding her Arabian stallion Kamazan with her son Christopher Healis "Kit" Bexley. (Jennifer Bexley.)

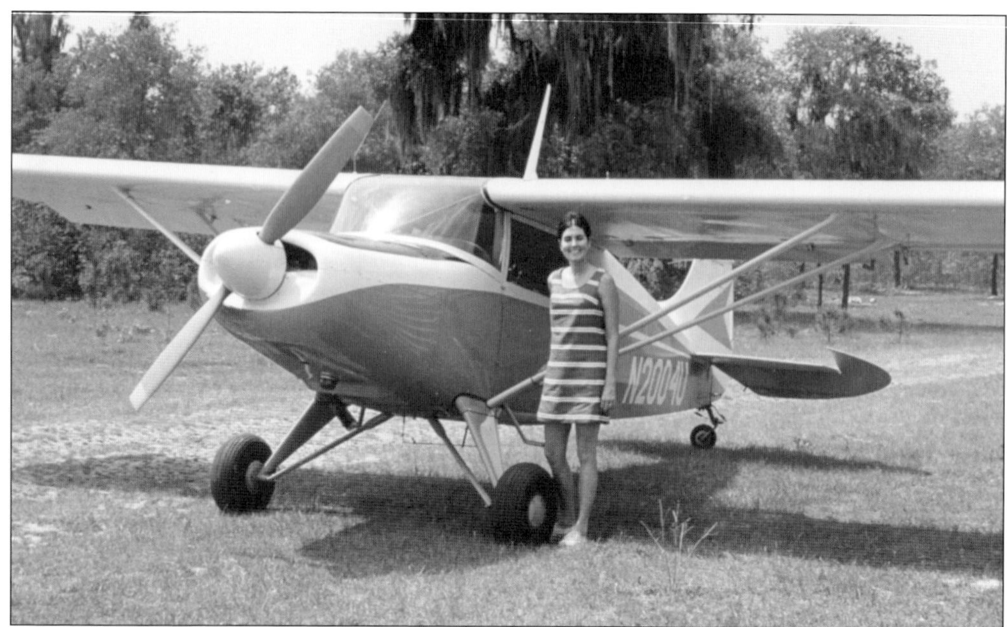

Mabel Healis Bexley lived life with exuberance. During the 1960s, she started a family, built a home in rural Land O'Lakes with her husband, and decided to obtain her pilot's license. She founded an aerial photography company. She later quipped, "It was the 1960s and the only way you could take the kids to work with you was to put them in the back of a plane." The photograph above shows Bexley in 1968 with her Maule Rocket aircraft, which she flew while taking aerial photographs. Always a fervent advocate for women and children, she later co-founded the Centre for Women in Tampa, which provided counseling and education and was eventually tapped for numerous awards, including Executive Woman of the Year from the Network of Executive Women and Outstanding Contribution to Women's Health Care from PBS station WEDU. (Above, courtesy of Jennifer Bexley; below, courtesy of The Spring of Tampa Bay.)

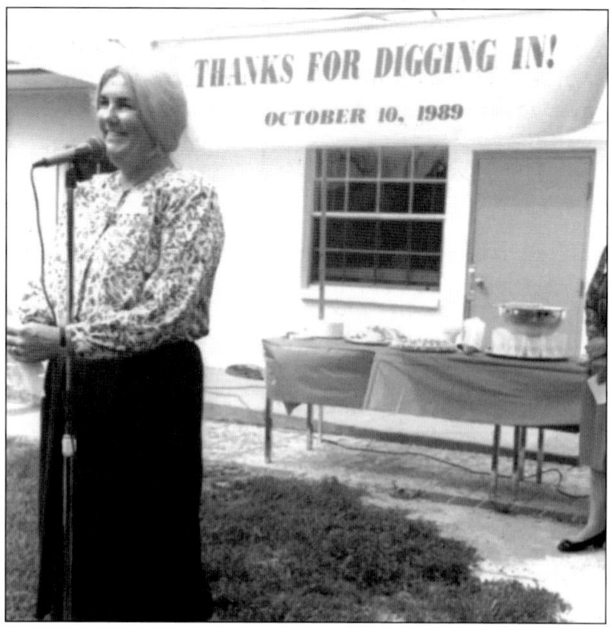

Eight

Educating the Masses

Early colonizers who arrived for settlement in Tampa Bay, motivated by the Armed Occupation Act and, later, the Homestead Act, prioritized education. Reflecting upon the history of Florida, the schoolhouse was one of the first buildings to be constructed in most Tampa Bay settlements. There was a strong mission and action for educating children in frontier Florida. Often, the schools were makeshift operations from an abandoned building or an antiquated abode, but the commitment to community schooling was a shared value.

Like in most states, the need for teachers led to the establishment of a scattered group of normal school institutes in bay area towns to train these early frontier teachers, who were initially men. Women began to be admitted to the typical two-year program by the mid- to late 19th century. The concept of normal school was to teach the norms of pedagogy and curriculum. Many women sought teaching jobs for the independence and purposefulness of impacting their communities and the future.

The school calendars accommodated agrarian schedules like strawberry and citrus harvests, and the early teachers were housed in the homes of their pupils' parents, but the commitment was strong for education, both public and private.

The so-called feminization of teaching during the 20th century occurred as the profession became increasingly dominated by women. This change impacted the role of both men and women in the growing population in ways that have not yet been fully recognized.

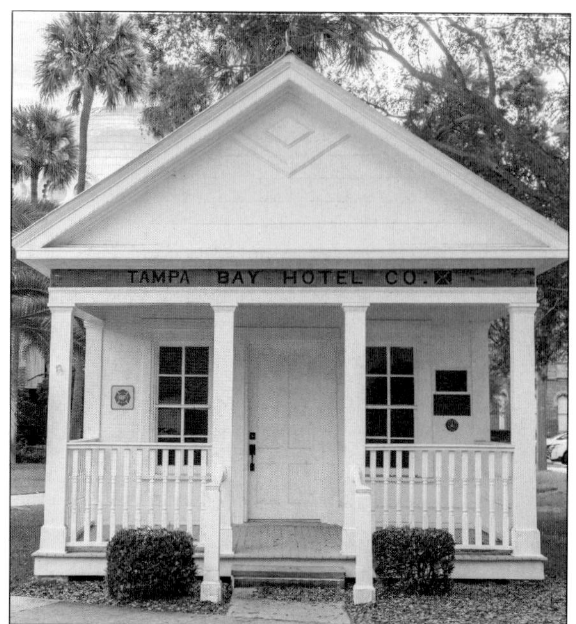

Structures and remnants preserved in museum locations offer a glimpse of early educational settings. The Old School House on the grounds of the University of Tampa, built in 1855, still stands and is maintained by the Desoto Chapter of the Daughters of the American Revolution. Gen. Jesse Carter constructed the tiny school building for his daughter and seven other female students: Josephine Carter, Janie Givens, Mary Lesley, Mary Kelly, Eugenia Spencer, Lizzie Spencer, and Hayden Porter. Other relics of early education are preserved at places such as the 1858 Castalia School House at Cracker Country at the Florida Fairgrounds and the 1930s Lacoochee School House at the Pioneer Florida Museum & Village. (Matthew Paulson.)

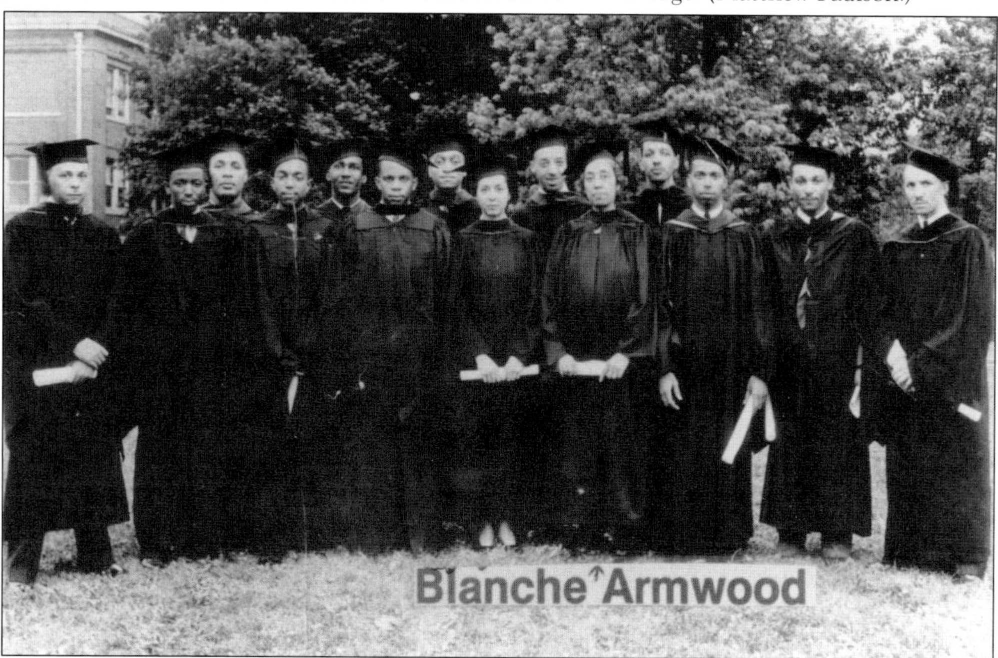

Blanche Armwood was a graduate of St. Peter Claver Catholic School and, at the age of 12, passed the state teacher exam. She later graduated from Spelman Seminary and taught for seven years in Tampa. In 1914, she was with Tampa Gas Company as a demonstrator in conjunction with the school board. In fact, several gas companies from around the country consulted with her on her presentations. In 1922, she was selected as the national campaign speaker for the Republican Party and executive secretary for the Tampa Urban League as well as supervisor of Black public schools. Still striving to make a change, she entered Howard University's School of Law in the 1930s and earned a law degree. In 1984, Armwood Comprehensive High School in Seffner was named for her. (Tampa Bay History Center.)

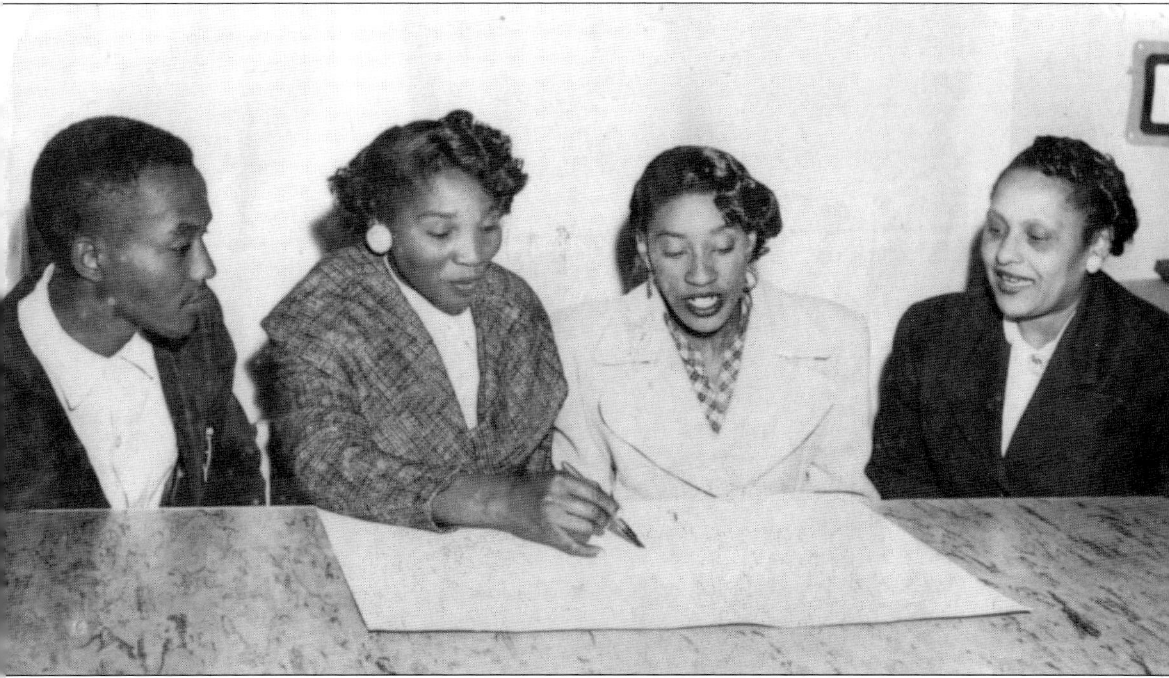

In 1981, Christine Peters Mickens became one of the first African American women in the rural south to be appointed to an elective position since Reconstruction when she replaced her late husband, Odell Kingston Mickens, as a member of the commission for Dade City. She served in the position until her death. She arrived in Dade City in 1933 during the Great Depression along with her husband. They had been referred by their mentor, Mary McLeod Bethune. Christine was born in Midway, Florida, and attended Bethune Cookman High School and Bethune College. She taught at the Dade City Colored School, Moore Academy, Mickens High School, and Pasco High School for a combined 40 years. When the boys' basketball team was without a coach in 1934–1935, she took an unprecedented move to step up and coach the team herself. As a lifelong educator who assisted with integration efforts in the Tampa Bay schools, she mentored Eunice Penix, who later served on the Dade City Council. In this photograph, Mickens (far right) leads a discussion about a community endeavor with, from left to right, Estes Smith, Rev. Cora Hill, and Dorothy B.T. Baker. (Moore-Mickens Education Center.)

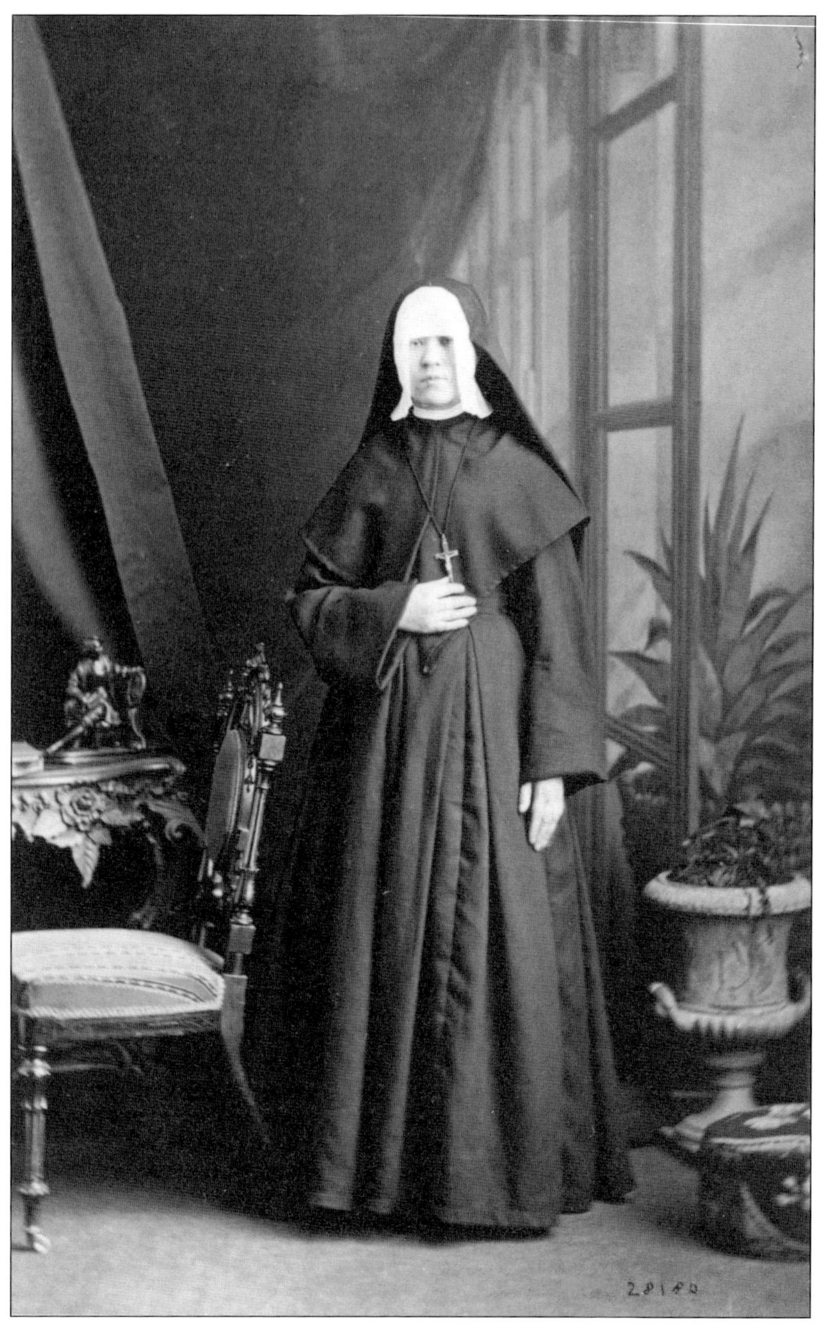

Elizabeth Crean, the president of the Academy of Holy Names in 1993, said, "Our heroes are all women." In 1881, Sisters Marie Maurice and Marie Augustine boarded a steamer from Key West for a journey to Tampa to start a school for their order, which was originated by a Canadian nun, Eulalie Durocher. An impetus for the action had come from a Tampa native, Kate Jackson, a recent graduate of the Key West Academy School who nudged her father to support the concept of a new school in Tampa. When the sisters were deposited at the Manatee River, they had to make their way to Tampa. One of the trailblazing educator/founders, Marie Maurice was born Elmire Lapointe in 1846 in Montreal and entered the religious community in 1866. (Geneviève Noël.)

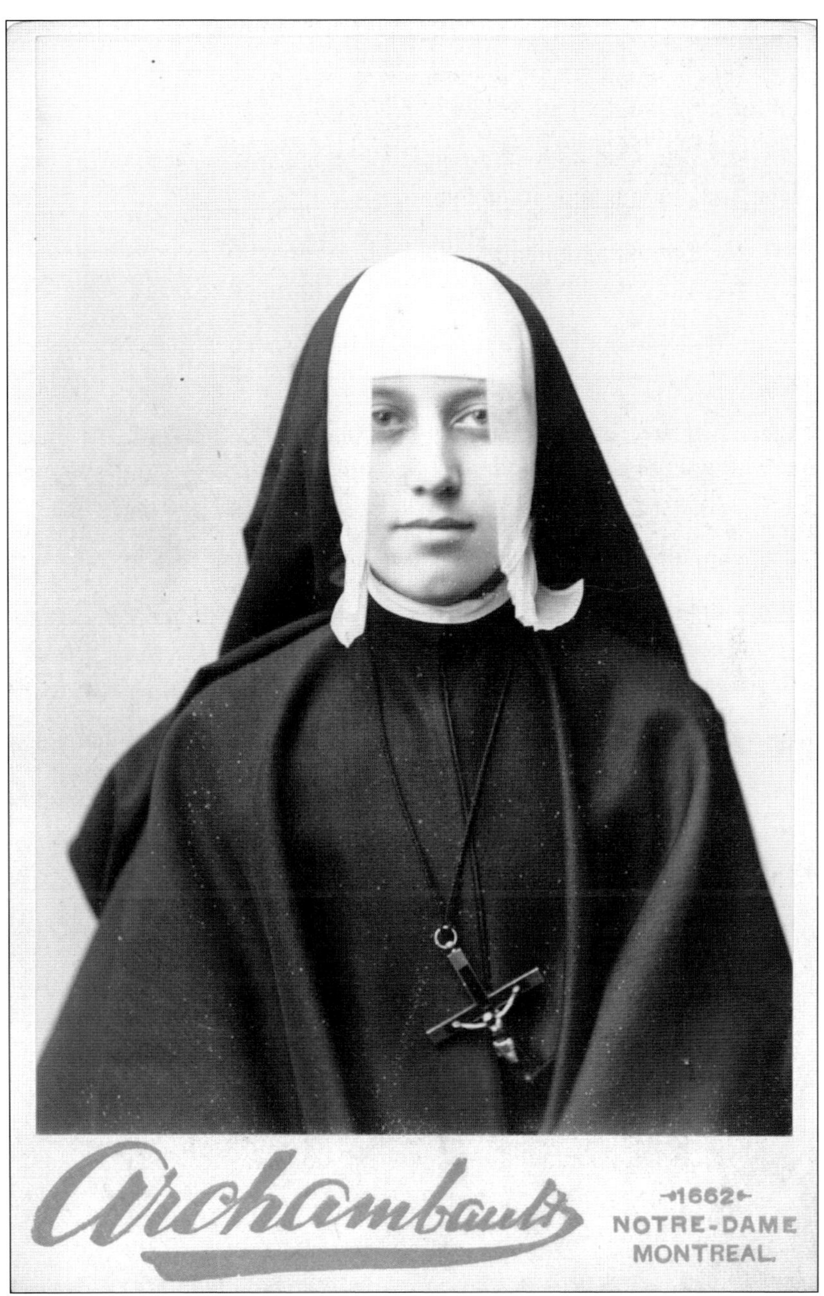

The other pioneering founder, Sr. Marie Augustine, was born in Quebec as Victoire Bergevin in 1833 and entered the religious community in 1851. After the journey to Tampa, the founders' initial school building (that was to evolve into the Academy of the Holy Names) was an abandoned forge. For furniture, they had a rusty stove, a shaky table, four chairs without backs, and no beds. Mosquitoes were unavoidable, and dengue fever did not spare them. Soldiers from Fort Brooke chipped in some modest funds to make the place habitable. Despite the incredible personal risk to body and constitution, the two courageous nuns persevered as true trailblazers in education. Sr. Anne Regan reflected that the school had educated a diverse population throughout time, including many immigrant children of various backgrounds and religions. (Geneviève Noël.)

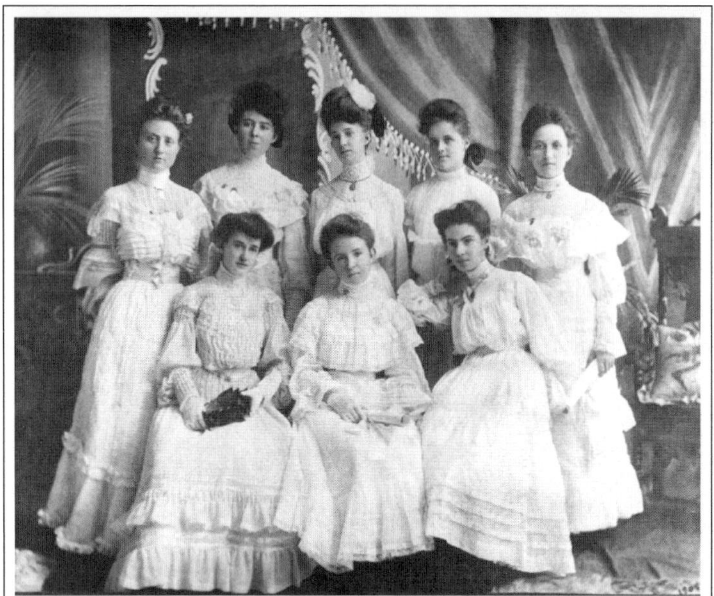

From the 30 students in the first class of students at the Academy of the Holy Names, thousands of students have attended. This portrait of the graduating class of 1904 is made up of eight graduates, namely Mabel Mendenhall, Edna Davis, Lulu Jackson, Grace Austin, Beatrice Parslow, Dreast Davis, Elvira Guerra, and Mercedes Clark. (Academy of the Holy Names.)

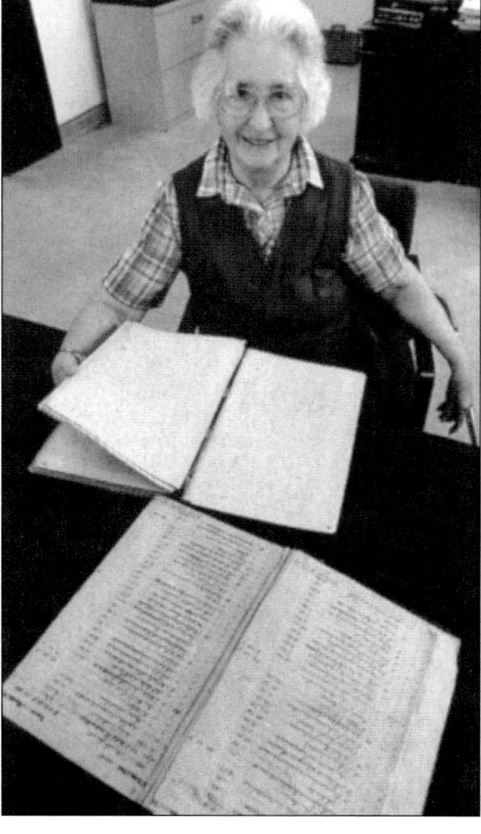

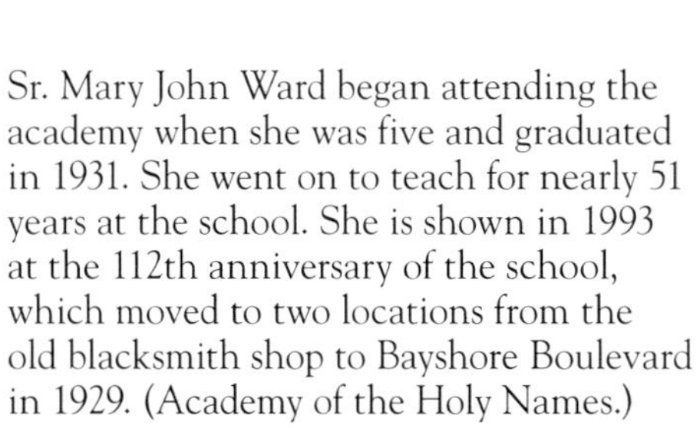

Sr. Mary John Ward began attending the academy when she was five and graduated in 1931. She went on to teach for nearly 51 years at the school. She is shown in 1993 at the 112th anniversary of the school, which moved to two locations from the old blacksmith shop to Bayshore Boulevard in 1929. (Academy of the Holy Names.)

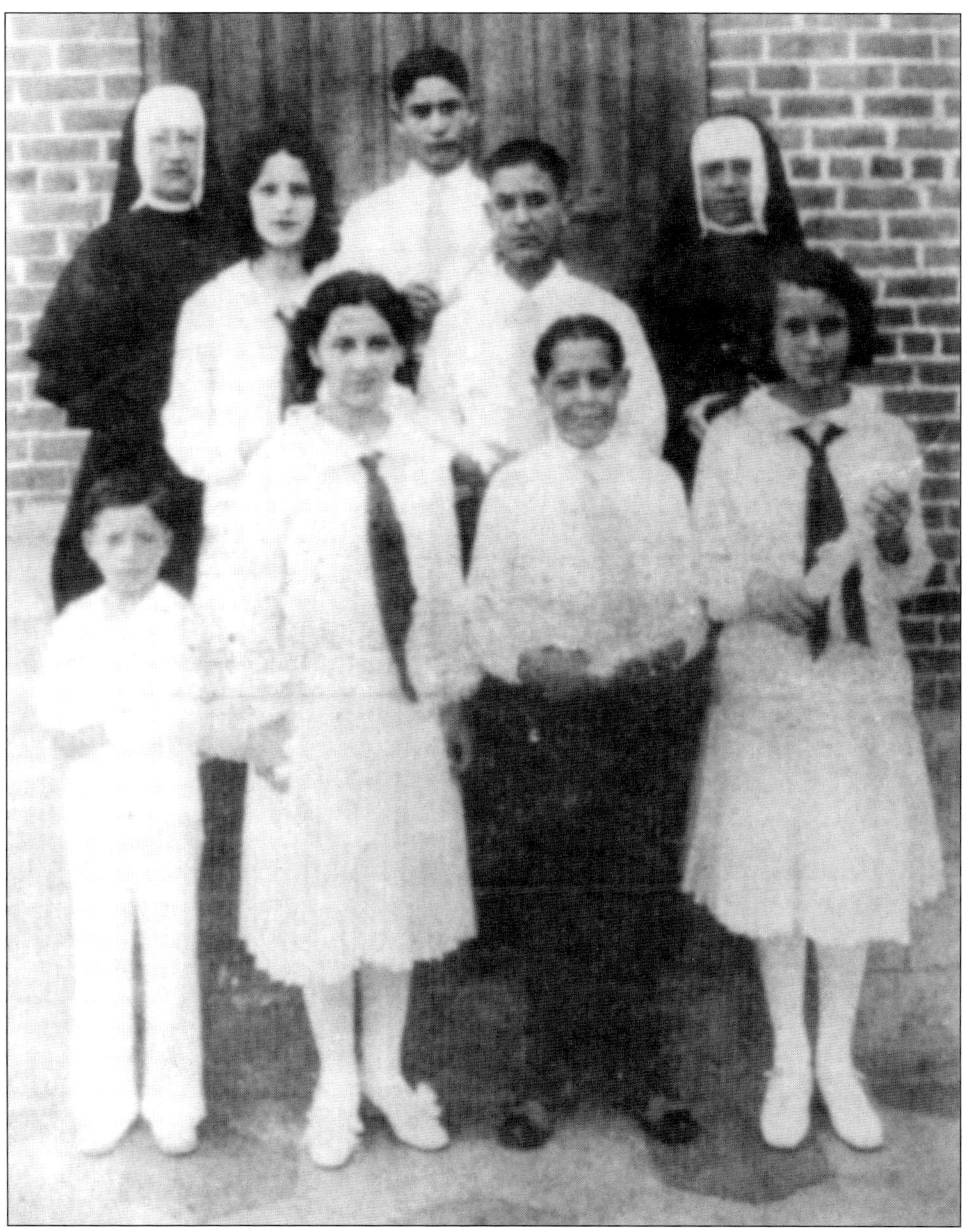

Recognizing a need for the education of African American children in Tampa in the segregated South, Sisters of the Holy Names opened a Black school in Tampa on February 2, 1894, spearheaded by trailblazers from Quebec, Sisters Marie-Aurélie (left, born Delphine Trudeau in 1857) and Marie Germaine (right, born Philomene Leblanc in 1830) soon joined by Sr. Catherine-Rici as the first teacher. Soeur Marie-Félicité, the sister who wrote the history of St Peter's Claver, was in mission there for many years and wrote, "Ten days after the opening of St. Peter Claver School in Tampa, Sister Marie Aurelie and Marie Germaine discovered the school building, a small house adjoining the old Methodist Church, was burned to the ground, and a post was affixed nearby that warned that any attempt to reopen would meet a like fate or worse. Not to be deterred, by October 8, 1894, a house in the Black section was purchased through the church and the school reopened for classes; by the end of the year, it boasted eighty students." (Geneviève Noël.)

Archives
De Sœur Marie-Félicité

SAINT PETER CLAVER'S SCHOOL

TAMPA, FLORIDA

In history,we read how as a result of the Civil War in the United States of America, the Negro race was freed and given equal rights with other citizens of that country. Such was added to the Constitution but examples could be multiplied to show that clauses written into the law had little or no practical meaning. In the States of Florida, petition after petition for educational provisions for the Negroes was met with refusal.

On February 2, 1894, the Sisters of the Holy Names opened a school for these unfortunate people of God. It is nor surprising, however, with the feeling that existed, that their act would meet with opposition and ten days after the opening, Sister Marie Aurélie and Sister Marie Germaine found the building, a small house adjoining the old Methodist Church, burned to the ground. A notice was fastened to a tree near the ruins. It warned against trying to operate a Negro school in that vicinity saying that the citizens would not submit to it. Any ather attempt to do so would meet a like fate or worse.

In 1916, St. Peter Claver met an ominous challenge as the Florida legislature acted upon a bill passed in 1913 that read, "White children and Negro children were not to be taught in the same school." If discovered, the punishment would include a hefty fine and six months' imprisonment. Fueled by Jim Crow radicals, Florida governor Park M. Trammel, (whose term was known for its blatant racism and endorsement of segregation and the overlooking of 21 lynchings) issued a warrant and arrested three teachers at St. Joseph School in St. Augustine for teaching Black children. St. Peter Claver closed during the legal battle, only to reopen several months later in May 1916 when Judge George Cooper Gibbs ruled the law unconstitutional. St. Peter Claver School has been educating children for 127 years. (Geneviève Noël.)

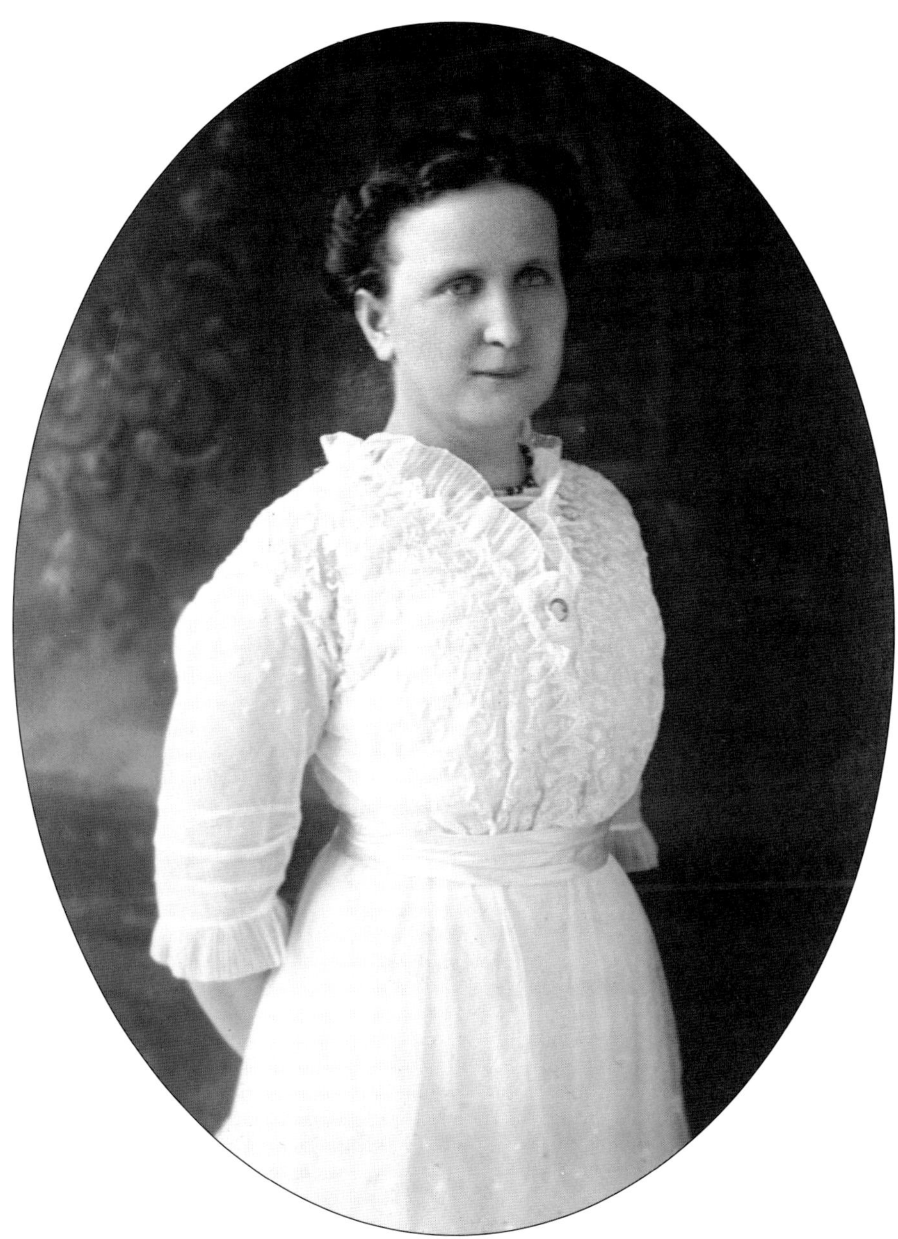

Born in Minneapolis, Minnesota, Frances Clayton passed the examination for high school entrance at age 10. She later graduated as class poet. Due to her mother's health, she moved with her family to Tampa. There, she had the unique opportunity of making the highest average in each of three competitive teacher exams at 99.75, beating out the previous record-holder, a male. She taught a variety of subjects and was an administrator at Hillsborough High School. She also served as a principal in Franklin County, then the highest salaried woman principal in the state. Urged by colleagues to open a private school and believing that Tampa had reached the size where such a school was justified, she opened Hillcrest Academy and later moved it to Davis Boulevard, naming it Sea-Born. "Here," said Clayton, "we shall combine the best principles of public-school education with the greater opportunities afforded in small classes, and pleasant social conditions." (Florida Memory.)

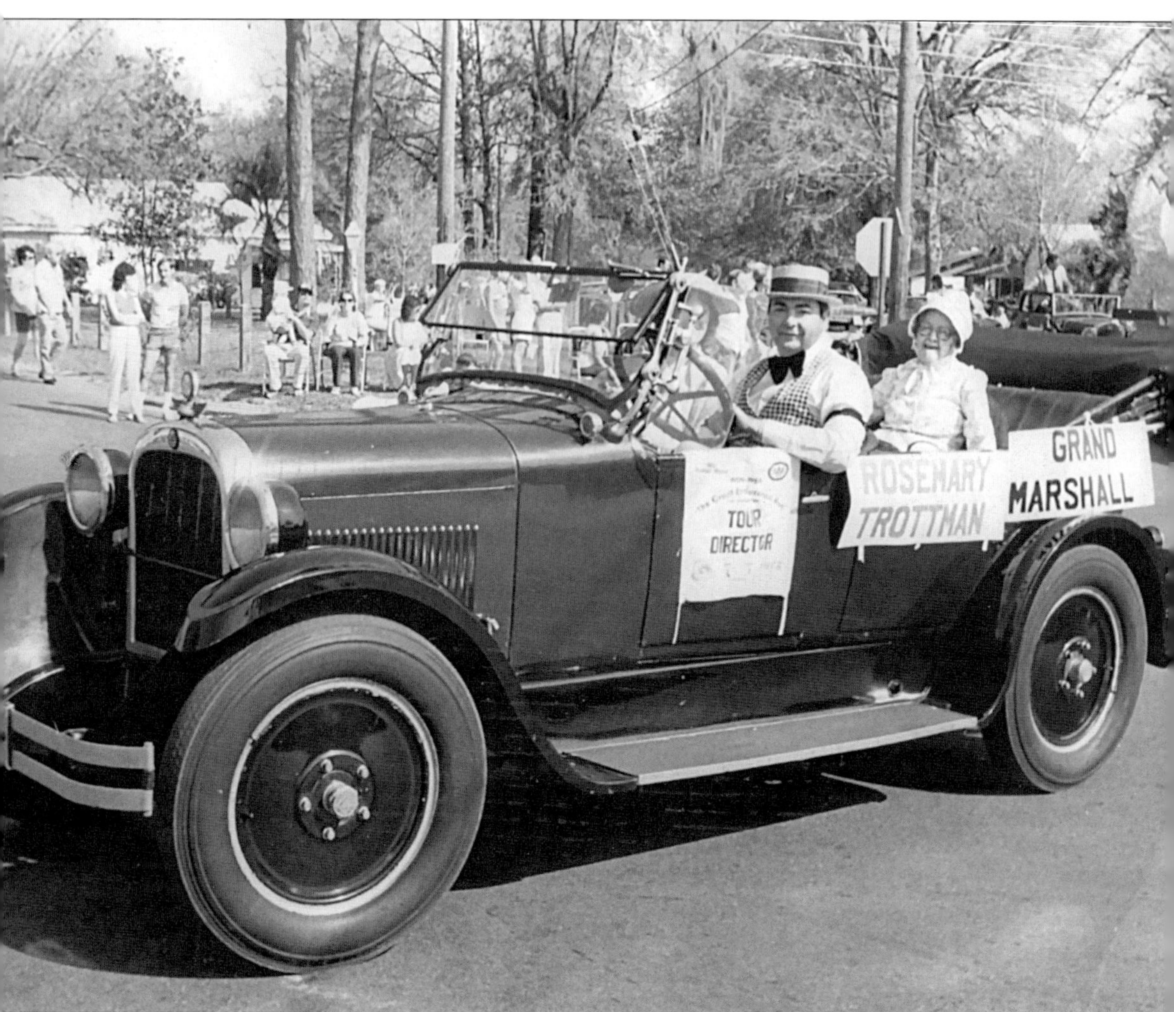

Rosemary Wallace Trottman was an educator in east Pasco from a pioneer family. Although two other books have been written about Zephyrhills, the study penned by Trottman is the definitive primary-sourced history that stands the test of time, as she chronicled history from 1821 to 1921. Trottman lived many of the frontier tales herself or listened to stories from the mouths of those who did. Her great-grandfather Willis Frank Smith was a soldier in the First Seminole War and claimed land under the Armed Occupation Act of 1842. Her grandfather James Goodwin Wallace was a North Carolina surgeon-lawyer who came to establish a new life in Florida after the Civil War. Trottman was a longtime educator and community activist. She is pictured here riding in a vintage vehicle as she was honored in the Founder's Day parade with her characteristic demure smile. (Zephyrhills Historical Association.)

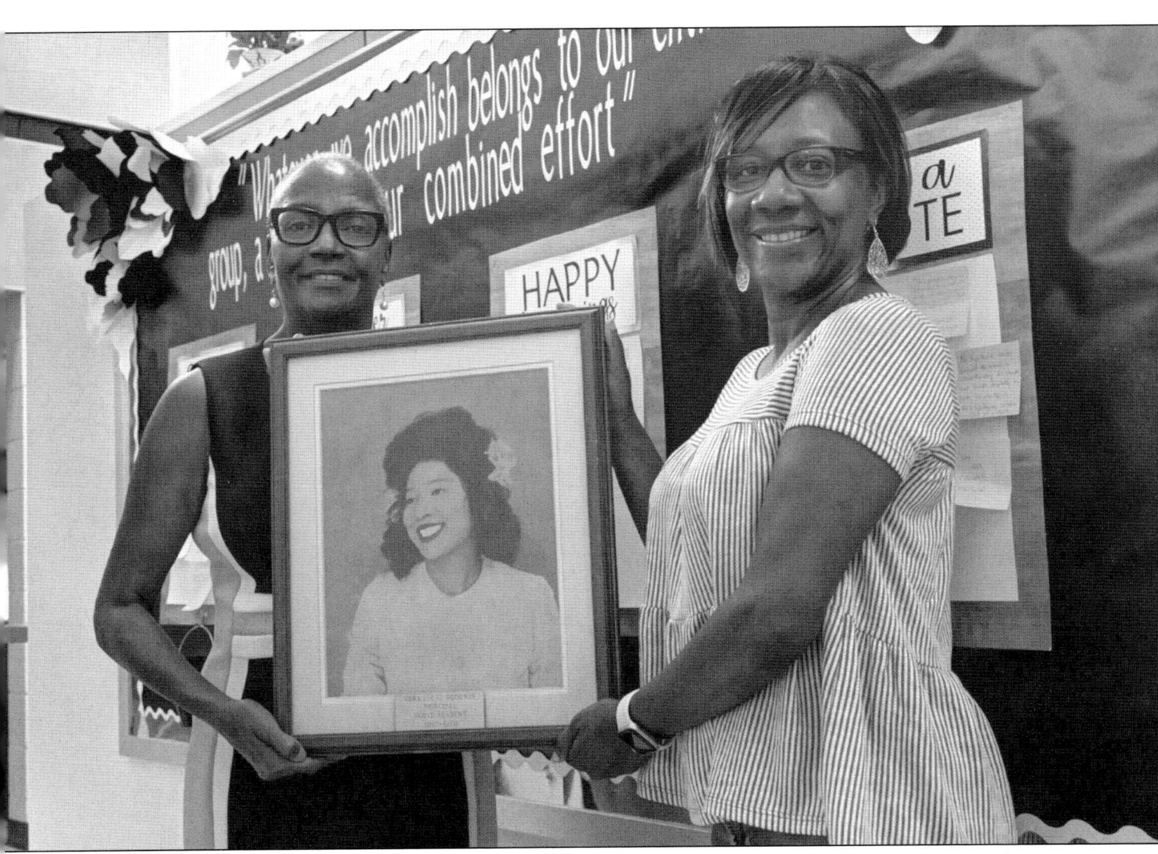

Vera Lucas Goodwin was one of Florida's outstanding educators for more than 30 years. She was an educator who used what she had and held the belief that all children could learn regardless of their beginning in life. Despite Jim Crow laws, she earned a master's degree in administration from New York University in 1952, when most schools were not admitting Blacks. After earning her bachelor's degree from Florida Agricultural and Mechanical College, she returned to Pasco County in 1931 with missionary zeal to not only teach Black students the basics, but also the finer points of life. As a teacher of penmanship and music and later as the principal of Floyd Academy for 22 years in Lacoochee, she taught music appreciation and chaperoned her students on field trips to perform throughout Tampa Bay. She demanded as much of herself as she did of students. She was the epitome of self-determination and high achievement. The portrait of her that hangs in Lacoochee Elementary is held lovingly by Rev. Cassie Coleman on the left, a former teacher and community leader/pastor, and Latoya Jordan on the right, current principal of the elementary school in the town that housed Goodwin's school. (Richard K. Riley.)

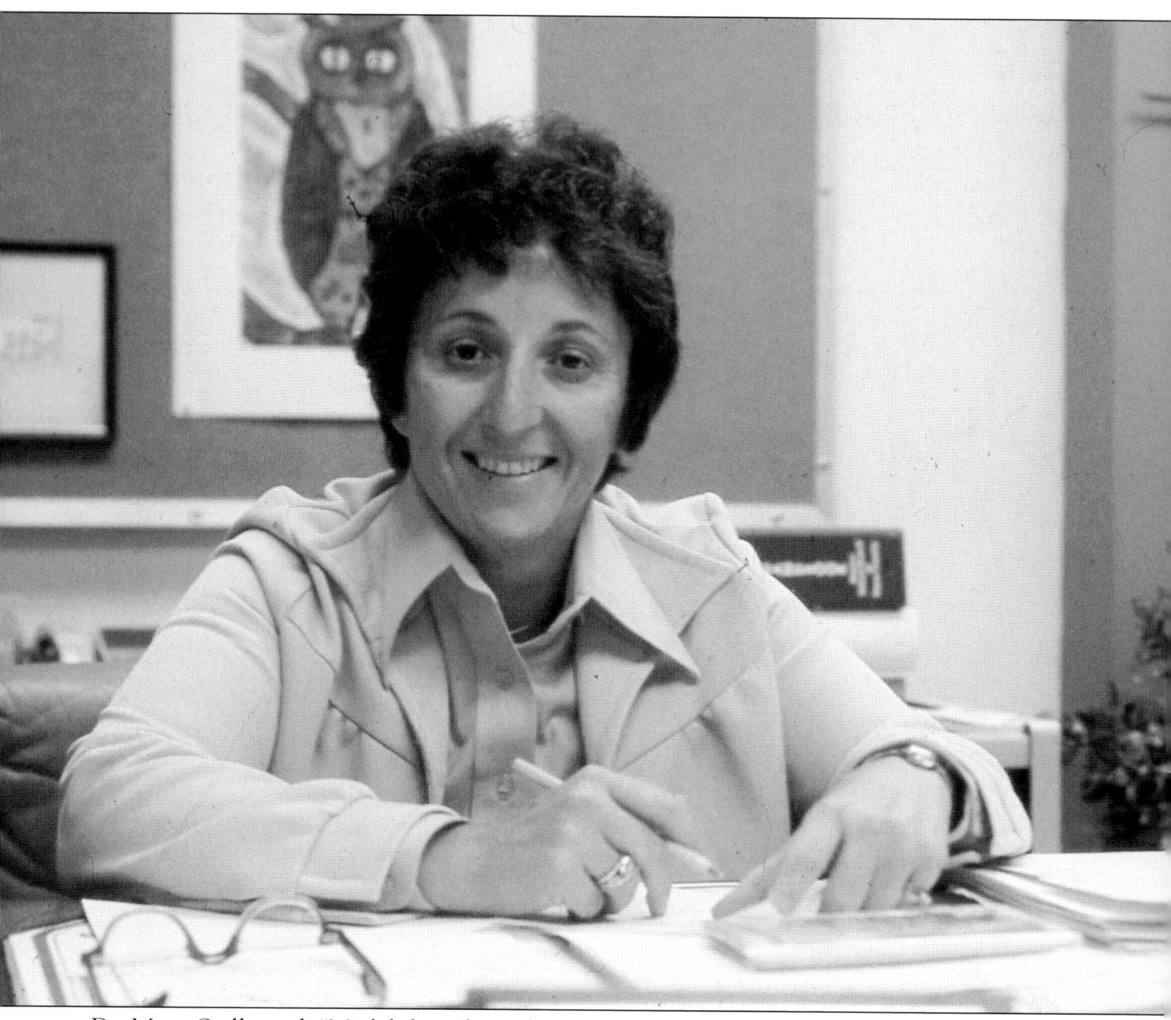

Dr. Mary Giella said, "My life has always been full of pleasant accidents." A graduate of Pasco High and the daughter of an Italian immigrant who decided to leave New York and move into the woodland north of Dade City when Pasco was still rural, Giella possessed a humble demeanor and instinctive insight into people and situations. Supt. Rodney B. Cox had the foresight to tap her as an assistant superintendent when she was in her early 30s. Skilled in in-depth knowledge of learning and curriculum, Giella steered the school district at a time of enormous growth and change and impacted education in the state of Florida for over 30 years. Keenly aware of diversity, she worked with the latest researchers, such as Dr. Karolyn Snyder, and mentored women in school administration. Even after retirement, she pulled together female leaders in honor of one of her favorites, Greta Adams, in a group called Steel Magnolias. Intuitive and empathetic with a toolkit of leadership techniques, she worked in a world that had been traditionally male and fostered hundreds of women in education. (Pasco County School Board.)

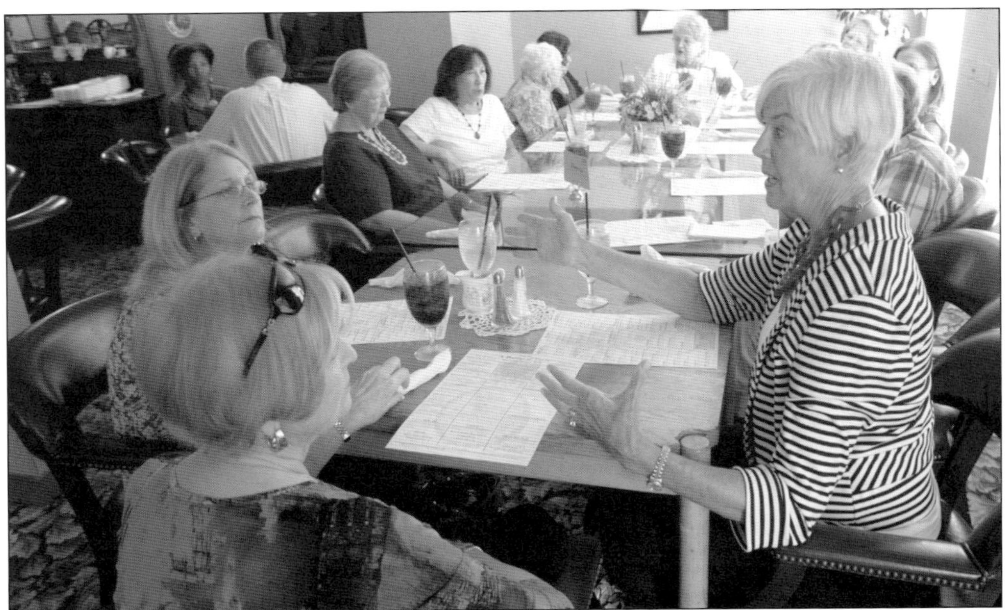

"As I watched them having a good time, it occurred to me that seldom will you see so many PhDs under one roof," wrote reporter Bill Stevens after he joined the Steel Magnolias for a luncheon; Dr. Myndy Stanfill had just retired as Pasco's assistant superintendent for human resources. Greta Adams wound up with a long career as the district's director of communications and community partnerships. Katherine "Kitty" Piersall retired as director of research and evaluation. They had all worked their way through the ranks, starting in classrooms. They had much in common, including their love for each other. "We wanted to stay connected," Giella said, "so we started having lunch at least once a month. It helped ease the transition from being so busy to having time to relax a bit. Myndy said, 'We need a name.' *Steel Magnolias*, a movie about strong Southern women was popular and they were feisty." (Above, photograph by Skip O'Rourke, *Tampa Bay Times*; below, Beatrice Pauls.)

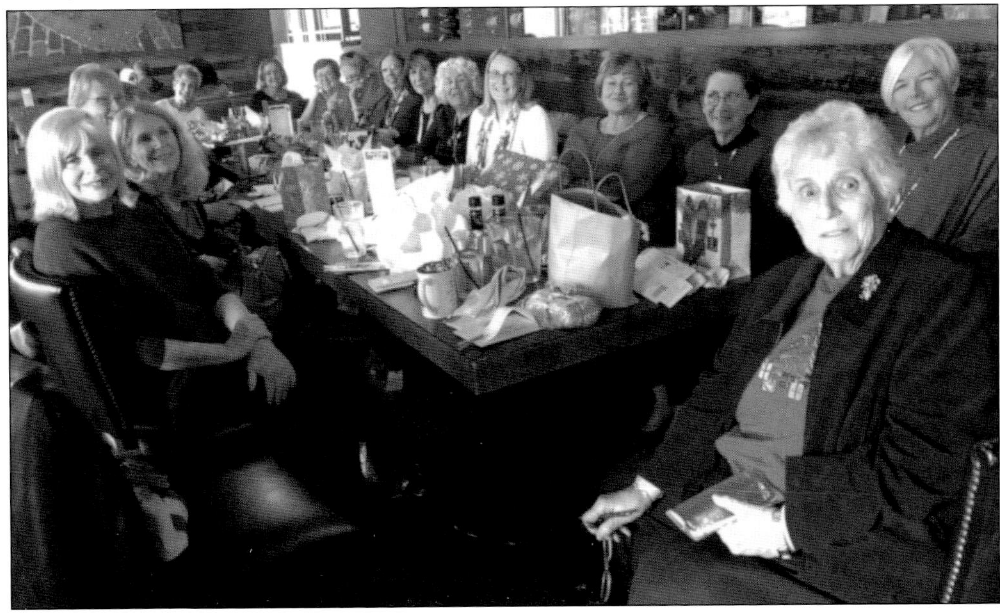

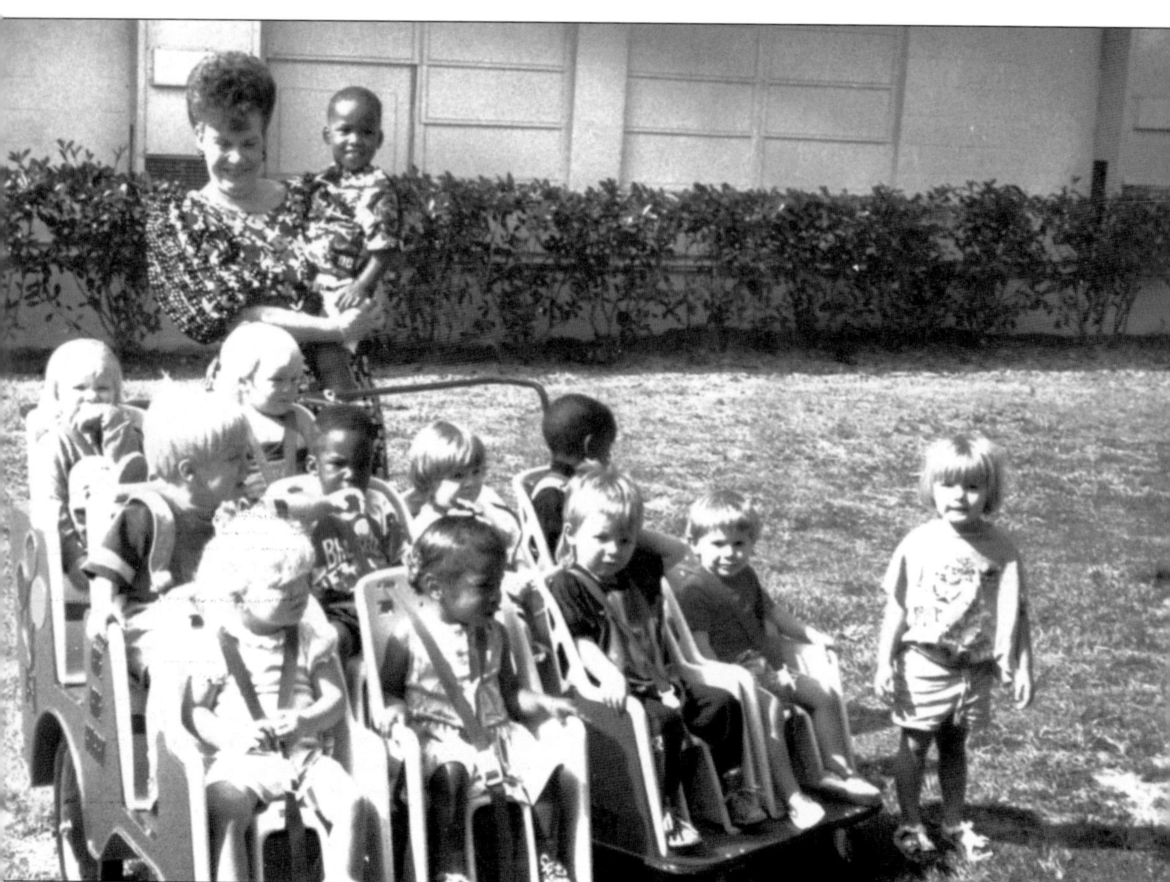

Greta Adams, a cherished teacher/principal and later director of communications for the district, had a 33-year career. This photograph shows Adams with the first Cyesis program she helped to create, a beloved project that caught national attention, including an interview on *Oprah*. Jeanette Thompson, the internationally acclaimed opera singer, said her teacher instilled in her "to strive for perfection and believe in herself. It was as if she could reach into your soul and take away the entire concept of mediocrity." Adams's 1964 teacher application read, "Every child has a need and desire to learn, and I, as his/her teacher, must be the one to meet the demands as completely and as understandingly as possible." With a lovely Southern drawl and the liveliest sense of humor, Adams taught for many years with her dear friend, Martha Walker. A community joy was attending their comedy show *The Hootenanny*. (Pasco High School.)

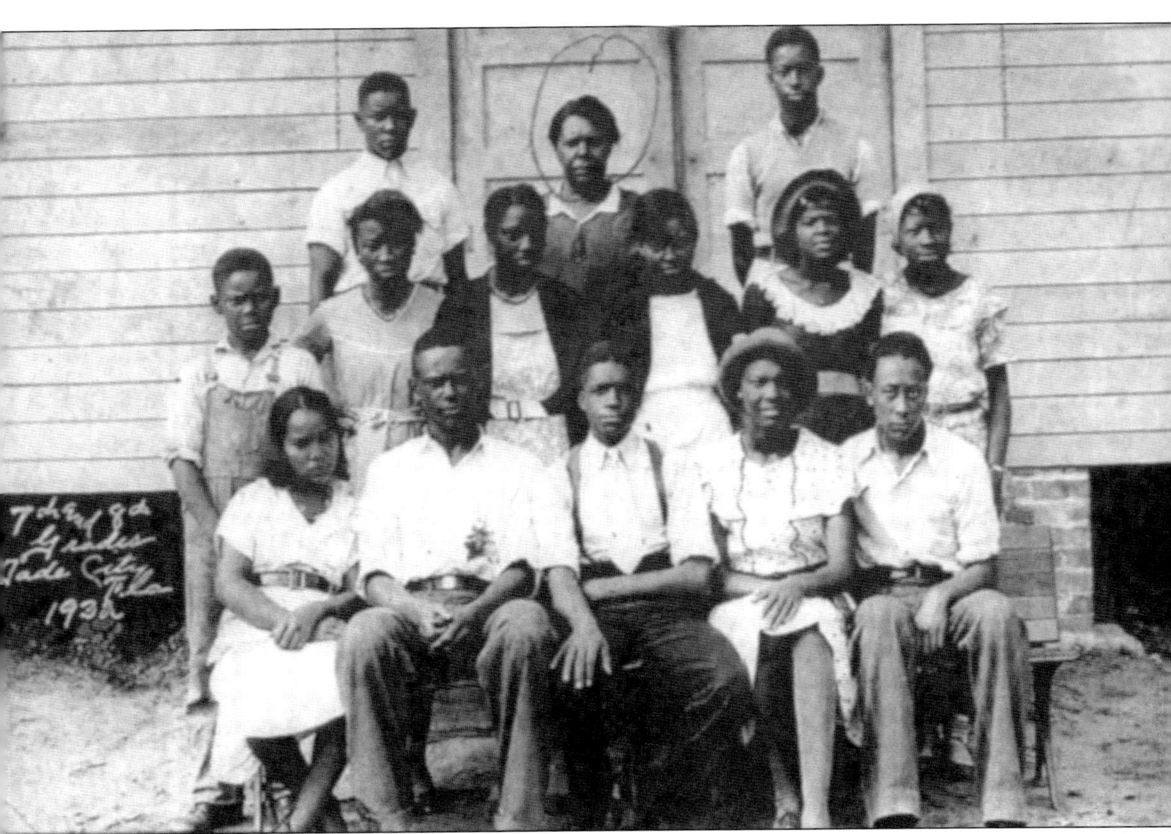

Etta Burt was a second-generation teacher and the first African American teacher in Pasco County to possess a bachelor's degree, which the Atlanta native earned from Atlanta University in 1904. After teaching in Marion County, she moved to Pasco, where she taught in Trilby, Blanton, and other locations for 40 years. She was appointed principal of the Dade City Colored School in 1931 and served in that capacity until 1935. "She did not allow other people's problems such as racism to distract from her love of teaching which she pronounced was her 'calling.' She was also the mother of eleven children, four of whom followed her into the teaching profession," said Imani Asukile. (Photograph by Martha Lewis, Imani Asukile.)

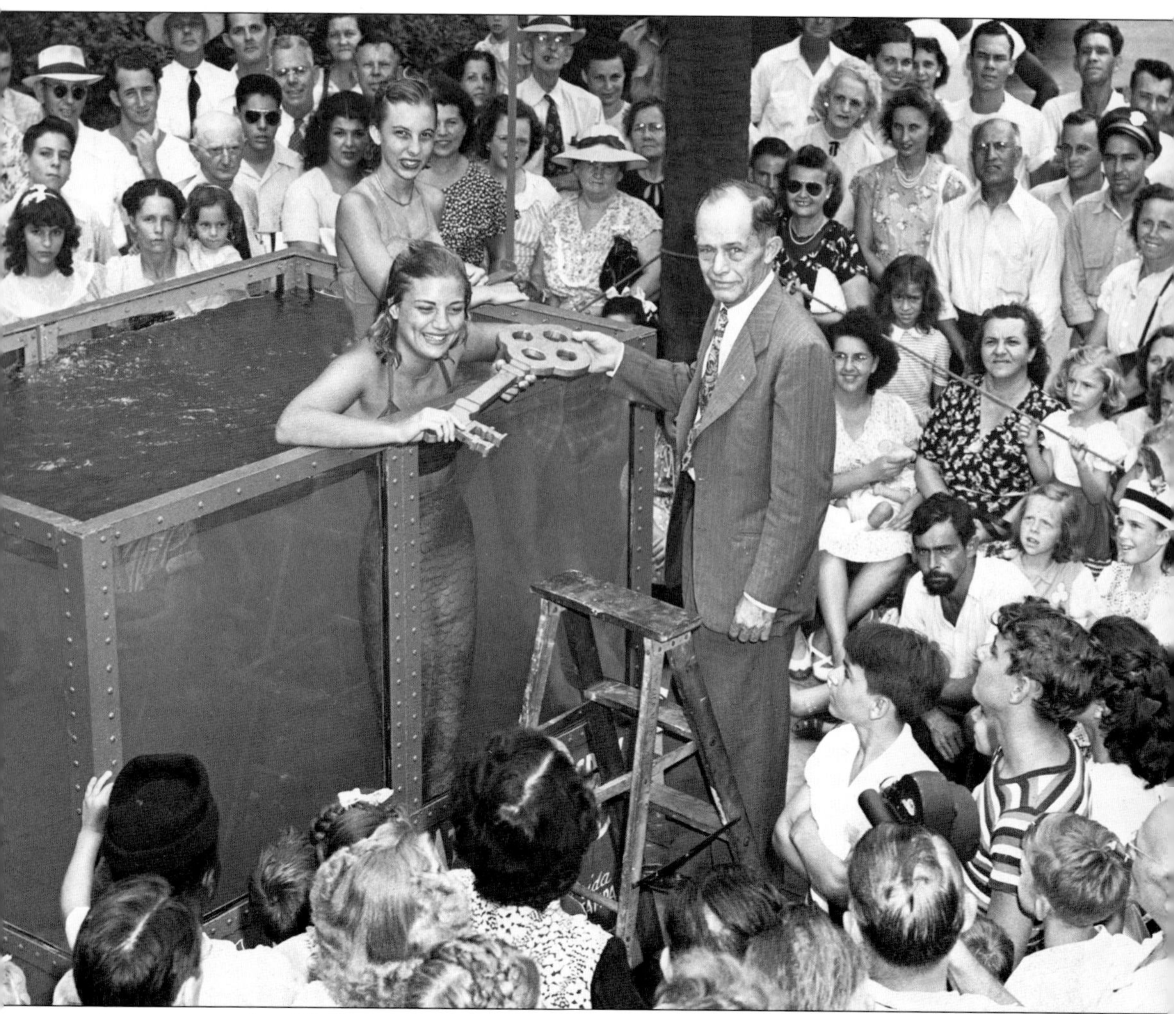

A star mermaid at Weeki Wachee Springs, Nancy Tribble Benda was one of the first mermaids at Weeki Wachee State Park, founded in 1947, and from that exposure went on to star in the television show *Miss Nancy's Store*. Later, she was tapped as the director of equal opportunity for the Florida Department of Education and oversaw enforcement of Title IX. She traveled the state investigating the disparities in athletic offerings. Seen here in 1948 on a promotional tour for the movie Mr. *Peabody and the Mermaid*, she receives a key to the city of Tampa from Mayor Curtis Hixon. (Florida Memory.)

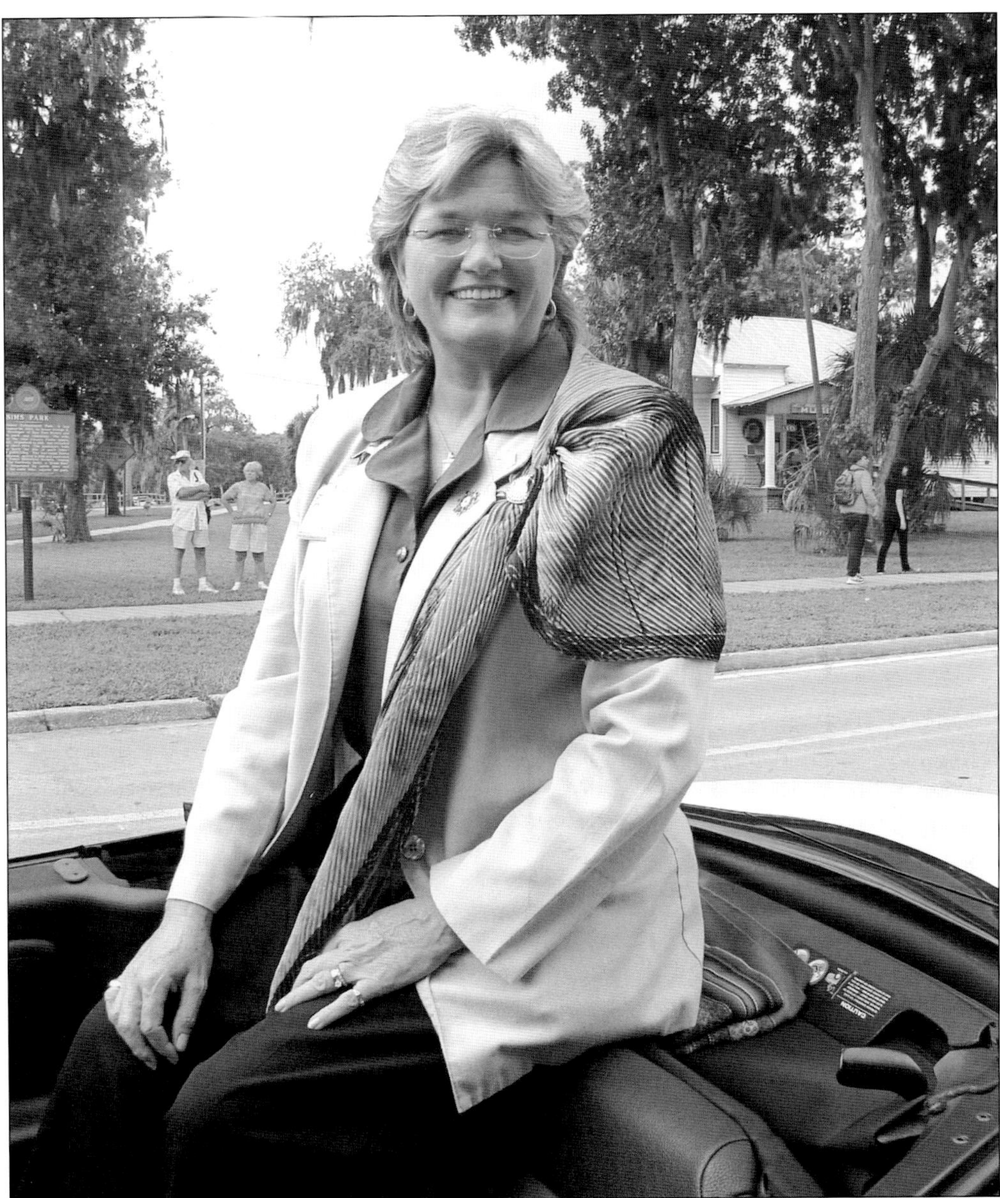

Heather Fiorentino was the first female school superintendent in Pasco and served two terms following a career in education that started in 1984 as a teacher. She was elected to the New Port Richey City Council, where she served five years, after which she won election for six years to the Florida House of Representatives. She was honored by Pasco Hernando State College as Alumni of the Year. Always the teacher, Fiorentino authored *An Emotional Journey—Humor and Hope Through Breast Cancer* in 2020 to help lighten up and support the journey of women. Dr. Paula S. O'Neil, the county clerk and controller, said, "The attitude Heather had was positive—like her attitude toward life. Her unique insight into life situations has been well-illustrated within her artwork for years." O'Neil is the author of *Fighting Cancer Like a Girl*. (Jeff Miller.)

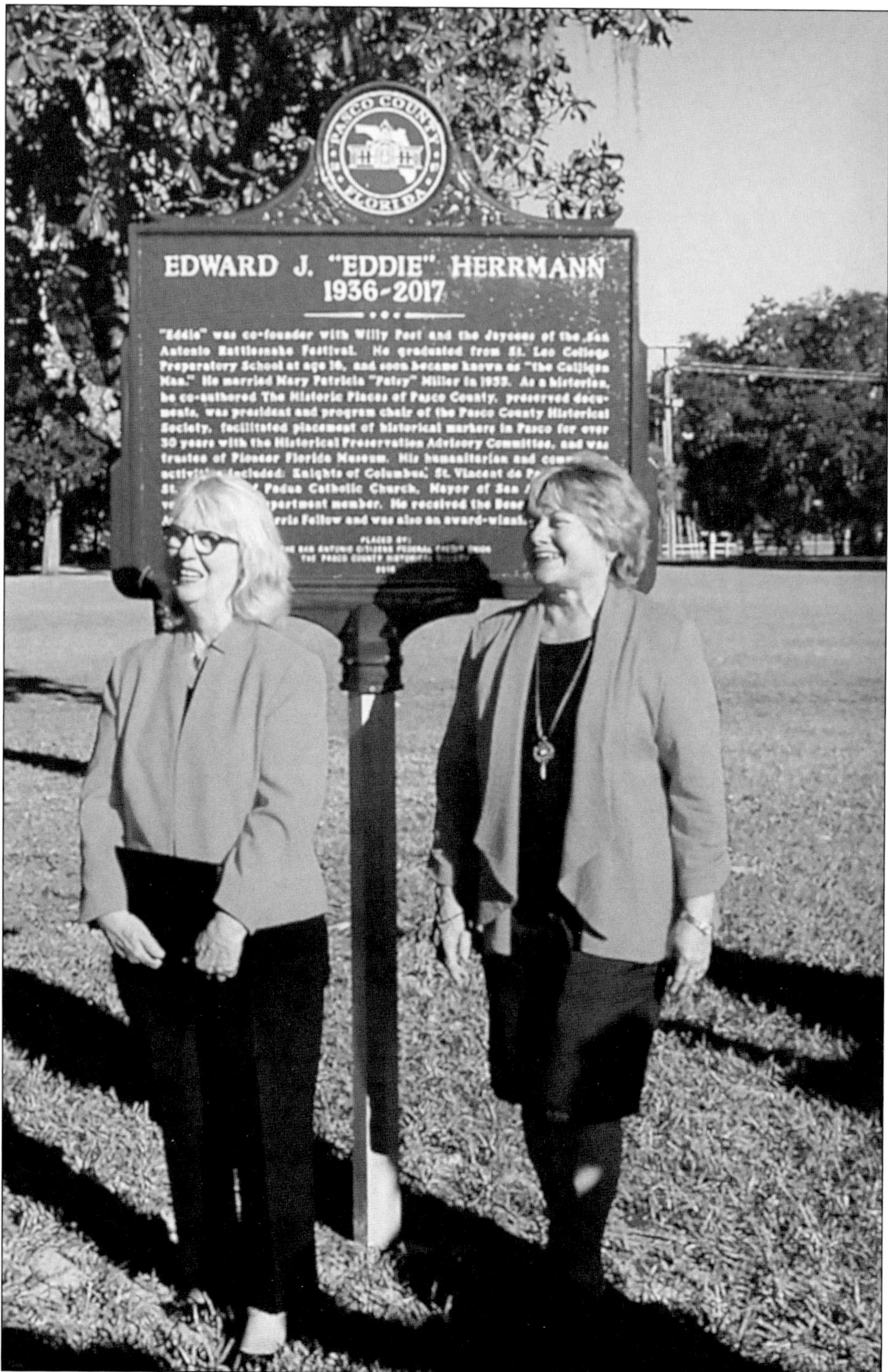

Dr. Susan MacManus (left) and author Madonna Wise were speakers at the dedication of the 2018 plaque to honor the Herrmann family in San Antonio, Florida. MacManus grew up in Lutz–Land O'Lakes and taught at the University of South Florida. She served as a political analyst for WFLA News Channel 8 and later ABC News. (Sally Redden.)

Nine

Addressing Sports with Zeal

In contemporary times, we recognize the body-mind-spirit connection, and for optimum health attempt to balance these aspects of our existence. In the 19th and early 20th centuries, a series of erroneous messages were given to females about exertion, appearance, and competition. The women in this section represent trailblazers of a different nature. For the most part, they excelled in sport and activity and did not put it aside because of superstition or societal expectations. Women were limited in the opportunity for team sports, which varied in different locales. Some schools had girls' basketball teams in the early 1900s but discontinued them later in the century when boys' sports were considered the moneymakers. Various businesses, grocery stores, and factories had girls' baseball teams and basketball teams as well. The All-American Girls Professional Baseball League, which gained acknowledgment from the 1992 movie *A League of Their Own*, was an opportunity for women from 1943 to 1954 to keep baseball in the public eye while World War II and its aftermath had temporarily shut down men's baseball. Tampa Bay did not have a team, but one of the prominent players, Betty Emry, settled in the area after her stint with the league and often shared stories of her phenomenal experience.

In this section are coaches, a professional team owner, and a trailblazing sports newscaster, all of whom have roots in Tampa Bay. Fortunately, with the passing of Title IX in 1972, which prohibited sex discrimination in the workplace and at schools, opportunities have opened up, and the sky is the limit.

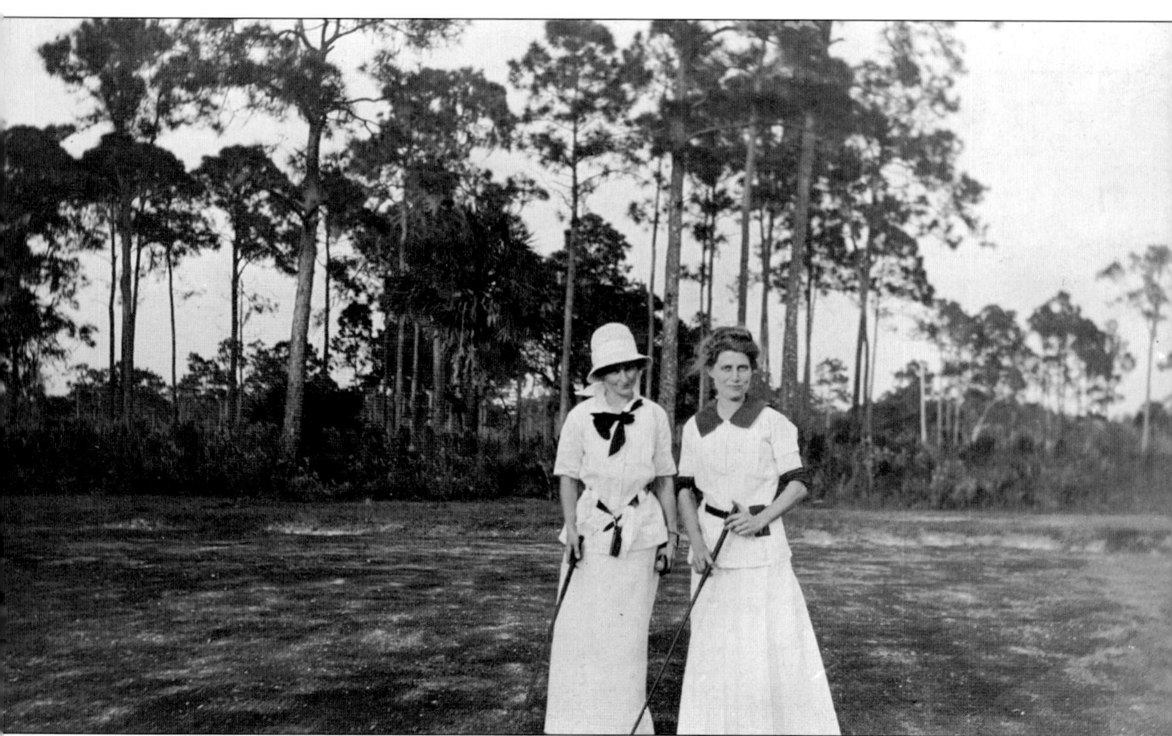

Pictured here in golfing attire holding golf clubs are Dora Lakeland Bonacker (left) and Katherine Lee Bitzer. In 1914, these names appeared regularly as high-ranking golfers at the Tampa Automotive and Golf Club, which changed its name to the Rocky Point Golf Course around 1918. Bonacker, a native of Lakeland, whose father, Captain W.B. Bonacker, was considered a founding member, worked with the Coca Cola Company for six years after graduation from Soule Commercial College in Tampa in 1919. (An advertisement in 1918 urged young women to take the telegraph course to obtain a high-paying government job). Bonacker married Dr. John S. Helms and remained active in the Tampa community throughout her life. Bitzer, who married Alvin Magnon in 1923, was still playing golf quite competitively some 50 years later in 1963 when she was a top finisher at the Silver Lakes Women's Golf Association, tying with a high score of 65. (Tampa Bay History Center.)

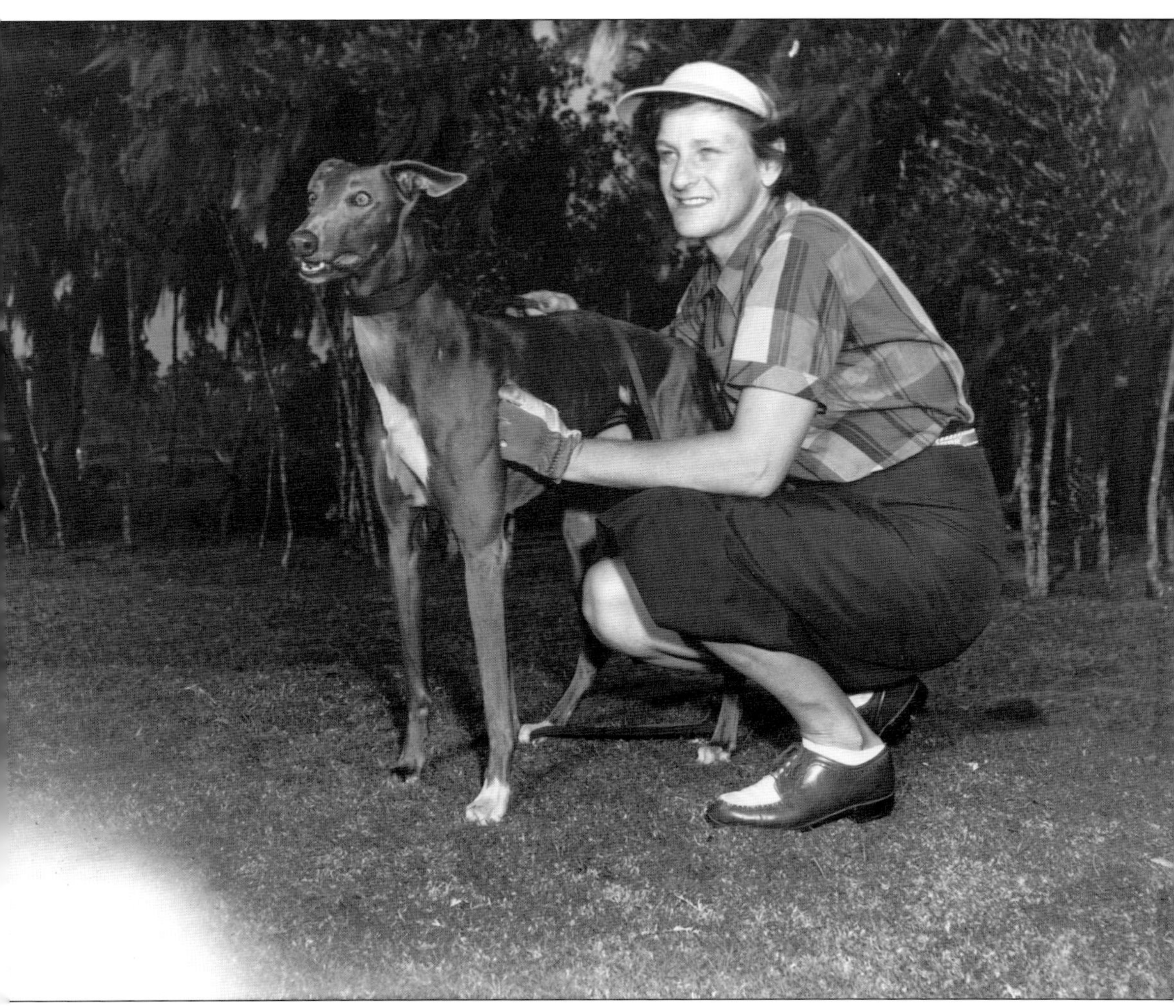

Mildred Ella "Babe" Didrikson Zaharias is an adopted daughter of Tampa Bay as she moved to the area in the 1950s. The sixth of seven children born to Norwegian immigrants, she is considered one of the greatest female athletes of all time. She was instrumental in organizing the Tampa Junior Golf Tournament and the Florida Seniors Tournament. She is the only woman to have played in the Professional Golf Association tournament in both 1938 and 1945. A co-founder of the Ladies Professional Golf Association (LPGA) with Patty Berg, Babe won 10 LPGA championships. She took gold medals in the 1932 Olympics in javelin and the 80-meter hurdles, setting records as well as earning silver in other track events. She played on the semipro basketball team the Golden Cyclones. A fierce competitor, she could run, jump, throw, play tennis, polo, basketball, soccer, lacrosse, and billiards. Because of her prowess as a hitter in baseball, she was nicknamed "Babe" after the famed Babe Ruth, and the name stayed with her throughout her career. Local golf celebrity Harry Root remembered playing with her on numerous occasions and recalled the first time he saw her hit a golf ball: "She hit the golf ball so far, we were aghast." (Burgert Brothers Collection, Tampa–Hillsborough County Public Library.)

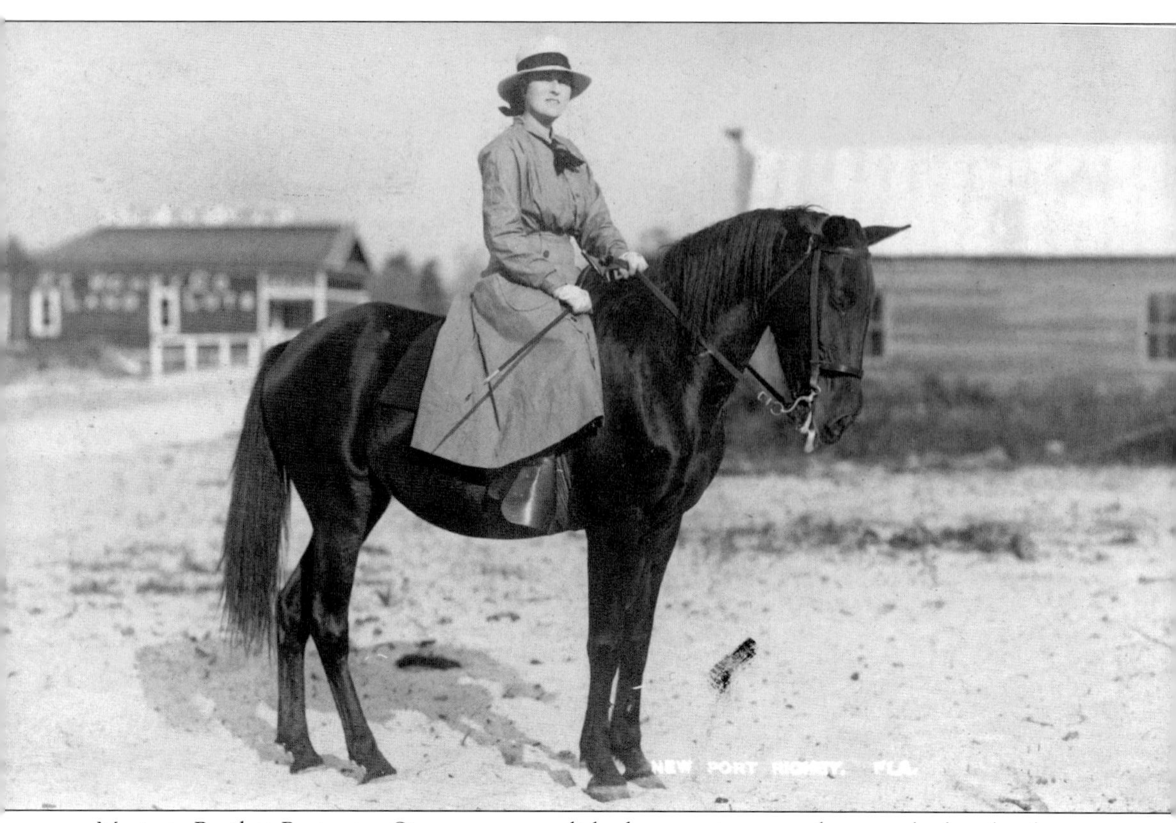

Marjorie Bartlett Bryington Sims, an accomplished equestrian, was photographed on her horse about 1915 in New Port Richey, with the land company building behind her. Known as the first lady of New Port Richey, she arrived in 1911 and assisted her husband, who is credited with the founding and early development of the New Port Richey area, where she infused culture and civic involvement. (West Pasco Historical Museum.)

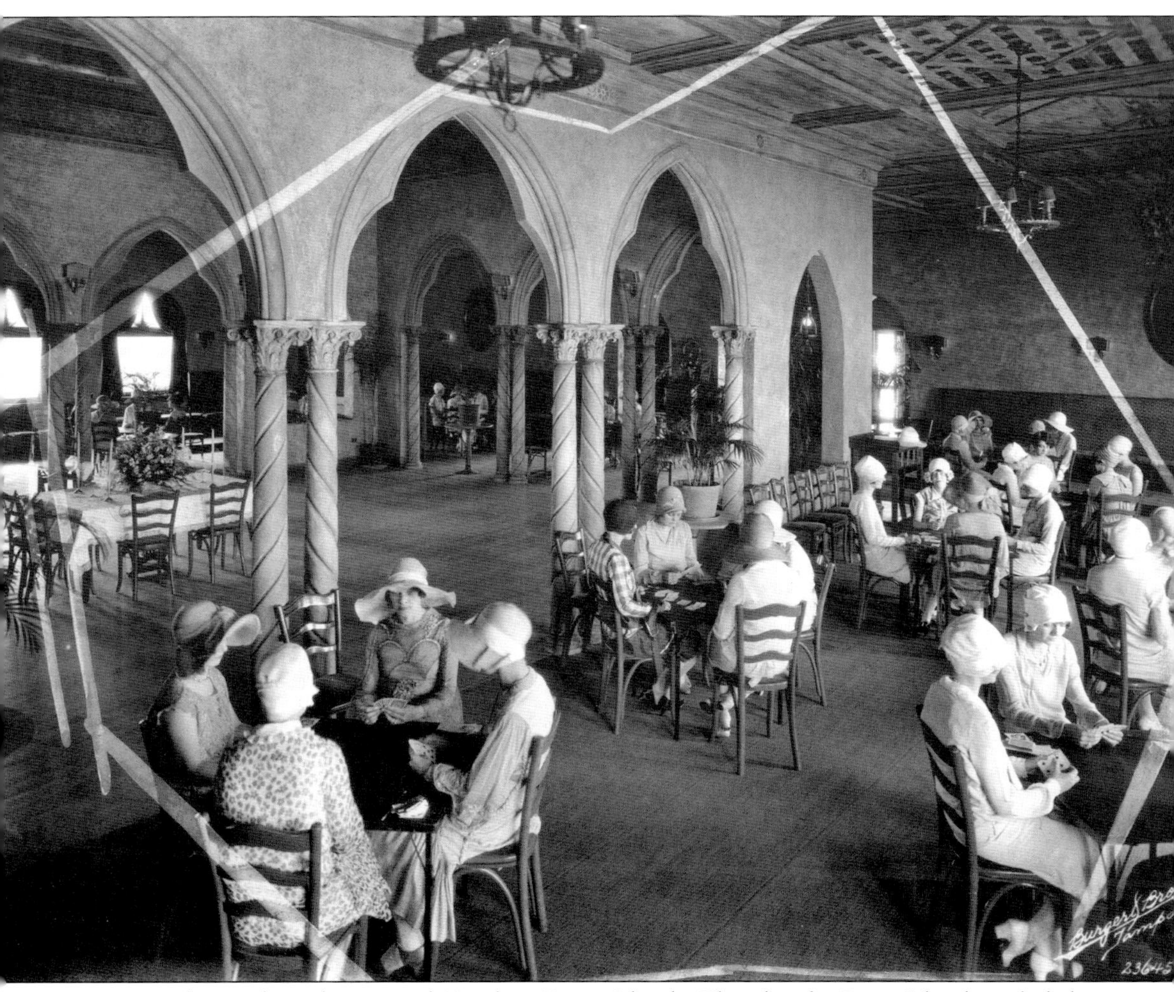

Women play cards at the Mirasol Hotel on Davis Islands. The plan for Davis Islands included several luxury hotels with fine Mediterranean architecture to act as a place for vacationers to escape and relax and for locals to socialize. The largest and finest of these hotels was the Mirasol. In 1924, inspired by a massive statewide real estate boom, the City of Tampa sold two mud flat islands to real estate developer D.P. Davis and work began to turn them into habitable land as the real estate development Davis Islands. At first, properties sold out, but poor management and cash flow problems meant that the city was making little money. In 1926, the real estate bubble popped, and Davis was forced to sell his company. On October 12, he went overboard from the ocean liner *Majestic* under mysterious circumstances, and his body was never found. While Davis Islands was initially a major financial loss for Tampa, the investment paid off in the long run, and today, Davis Islands remains some of the city's finest and most sought-after real estate. (Tampa Bay History Center.)

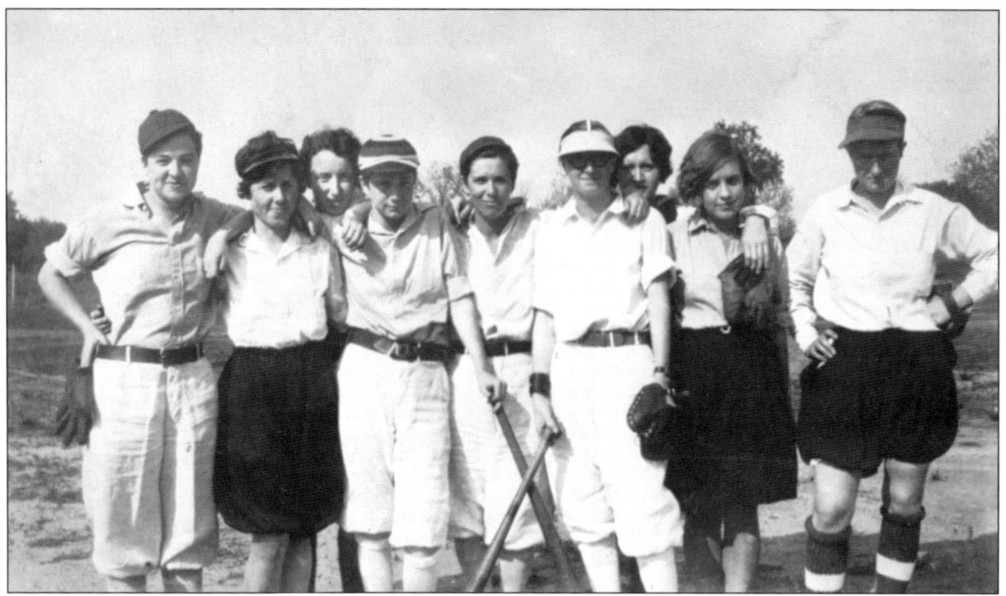

Pictured here is the Florida State College For Women (FSCW) 1928 baseball team. Softball was not widely recognized until the 1930s. Baseball was commonly referred to as too masculine and was played on the FSCW campus as an intercollegiate sport. Bernice Conklin from Tampa was recognized as the best athlete at FSCW. One of their debut athletic events was the Odds and Evens match in basketball and volleyball on Thanksgiving morning for the intercollegiate championship. (Florida Memory.)

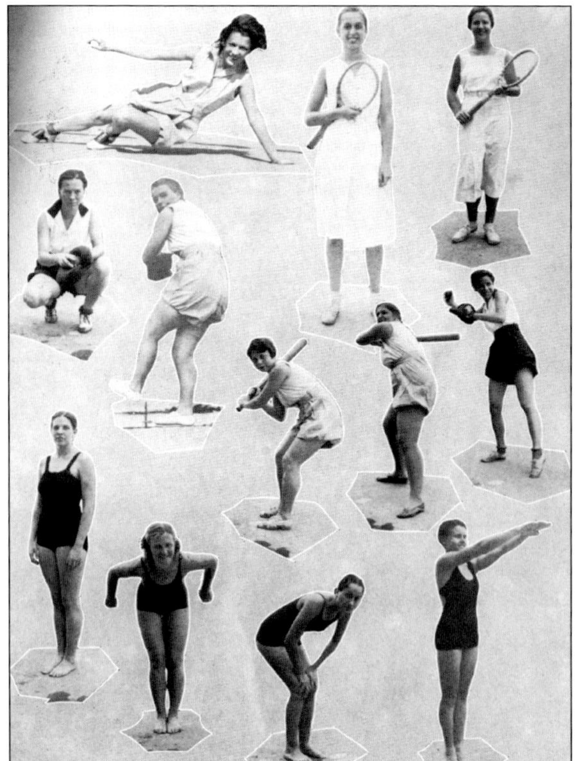

This photo collage of women's sports in 1935 shows the attire for the various acceptable female sports, including golf, tennis, baseball, swimming, track, and diving. Women first participated in the Olympics in 1900, and in addition to golf, the events were croquet, sailing, and tennis. Perceptions were changing as recognition of women's athletics were slowly growing over time. (Florida Memory.)

On December 27, 1987, Gayle Sierens became the first woman to call play-by-play of an NFL game when she was in the booth for NBC's broadcast of the Seattle Seahawks–Kansas City Chiefs. Sierens also co-anchored NBC's *NFL Live* pregame show during the Seoul Olympics. (Tampa Historical Society.)

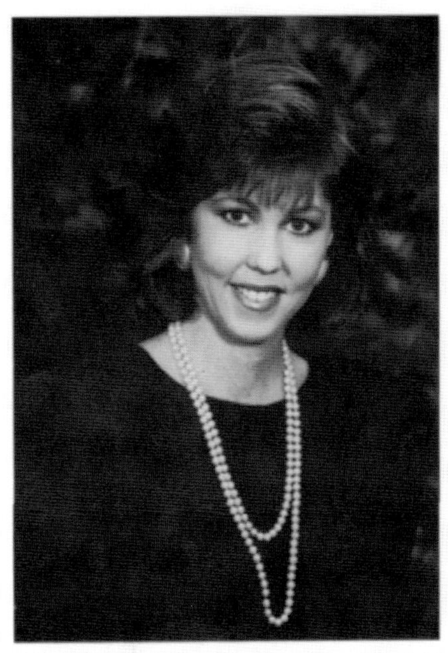

Journal of the Tampa Historical Society

TAMPA HISTORY MAKER IN 1988

CHANNEL 8's CO-ANCHOR GAYLE SIERENS

First Woman To Telecast Network Football Play-By-Play

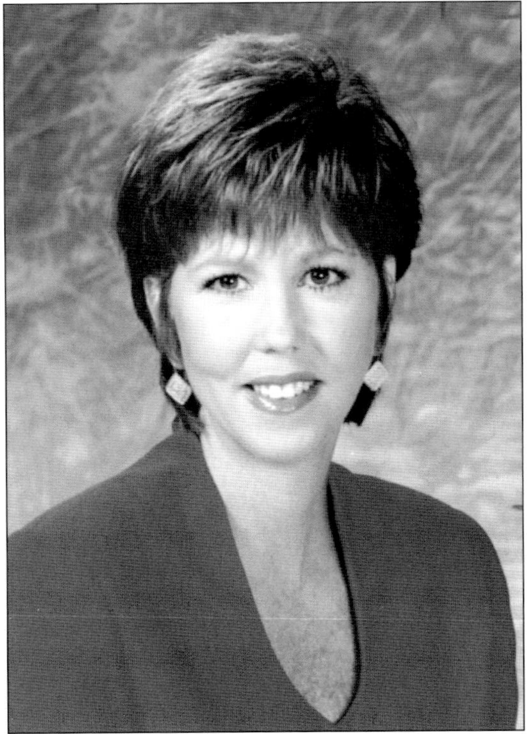

Gayle Sierens co-anchored the *NewsWatch* 6:00 p.m. and 11:00 p.m. newscasts and made her move from sportscaster in 1985. She received an Emmy for a sports feature. Prior to joining TV-8, Sierens was with WFSU-TV in Tallahassee, where she co-anchored and coproduced a morning newscast and talk show. She retired in 2015 after 38 years in broadcast journalism. Active in a variety of charitable causes such as funding for Alzheimer's, Sierens remains an active part of the Tampa Bay community. (WFLA-TV.)

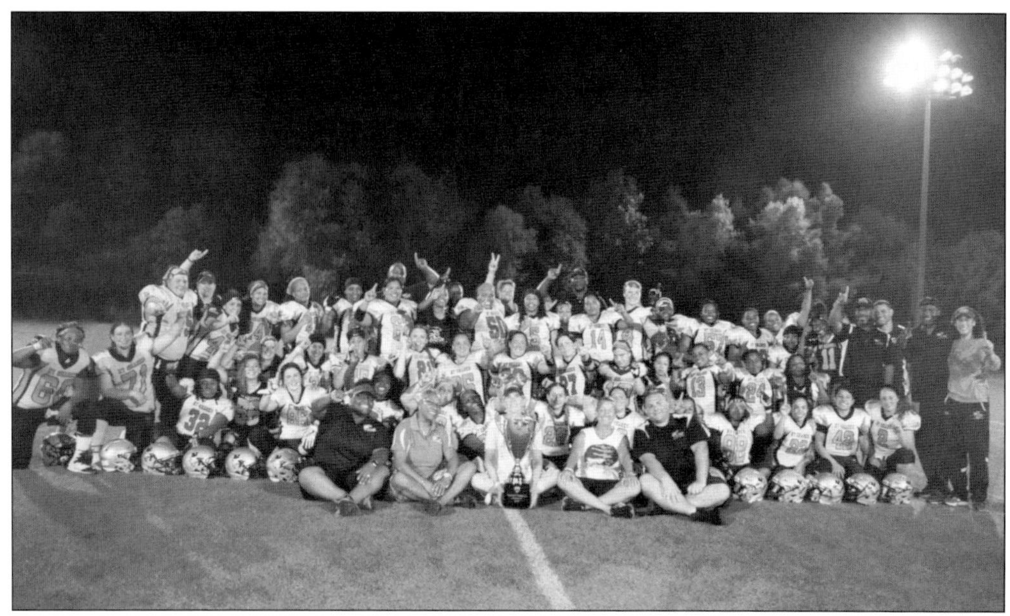

The New York Sharks won the 2018 Women's Football Alliance national championship and were Pro-Cloud Tournament international champions in Atlanta, Georgia, on July 27, 2018. The owner and former team quarterback, a graduate of FSU and a two-time national champion women's rugby team member who later played semiprofessional golf, Andra Douglas was a sports phenom from the Tampa Bay area, where she excelled at every female sport available in her high school in the pre–Title IX era. She penned a biography, *Black & Blue: Love, Sports and the Art of Empowerment*. (Both, New York Sharks.)

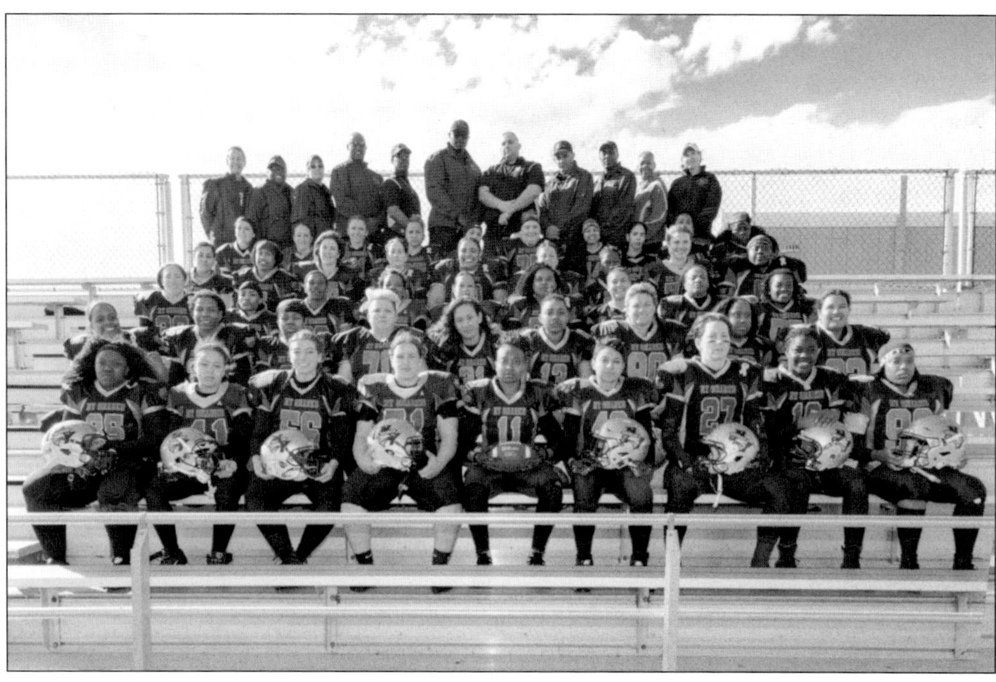

The New York Sharks won their second national title, this one for the Women's Football Alliance in Atlanta on July 27, 2018. Owner/manager Andra Douglas is hoisted by the players in celebration. She has created and exhibited extensive artwork and written about female athletes, including the 100-plus women's tackle football teams throughout the world who acted upon their passion for the game. (New York Sharks.)

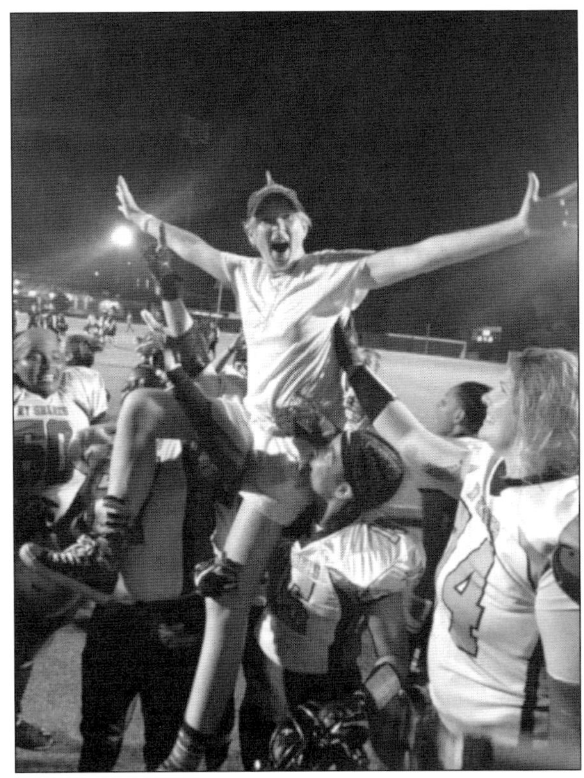

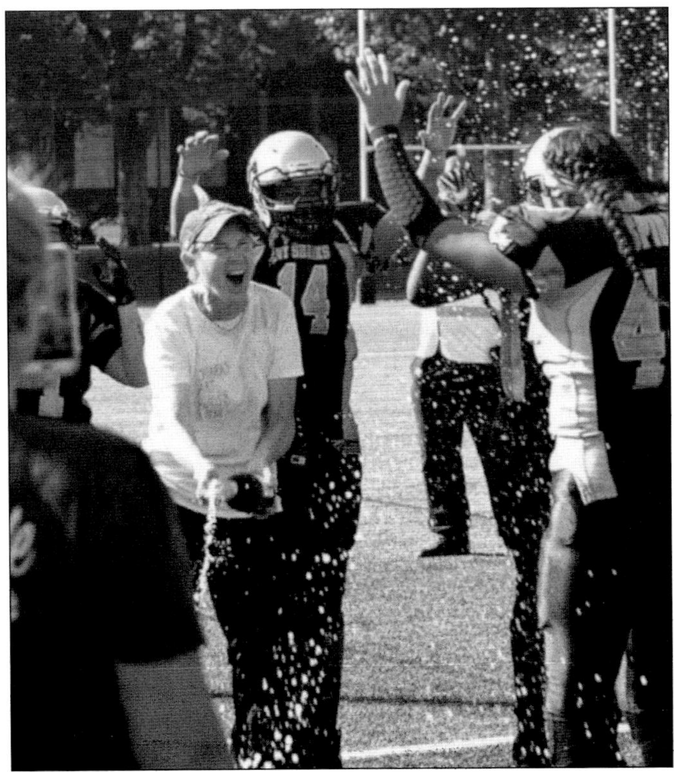

The New York Sharks won the first-ever International Women's Football Tournament hosted by the Birmingham Lions in Birmingham, England, on September 2, 2018. A fierce believer in teamwork and perseverance, the pride of Douglas's team is shown here with Douglas spraying celebratory champagne. (New York Sharks.)

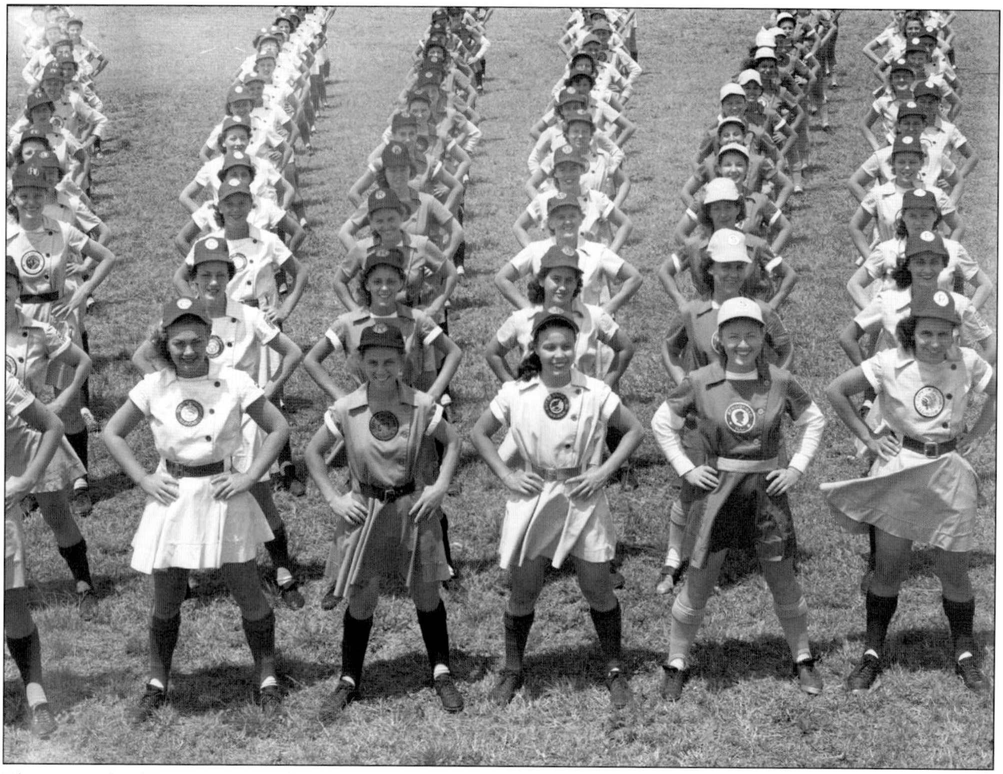

Photographed here on April 22, 1948, members of the All-American Girls Professional Baseball League line up at a practice in south Florida. Teams included the Springfield Sallies, Rockford Peaches, Peoria Redwings, Fort Wayne Daisies, Chicago Colleens, and the South Bend Blue Sox performing group calisthenics. (Florida Memory.)

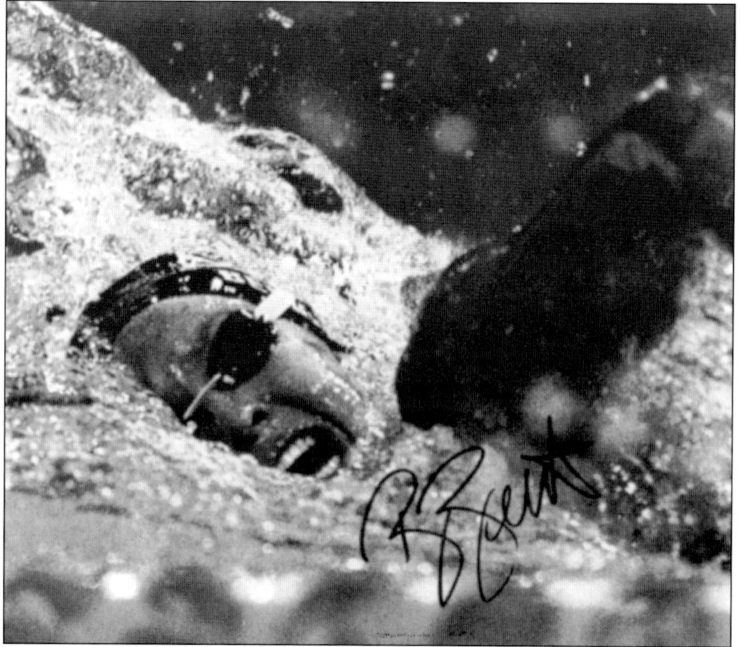

Tampa Bay claims Brooke Marie Bennett as an Olympic star. She earned three Olympic gold medals and 14 US championship titles. In the 2000 Sydney Olympics, she won gold in the 400-meter freestyle and 800-meter freestyle, while at the 1996 Olympics in Atlanta, she won gold in the 800 meters. (Author's collection.)

Ten

Reflecting on the Impact

The 20th century was a remarkable time of opportunity for women. Contemporaries recount the stories of parents and grandparents and identify the complexity of modifications in lifestyles and attitudes. Trailblazers like Ella Chamberlain and Elizabeth Robbins opened the doors. Risk-takers such as Sisters Marie Maurice and Marie Augustine, who undertook enormous personal risks to sail across Florida, were followed by intellectuals who sacrificed and fought to make inroads; generations of women have grown and thrived. The female artists and sports stars offered inspiration as well. Women, the nurturers, continued with their loving guidance and camaraderie.

Dr. Janet Denlinger, the world-renowned co-founder of Matrix Biology Institute from Tampa Bay, graduated from a local high school and later taught high school; she remains a quiet benefactor. With her husband, Dr. Endre A. Balazs, she perfected a process to obtain an acid from rooster combs that provides inflammatory relief and is used in joint and eye surgery treatment across the globe.

In the range of time represented in this collection from the 19th century to the 21st century, the value of women and their potential morphed into recognition of their authentic contributions in intellectual and leadership pursuits. This final chapter presents a sample of images of women in Tampa Bay. With enormous gratitude, those who follow are humbled by all that these trailblazers have given and hope that their influence will continue to inspire women of the future.

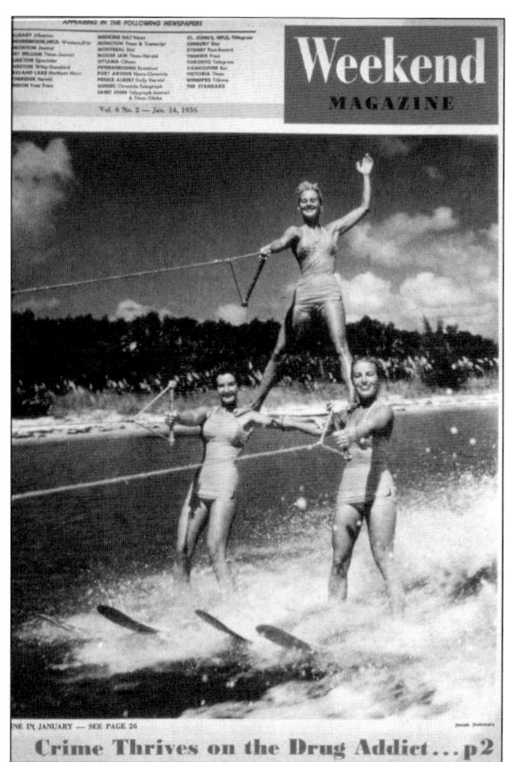

This *Weekend Magazine* cover from January 14, 1956, shows women water skiers in formation; such images were a popular promotion for Florida tourism for many decades. Peter Schall of the Florida Attraction Association reported in 1951 that Florida's tourist attractions were up in attendance by over 30 percent; those attractions included Turner's Sunken Gardens in St. Petersburg, Sarasota's Jungle Gardens, Ringling Museums, Homosassa Springs (Giant Fishbowl), Weeki Wachee's Spring of Mermaids Show, Cypress Gardens Rainbow Springs, the Alligator Farm in Sarasota, and Muse Island Indian Village. In this era, advertisers used sex appeal with elaborate athletic displays of water skiers in costume, Southern belles, and attractive women hosting exhibits (Photograph by Joseph Steinmetz, Florida Memory.)

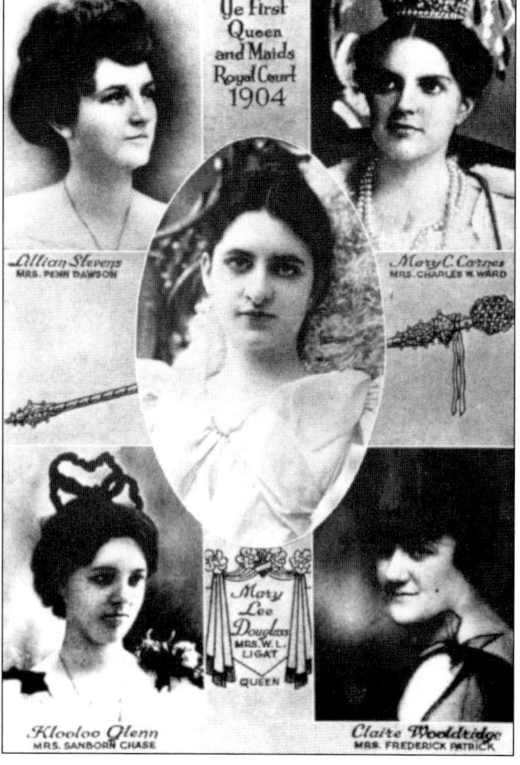

The first Gasparilla queen and maids in Tampa were revealed in 1904. Whatever the motivation, costume, appearance, and demeanor are judged in the many beauty contests and pageants. The Gasparilla court included queen Mary Lee Douglas Ligat (center). Clockwise from upper left are Lillian Stevens Dawson, Mary Carnes Ward, Claire Wooldridge Patrick, and Klooloo Glenn Chase. (Florida Memory.)

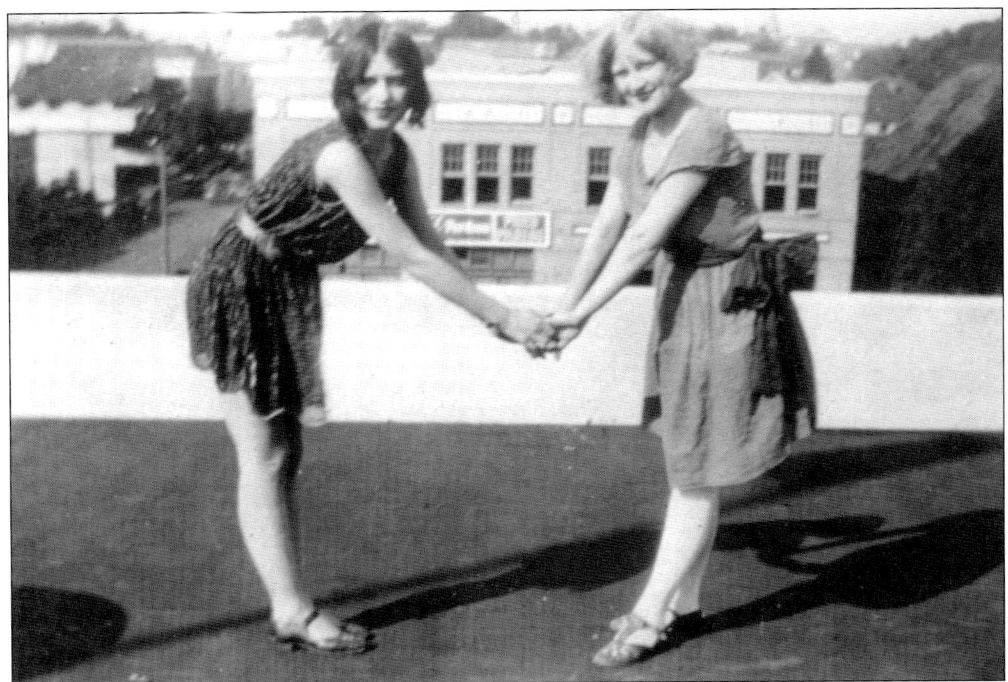

Two women friends reveal their friendship in their casual handholding on a Tampa rooftop. Manners and etiquette in Victorian times allowed for all types of protocol on glove attire and behavior, but the practice of holding hands among friends was commonplace. (Tampa Bay History Center.)

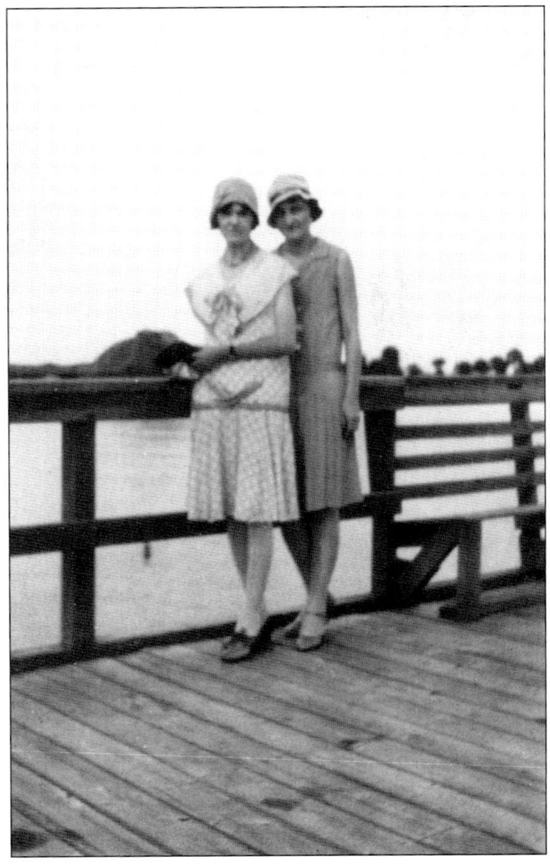

At the onset of the Great Depression, Blanche Alcock from Frederika, Iowa, and Margaret McDowell from Sumner, Iowa, were hired to teach school in Frostproof and Lakeland, respectively, for the school term of 1929–1930. They returned home to Iowa for summer 1930 and then traveled back to Florida in September 1930 to resume their teaching positions, this time in Tampa. Along the way, the two teacher friends enjoyed an excursion to the beautiful Municipal Pier in Clearwater. With traditional careers as educators, these adventurous women traveled across the country for their work and enjoyed the Joy Land Pavilion, which was considered the hippest dance pavilion in Florida at the time and a haven for "tin can tourists." (Tampa Bay History Center.)

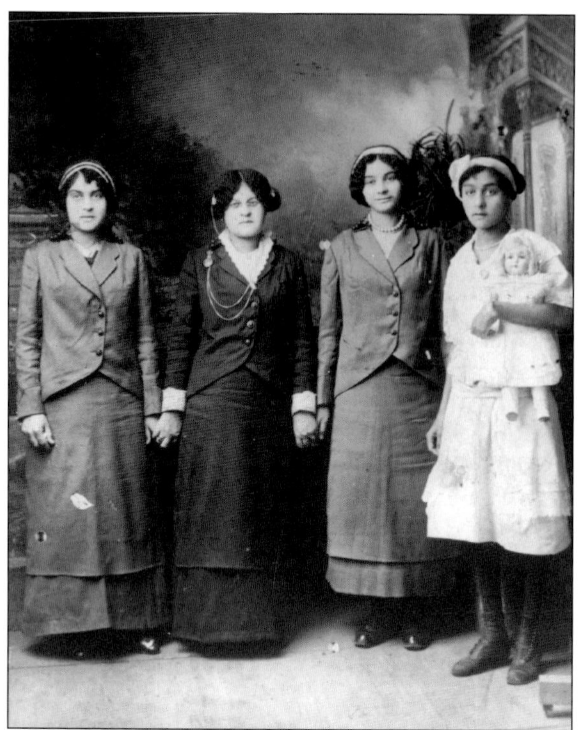

Many women with Cuban heritage have shaped Tampa Bay. According to *Florida Trend*, Cubans comprise the largest Hispanic group in Florida. With the influx of both white and Black Cubans in the early 20th century, influences of the Jim Crow South created a hierarchy that caused conflict and resulted in extraordinary art, music, and culture. This photograph captures four unnamed Afro-Cuban women in the early 1900s in Tampa. A shining example of the contributions of this group is Sylvia Rodriguez Kimbell, who became the first Afro-Cuban American woman to win a major office when she was elected to the Hillsborough Commission and later served as chair. A descendant of Afro-Cubans and born in Tampa, Kimbell completed her doctorate at FSU. (Tampa Bay History Center.)

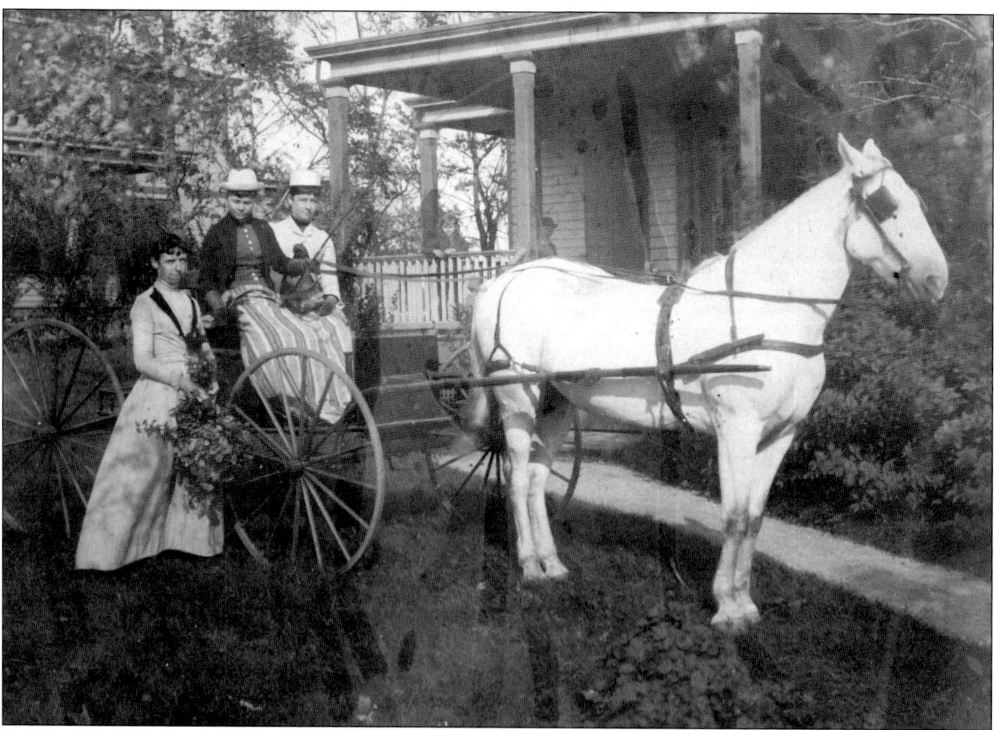

Women pose on a horse and buggy holding a basket of ivy. Though they remain nameless, this c. 1900 photograph in the Tampa Bay History Center is symbolic of the many anonymous women throughout Tampa's history. (Tampa Bay History Center.)

Three women in bathing costumes appear lakeside. One can only imagine the joy of the experience, probably during the Great Depression. (Tampa Bay History Center.)

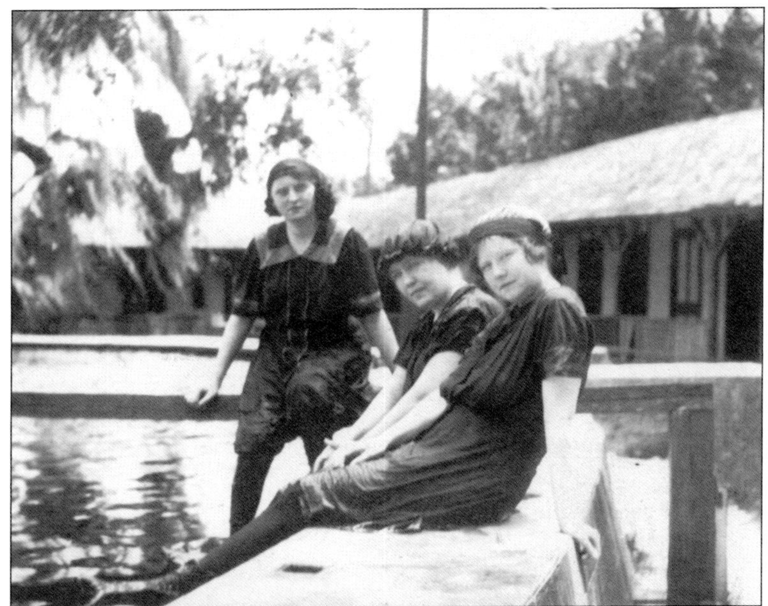

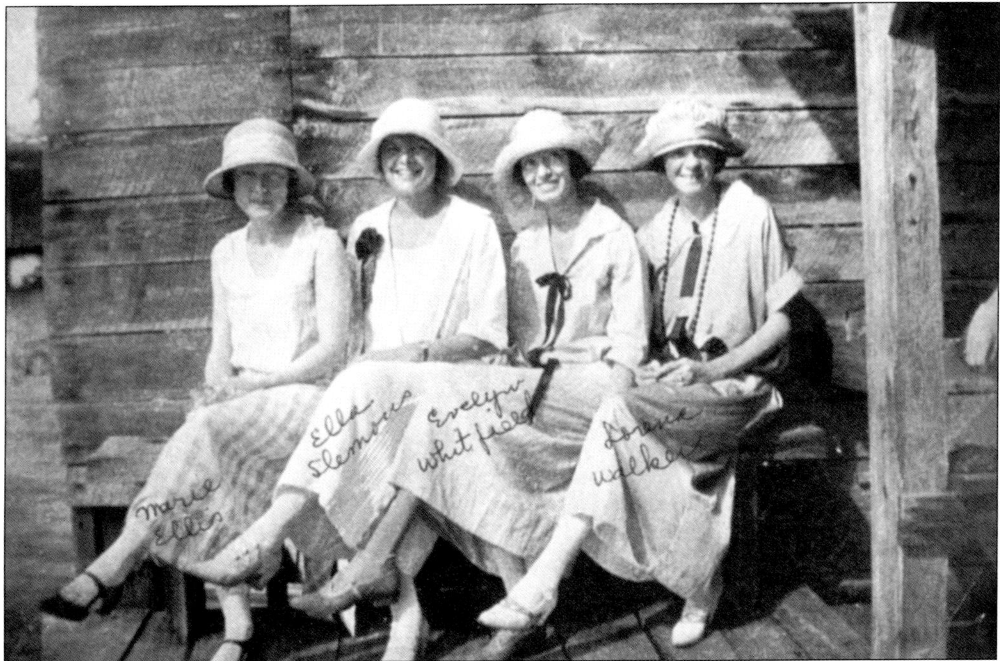

Spanx founder Sara Blakely grew up in Clearwater and graduated from Florida State University. She auditioned for the character of Goofy at Disney World but was found to be too short. She went on to sell office equipment before she had the innovative idea for Spanx. Using her meager savings, she started her line of underwear and leggings at age 27. A billionaire by 2012, she appeared on the cover of *Forbes* magazine and was inducted into the Florida Inventor's Hall of Fame in 2018 as the only woman among seven honorees. Showing off their own vintage stockings at FSU, Blakely's alma mater (then the Florida State College for Women), in 1924 are, from left to right, Marie Ellis Clark, Ella Slemons Bisbee, Evelyn Whitfield Henry, and Lorena Walker at the school's recreational facility Camp Flastacowo. (Florida Memory.)